*Oral Performance,
Popular Tradition, and
Hidden Transcript in Q*

Society of Biblical Literature

Semeia Studies

General Editor:
Gale A. Yee

Editorial Board:
Roland Boer
Elizabeth A. Castelli
Musa Dube
Richard A. Horsley
Cheryl Kirk-Duggan
Tat-Siong Benny Liew
Tina Pippin
Ilona N. Rashkow
Erin Runions
Fernando Segovia
Yvonne M. Sherwood
Abraham Smith

Number 60

Oral Performance,
Popular Tradition, and
Hidden Transcript in Q

edited by
Richard A. Horsley

Oral Performance, Popular Tradition, and Hidden Transcript in Q

edited by
Richard A. Horsley

Society of Biblical Literature
Atlanta

Oral Performance,
Popular Tradition, and
Hidden Transcript in Q

Copyright © 2006 by the Society of Biblical Literature

All rights reserved. No part of this work may be reproduced or transmitted in any form or by any means, electronic or mechanical, including photocopying and recording, or by means of any information storage or retrieval system, except as may be expressly permitted by the 1976 Copyright Act or in writing from the publisher. Requests for permission should be addressed in writing to the Rights and Permissions Office, Society of Biblical Literature, 825 Houston Mill Road, Atlanta, GA 30333-0399, USA.

Cover photo of Pesher Habakkuk, Qumran, courtesy of the D. Samuel and Jeane H. Gottesman Center for Biblical Manuscripts, The Israel Museum, Jerusalem.

Library of Congress Cataloging-in-Publication Data

Oral performance, popular tradition, and hidden transcript in q / edited by Richard A. Horsley.
    p.   cm. — (Society of Biblical Literature Semeia Studies ; v. 60)
Includes bibliographical references.
Two source hypothesis (Synoptics criticism)
ISBN-13: 978-1-58983-248-0 (paper binding : alk. paper)
ISBN-10: 1-58983-248-5 (paper binding : alk. paper)
    1. Q hypothesis (Synoptics criticism) 2. Bible. N.T. Gospels—Criticism, interpretation, etc. 3. Public speaking—Religious aspects—Christianity. 4. Oral tradition. I. Horsley, Richard A.

BS2555.52.O73 2006
226'.066—dc22   2006032937

---

13 12 11 10 09 08 07 06   5 4 3 2 1

Printed in the United States of America on acid-free, recycled paper conforming to ANSI/NISO Z39.48-1992 (R1997) and ISO 9706:1994 standards for paper permanence.

Contents

Abbreviations　　vii
Introduction
Richard A. Horsley　　1

Part One
Oral Performance and
Popular Tradition in Q

Essays

The Verbal Art in Q and *Thomas*:
A Question of Epistemology
Werner H. Kelber　　25

Performance and Tradition:
The Covenant Speech in Q
Richard A. Horsley　　43

Jesus' "Covenantal Discourse" on the Plain (Luke 6:12–7:17)
as Oral Performance: Pointers to "Q" as
Multiple Oral Performance
Jonathan A. Draper　　71

Responses

Response to Kelber, Horsley, and Draper
Joanna Dewey　　101

Oral Performance in Q: Epistemology, Political Conflict, and Contextual Register
Vernon K. Robbins   109

The Riddle of Q: Oral Ancestor, Textual Precedent, or Ideological Creation?
John Miles Foley   123

Part Two
Moral Economy and Hidden Transcript: Applying the Work of James C. Scott to Q

Essays

Moral Economy and Renewal Movement in Q
Richard A. Horsley   143

The Jesus Movement in the Villages of Roman Galilee: Archaeology, Q, and Modern Anthropological Theory
Milton Moreland   159

Going Public with the Hidden Transcript in Q 11: Beelzebul Accusation and the Woes
Alan Kirk   181

Communities Resisting Fragmentation: Q and the Work of James C. Scott
Melanie Johnson-DeBaufre   193

Response

The Work of James C. Scott and Q: A Response
William R. Herzog II   211

Bibliography   217

Abbreviations

ANRW	*Aufstieg und Niedergang der römischen Welt: Geschichte und Kultur Roms im Spiegel der neueren Forschung.* Edited by H. Temporini and W. Haase. Berlin. 1972–
ASNU	Acta seminarii neotestamentici upsaliensis
AThR	*Anglican Theological Review*
BASP	*Bulletin of the American Society of Papyrologists*
BJS	Brown Judaic Studies
BTB	*Biblical Theology Bulletin*
CBQ	*Catholic Biblical Quarterly*
CurBS	*Currents in Research: Biblical Studies*
HTS	Harvard Theological Studies
IEJ	*Israel Exploration Journal*
Int	*Interpretation*
JAAR	*Journal of the American Academy of Religion*
JBL	*Journal of Biblical Literature*
JSNT	*Journal for the Study of the New Testament*
JTSA	*Journal of Theology for Southern Africa*
Neot	*Neotestamentica*
NovTSup	Novum Testamentum Supplements
SBLDS	Society of Biblical Literature Dissertation Series
SemeiaSt	Semeia Studies
SNTSMS	Society for New Testament Studies Monograph Series
STRev	*Sewanee Theological Review*
ZTK	*Zeitschrift für Theologie und Kirche*

Introduction

Richard A. Horsley

Two originally separate lines of investigation of the earliest Gospel literature have recently begun to converge. Pioneering scholars such as Werner Kelber, recognizing just how inappropriate were the assumptions of print culture still being followed in classical form-critical analysis, sought ways to understand the sayings of Jesus more adequately as oral performance (1983). It is now being recognized in Gospel studies as in the study of ancient literature generally that whether or not they existed in written form, texts were recited aloud before groups of people. Meanwhile, interpreters of the speeches of Jesus that appear parallel in the Gospels of Matthew and Luke, but not in Mark—known as "Q"—began investigating the social context they presupposed and addressed (e.g., Horsley 1989; Kloppenborg 1991). Among the factors that bring these two lines of investigation together are the implications of considering texts such as Q in oral performance. If a text was usually recited orally before a group, then it must be understood less as an artifact in the abstract and more as communication of a message by performers to audiences in their historical-social context. Performance was "always already" a dynamic communication situated in a social context.

This volume of Semeia Studies presents some further "soundings" in these interrelated aspects of Gospel literature, particularly the speeches of Jesus in Q. These soundings were initially voiced in recent sessions at the Society of Biblical Literature Annual Meetings, sessions that embodied fruitful interaction among three very different program units. Kelber's article in Part One below is a further development of his response in a 1999 session of the Q Section to presentations by Jonathan Draper and myself exploring a recently developed approach to Q speeches as oral performance in historical-social context. Members of the Bible in Ancient and Modern Media Group in attendance at that session devoted one of their sessions the next year to consideration of the approaches developed by Draper and myself with the "sound map" approach previously tried out on Matthew's Sermon on the Mount by Bernard Brandon Scott and Margaret

Dean (Scott and Dean), with responses by Joanna Dewey and Vernon Robbins. The articles by Draper and myself and two of the responses in Part One of this volume are further developments of papers from that session. Since his work had been so influential in these papers and responses, John Miles Foley was invited to respond to the whole discussion as a prominent theorist of oral performance and oral-derived texts.

The articles in part two derive from another session of the Q Section, at the 2001 SBL Annual Meeting. Douglas Oakman, chair of the Social Scientific Study of the New Testament Group, had invited to the Annual Meeting the distinguished political scientist and anthropologist James C. Scott, who has been increasingly influential in studies of the historical Jesus and popular movements of the time (Scott 1977; Horsley with Hanson 1985; Crossan 1991a). Given the opportunity, the Q Section focused a session on applying Scott's work to the social context and implications of Q, a session in which Oakman and his colleagues in social-scientific approaches participated actively. The revised papers from that session by Alan Kirk, Milton Moreland, and myself are supplemented in part two by an article written specially for this volume by Melanie Johnson-Debaufre, with William Herzog, one of the New Testament scholars most familiar with the work of Scott, responding to the papers. Scott's work also figures prominently in the approaches to Q as oral performance in Part One.

As background and context of the articles below it will help to be aware of several recent developments in analysis of Q, in scholarly research on the historical-cultural context of Gospel literature (especially on orality and literacy), and in the comparative investigations and theory of nonbiblical scholars such as James C. Scott.

The Form and the Social Location of Q

Several important developments in literary analysis of Q or in scholarly investigation of key aspects of the historical-social and cultural context of Q are leading to significant shifts and innovations in approach to Q and the people who produced it and heard it performed.

Q as a Series of Speeches, Not a Collection of Sayings

Q, the sequence of Jesus speeches paralleled in Matthew and Luke but not in Mark, has standardly been understood as a "collection of sayings," despite the fact that in both Matthew and Luke most of the sayings appear in clusters of sayings in the same order (Taylor). Discovery of the *Gospel of Thomas*, which is organized precisely as a collection of Jesus sayings, and which also displays a great number of parallels to sayings in Q, appeared to confirm this understanding of Q as a sayings collection. In a close analysis of the composition of Q John Kloppenborg concluded that Q took the form of clusters of sayings, that is, short discourses or speeches or *chreiai* (1987). Many interpreters of Q nevertheless persisted in treating the material as individual sayings. They continued to label Q as a collection of sayings or even as a "Sayings Gospel." The International Q Project constructed a "critical edition" saying by saying, without much attention to how a "cluster" of several sayings formed a discourse with an inherent structure. Even Kloppenborg's composition criticism began from a classification of individual sayings according to "sapiential" versus "apocalyptic." The elaborate hypothesis that Q was composed in layers, an original "sapiential" stratum to which was added a secondary "apocalyptic" or judgmental stratum, and so on, was constructed on the basis of this classification of individual sayings. This "stratigraphy" of Q, which figures prominently in recent North American discussion of Q, has not proven persuasive to European interpreters. Yet whether based on the hypothesis of different strata (American) or not (European), most discussions of themes or issues or "theology" in Q proceeded from analysis of individual sayings, not from analysis of clusters of sayings or discourses (even Kloppenborg Verbin 2000; Arnal).

Recognizing that most materials in Q take the form of shorter or longer "speeches" makes a considerable difference in how the materials are analyzed and interpreted. As in any verbal communication, the function and meaning of any particular component saying of a speech in Q depends on its literary context, both in that speech and in the sequence of speeches as a whole. Since Kloppenborg's pioneering "composition criticism," further analyses have confirmed and strengthened his conclusion that Q, as evident through its incorporation into Matthew and Luke, had the literary structure of a sequence of discourses or speeches by Jesus on a series of issues such as mission or prayer or woes against the Pharisees (Q 10:2–16; 11:2–4, 9–13; 11:39–52, respectively; Horsley 1991; Kirk; Horsley and Draper: 61–93). One could even say that a consensus might be forming in this respect (Robinson 2000:lxii–lxvi). The implication of the perception that Q consisted of a series of speeches, not a collection of sayings, is that those larger and smaller speeches (not individual sayings) were the units of communication, intelligibility, and meaning, indeed that those speeches must be understood in the context of the whole sequence of speeches. Adhering to this principle, most of the essays in this volume focus on particular discourses in Q, and not individual sayings, as the unit of communication and meaning.

Elite and Popular Culture

The second major consideration leading to the exploration of Q as oral performance and more precise investigation of the social context of Q is recent recognition of the difference between elite and popular culture. Not only was society in ancient Palestine and surrounding areas in the Roman Empire divided politically and economically between rulers and ruled, taxers and taxed. It was divided culturally as well between a scribal elite supported by the ruling families and the vast majority of people, the peasants (including fishing people and some non-farming craftspeople as well as free-holding and tenant agrarians living in village communities). The standard conceptual apparatus of New Testament studies has been dominated by synthetic essentialist modern scholarly categories, often in dichotomous pairs, such as "Jewish" versus "Hellenistic" or "Judaism" versus "Christianity" or "sapiential" versus "apocalyptic." These synthetic constructs have, in effect, blocked discernment of the differences between elite and popular culture and channeled investigations into theological issues and the emergence of one religion, Christianity, from another, Judaism. It was simply assumed that Q originated in (an essentialist) "Jewish" culture. Hence if a Q saying seemed different, then it must somehow have been against the standard Jewish cultural conventions, that is, "unconventional" or "counter-cultural" (Mack; Kloppenborg 1987).

The fields of New Testament studies and Jewish history, however, are beginning to recognize the difference, and indeed conflict, between the Herodian rulers, priestly aristocracy, and "leading Pharisees," on the one hand, and the Judean and Galilean people, on the other (as portrayed in the histories of Josephus). Such conflicts figure prominently in the histories of Josephus and other sources. Analysis of some of the popular movements that took action against the established order, moreover, indicated that they were fairly clearly informed by Israelite traditions of resistance to oppressive rulers (Horsley 1984, 1985). These movements suggested that there must have been competing versions of Israelite tradition, one version serving to authorize the established order, and the other serving to authorize resistance.

The early work of James C. Scott was instrumental in the framing and investigation of such issues well before implications were drawn for interpretation of Q. Besides having read widely in historical and ethnographic studies of various peasant societies, Scott had done extensive field work in Malaysian villages where peasants were struggling with the impact of outside forces on their traditional economy and culture. His programmatic early article, "Protest and Profanation: Agrarian Revolt and the Little Tradition" (1977), has important implications for how the Q discourses are understood in their broader historical context.

Robert Redfield and other anthropologists had established a basic distinction between the "great tradition" and the "little tradition" to distinguish the interrelated lines of culture carried by the urban elite and ordinary people in the countryside, respectively. Focusing on agrarian societies, Scott believes that "more or less in keeping with Redfield's concepts, we may define the little tradition as 'the distinctive patterns of belief and behavior which are valued by the peasantry of an agrarian society'; the great tradition is the corresponding patterns among the society's elite" (1977:8). The great tradition was sometimes and to a certain degree written, whereas the little tradition was almost always cultivated orally. Scott widened the focus from mainly religion, ritual, and myth to issues of economic organization and political authority and added the word "valued" since much peasant behavior may be coerced and not a normative aspect of peasants' own culture. Scott also found in the "little tradition" far more than simply "a parochial version of cosmopolitan forms and values."

There are differences between elite and popular culture even in modern society, with its highly effective integrative mechanisms in the mass media. Even more than in ancient societies, "in the absence of these integrative factors, the contours of non-elite beliefs are likely to diverge more strikingly from elite beliefs and the variety of beliefs *among* non-elites is also likely to be greater" (Scott 1977:7). Indeed, one can discern "what amounts to 'a shadow society'—a pattern of structural, stylistic, and normative opposition to the politico-religious tradition of the ruling elites" (4). "The material and symbolic hegemony normally exercised by ruling institutions does not preclude, but rather engenders, a set of contrary values which represent in their entirety a kind of 'shadow society'" (19). In some societies the folk culture functions, "both in form and content, as a symbolic criticism of elite values and beliefs.... Under certain circumstances... such forms of symbolic conflict may become manifest and amount to a political or religious mobilization of the little tradition" (12).

This distinction between the "little tradition" and the "great tradition" and its profound implications for study of Jesus and the Gospels in historical context have gradually worked their way into New Testament scholarship, even into interpretation of Q, mostly on the basis of Scott's programmatic comparative article. This basic distinction was helpful in explaining the popular Judean, Samaritan, and Galilean "messianic" and prophetic movements in late-second-temple times that appeared to be informed by Israelite traditions of popular kings such as Saul, David, and Jehu, and prophetic leaders such as Moses and Elijah (Horsley 1984, 1985). As Scott comments, "[T]he little tradition achieves historical visibility only at those moments when it becomes mobilized into dissident movements which pose a direct threat to ruling elites" (1977:240). The "little tradition" concept is implicit throughout my treatment of Jesus and the Jesus movement, and explicit at certain points (Horsley 1987: esp. ch. 5; and 1989: chs. 6–7). The distinction has since been used for popular movements and/or Jesus and Gospel materials by others such as Burton Mack (1988) and John Dominic Crossan (1991a). The distinction played an important role in my tentative explanation of Galilean culture that resulted from a regional history different from that of Jerusalem and Judea (Horsley 1995: esp. chs. 2, 6). I drew heavily on Scott's article in attempting to come to grips with the prominent appearance of Israelite traditions in Q discourses, particularly insofar as these traditions are clearly contested (Horsley and Draper: 99–122). And Kloppenborg Verbin offered a qualified acceptance of Scott's treatment of the "little tradition" for the interpretation of what he sees as the "main redaction of Q" (2000:206–8).

A survey of Israelite "little tradition" in Q informed by Scott's article is already available (in Horsley and Draper: 104–22), along with fuller explorations of Israelite popular tradition in many of the speeches of Q (Q 6:20–49; 7:18–35; 9:57–10:16; etc.; in Horsley and Draper: chs. 9–13). A few general observations may be appropriate in this introduction to the use of Scott's work on Q.

First, both in terms of their occurrence in several Q discourses and by comparison with biblical materials and contemporary Judean texts such as certain Dead Sea Scrolls, certain themes are strikingly prominent in Q, some previously given little attention in Q studies: renewal of Israel (Q 3:7–9, 16–17; 7:18–35; 9:57–10:16; 11:2–4; 22:28–30), covenant, covenant law, and covenant renewal (6:20–49; 11:2–4; 12:22–31; 16:16–18), and prophets and prophetic forms (3:7–9, 16–17; 7:18–35; 9:57–10:16; 11:39–52; 13:28–29, 34–35).

Second, by comparison and contrast with Judean texts produced by scribal circles, differences are apparent between Q's versions and uses of Israelite traditions and scribal texts' versions and uses, and those differences correlate with differences in social location.

Third, in the latter connection, it is evident that some of those cultural traditions operative both in Q and in contemporary scribal literature were of broader scope than the "verses" or "lines" that we usually consider (given the standard scholarly focus on individual "sayings")—for example, broader patterns of covenant (renewal), series of prophetic woes, and prophetic roles. For us to recognize such broader patterns may require a conscious effort to counteract the influence of modern print culture that resulted in the printing of individual "verses" of the scripture in separate sentences/paragraphs (as in the King James Bible; see Kelber 1994).

Fourth, differences between elite culture, as evident in certain scribal literature such as the Dead Sea Scrolls, and the popular culture that comes to articulation in Q (and Mark, etc.), may better account for distinctive expressions found in Q speeches more appropriately than standard older interpretative concepts such as the dichotomies between "Jewish" and "Christian" and "cultural/conventional" versus countercultural/unconventional."

Finally, recognition of the eclectic character of popular culture should make us cautious in our reception and analysis of Q materials; for what appear to us as eclectic elements that do not fit our conception of sayings or discourses may have been part of an eclectic popular culture, not the result of deliberate editing by an editor or redactor.

Literacy, Performance, and Composition

Questions about Literacy and the Case for Q as a Written Composition

Biblical studies developed as a field devoted to the interpretation of Scripture, that is, the sacred *written* texts of Judaism and Christianity. Just as "the Jews" had in ancient times been a "people of the book," so also "Christianity" quickly produced its own written texts. Biblical scholarship has simply proceeded on the assumption of general literacy and availability of written texts. It was even assumed that Jesus, who presumably spoke Aramaic, was fully literate (in Hebrew) and that he, like everyone else, had access to written texts of the Scripture. After all, according to Luke, when he entered the synagogue in Nazareth he was handed "the scroll of the prophet Isaiah," which he unrolled and "found the place where it was written..." (Luke 4:16–21). Similarly, it was assumed that the written text of Scripture was stable and that nascent Christian literature featured literate interpretation of "The Law and the Prophets."

An ever-widening stream of recent scholarship has been challenging such assumptions. During the 1980s scholarly investigations clearly demonstrated that literacy in the Roman Empire was limited to a small percentage of the population even in the cities, and was rare in the countryside. Written scrolls were extremely cumbersome to handle and read as well as extremely costly to possess. Scrolls were rare in Judea, confined mainly to the Temple and to scribal communities such as that at Qumran. Communication, including most transmission of culture, was predominantly oral, with literacy simply being unnecessary for most people (e.g., Harris; Niditch; Achtemeier; Botha 1992). Pioneering biblical scholars explored the features of Jesus-tradition, including Q materials, as oral performance (Kelber 1983) and detected traits of oral performance in the Gospel of Mark (Botha 1991; Dewey). An early issue of *Semeia* (vol. 5, 1976) was devoted to orality in the Bible, another (vol. 39, 1987) to orality and literacy mainly in the Gospels. The Bible in Ancient and Modern Media Group was formed in the SBL to further explore oral performance, and produced another issue of *Semeia* (vol. 65, 1994) with suggestive analysis of features of orality and the relation of orality and literacy in Jesus' teachings, the Gospels, and the letters of Paul. Many of these scholars mediated the burgeoning and increasingly sophisticated investigations of oral performance in other times and places and academic fields, including the developing theory of John Miles Foley (1991; 1995; 2002). Drawing on these investigations of literacy and orality and of texts in oral performance, Horsley and Draper explored how the speeches of Q can be appreciated as oral performance in their historical-social context.

Meanwhile, representatives of what had become the "mainline" North American interpretation of Q dominant in the Q Section of the SBL continued to argue that Q must be considered as a written composition. John Kloppenborg Verbin (2000) and his student William Arnal (2001), on the assumptions standard in biblical studies, reasserted that Q was composed in writing and that it can be analyzed according to criteria for authorship in literate culture. (They completed their books prior to the publication of Horsley and Draper.) Different from most previous studies, however, they were aware that in ancient Galilee, where they place Q and those who produced it, literacy was limited to a minority of people with at least some level of education and training. They therefore looked for appropriate candidates for the authorship of Q: people who were literate and educated yet who could have been attracted to Jesus and/or a Jesus movement in the villages of Galilee. Insofar as they represent the view most prominent in North American interpretation of Q, we should summarize Kloppenborg Verbin's and Arnal's hypothesis about the authorship of Q as a written composition in order to appreciate the view, assumptions, and approach to which the articles in Part One below attempt to provide alternatives.

In *Excavating Q* (2000), Kloppenborg Verbin repeats the hypothesis he had laid out a decade earlier (1991) about the authors who initially composed Q as a written document. That in turn built on his earlier argument that Q can be analytically separated into layers of different types of sayings (Kloppenborg 1987). This procedure depends heavily on the susceptibility of synoptic Gospel materials to literary analysis such that their (written) documentary sources can be isolated and reconstructed. Not only is Q reconstructed from parallel passages in Matthew and Luke, but Q itself is then separated into a literarily identifiable "formative layer" and literarily identifiable subsequent strata. The assumptions and criteria of modern literature and literary criticism are evident repeatedly in such analysis. Most important, of course, for the kind of control necessary to conduct all these analytical operations is that Q was definitely a written document that can be reconstructed with some confidence. An oral Q would be unstable, making such intricate surgeries risky if not impossible. Kloppenborg accordingly devoted a section of one chapter to establishing that Q was written, not oral (1987:42–51). Working from the less complicated understanding of oral tradition available earlier in the twentieth century, including the early work of Milman Parry on the formulaic diction of Homeric style (1930), he claimed that four types of evidence confirm Q as a written document: stronger verbal agreements between Matthew and Luke than could (supposedly) be explained from oral reproduction, the survival of peculiar formulations, significant agreements in order, and doublets reproduced by Matthew and Luke from Mark (clearly) and Q (apparently) that must come from written sources. (See further Draper's evaluation of these arguments below on the criteria of more recent comparative study and analysis of oral tradition and performance.)

Having secured Q as a document composed in writing, and after intricately sorting out the formative sapiential layer of Q, Kloppenborg then argued that it fits the broad general ancient Near Eastern genre of instruction. Since the instruction genre presupposes a fairly high level of educational sophistication, Kloppenborg looked for authorial candidates of a corresponding educational level for Q. Accordingly he found that the appearances of a peasant ethos in Q that others have detected are deceptive. The "wealth of agricultural imagery" in Q might suggest a peasant audience, but "the selection of a relatively learned and characteristically scribal genre" means that the document was written in a different social location (Kloppenborg 1991:85). Although "some of the contents of Q are not paralleled in near Eastern instructions," the sayings should be interpreted similar to the more reflective and theological sapiential piety of Prov 1:20–33 and Sir 51:23–30. The beatitudes (Q 6:20–22) present a "balanced and anaphoric synkrisis on the nature of true blessedness" (81). The composer of the following admonitions (Q 6:27–35) "has adopted a deliberative posture" (82). The saying in Q 12:2 suggests a "process of research and discovery" (83). Sapiential sayings such as Q 12:4–7; 12:22–31; 14:26–27; and 16:13 do not address people in concrete situations such as repression by the authorities or anxiety about economic subsistence, but rather "recommend a lifestyle that does not invest in the ordinary channels of personal security.... These are the views of intellectuals who utilize such idealizations [of poverty and detachment] as a counterbalance to what is perceived as a bankrupt or failing culture" (88). "The selection of a relatively learned and characteristically scribal genre by which to convey the sayings of Jesus does not accord well with a peasant setting" (85). The determination of genre in turn determines the social location of the framers of Q as literate and educated.

Kloppenborg thus looked for a "sufficient density of scribes" with some degree of education in and around Galilee where, by increasing consensus, Q is located. But since Q 10:21–24 and 11:39–52 are rather sharp in polemic against scribes and Pharisees, such elite scribal circles are excluded by Q itself. He looked rather in "the lower administrative sector of the cities and villages.... Villages in Galilee, the region of the Decapolis, Peraea and Ituraea all undoubtedly had administrative infrastructures which saw to the collection and disbursement of various revenues and to the administration of justice" (1991:85). Even "the villages of lower Galilee that depended on a polis . . . undoubtedly had a bureaucratic structure." Moreover, "the toparchic centers of Tiberias, Sepphoris, Tarichaeae, and probably Gabara would certainly have had a sufficient density of scribes and administrators." And the larger towns like Capernaum or Bethsaida had "commercial interests" that "would have supported a relatively substantial bureaucracy" (86). These "lower levels of the administrative and scribal classes" would have been the people with whom the Sayings Gospel struck a resonant note and who would have been capable of its composition in writing in the genre of instruction. "It is plain from Egyptian evidence that it is precisely within these sectors that the instructional genre was cultivated" (85).

Arnal further develops one of his teacher's arguments for the presence of such educated and literarily creative figures in Galilee. Villages and towns supposedly "required various officials [who] witnessed bills of sale, petitions, contracts, marriage agreements, wills, and so forth, as well as an apparatus for the administration of justice. Thus, in addition to local strong men and affluent families, a small class of literate administrators was essential... even prior to Roman-Herodian city building. Such a role was normally filled by the so-called village clerk, the *komogrammateus*" (151). Arnal cites evidence from papyri found in Egypt and "some indications" that such literate administrators were a feature of Palestinian village life (Josephus, *War* 1.479; *Ant.* 16.203). "As their title indicates, their primary task was writing: composing various official documents for those unable to write; forwarding petitions to appropriate officials; ensuring the execution of legal responsibilities; and serving as witnesses, middlemen, or accountants for persons with extensive business dealings" (151–52).

The Limits and Functions of Literacy

These arguments for lower administrators and "village scribes" as authorial candidates for Q as well as its pool of recruits, however, do not appear to be supported by the literary and inscriptional evidence adduced or by evidence for and analyses of political-economic patterns in Galilee. More comprehensive recent studies of the level and functions of literacy in Roman Palestine and the Roman Empire generally, moreover, make these arguments difficult to sustain.

Even prior to extensive recent studies of literacy in Roman Palestine, the argument for a "sufficient density" of lower-level administrators and scribes, hedged about as it is with caveats, appeared conjectural and based on questionable assertions (Horsley and Draper: 293–94). In the late antique epigraphic evidence cited from villages in Hauran and Trachonitis, the Greek terms used for village leaders parallel those used for Greek city officials. The duties and activities they carry out, however, parallel those of the leaders of village assemblies in rabbinic and other Jewish literature (Horsley 1995:227–33). In any case, inscriptions attesting a *protokometes* or multiple *dioiketai, pistoi, pronoetai, episkopoi,* or *oikonomoi* who attend to such tasks as the upkeep of the village water supply, as delegated by the village assembly, do not appear to provide evidence for scribes sufficiently educated that they could compose instructional literature. The inscription (Waddington 2143) indicating that a "community-minded pious high priest" named Alexander of 'Aqraba(n) apparently traveled with the imperial financial officer in western Hauran as his "interpreter" suggests that those village leaders did not constitute a "sophisticated rural administrative system" in late Roman times (vs. Macadam: 106–8; Kloppenborg 1991:85–86). The literary evidence for intellectuals adduced from Josephus's narratives of the great revolt in Galilee in 66–67 all pertains to Herodian officials (of Agrippa II) and other elite of Tiberias who stood in sharp conflict with both surrounding villagers and ordinary residents of the city. Evidence for lower-level administrators and scribes in Egypt indicates that, as often as not, their level of literacy was minimal, barely functional (see further below). In fact, there is to date no clear evidence for the existence of lower-level administrators located in Galilean villages. Nor was any evidence adduced (since none is yet available for Galilee) that the hypothesized lower-level administrators in the cities (Tiberius, Sepphoris, or Tarichaeae) were literate, much less capable of cultivating instructional wisdom.

Nor does the argument for "village scribes" and a local demand for written documents appear to be supported by historical evidence from antiquity. This argument leaves unaddressed the particular power-relations that developed in Galilee as the political circumstances changed in the early period of Roman rule. More important, recent studies of evidence for the level and function of literacy in Palestine, Egypt, and the Roman Empire in general do not support it.

Previous estimates of the extremely limited presence and function of literacy, documents, and scribes in Galilee (and Judea) based on broader studies of the Roman Empire generally (e.g., Horsley and Draper: ch. 6) have recently been confirmed by far more extensive and detailed investigations, particularly of evidence in rabbinic literature (see especially Hezser; and earlier Cotton; Satlow). In contrast with Egypt, precious few documents survive from ancient Palestine. The rabbis do make references to both documents and scribes. But it is clear that documents were optional and scribes were few and late, particularly in Galilean villages.

In cases of marriage contracts, testaments, and deathbed donations, only those with considerable property bothered with written documents (Hezser: 111–12, 297–99). The writing of marriage contracts was not the norm in the second century C.E. (Cotton 1998:178). Written marriage settlements may have been the invention of the rabbinic period (Satlow: 133ff.); a number of the rabbis were themselves possessed of considerable property. The Babatha letters found in the Judean wilderness attest the concerns of a local affluent and "materialistic, litigious coterie" (Lewis: 22–24) whose use of Greek reflected the snobbery of the local Jewish aristocracy (Goodman 1991:172). Transactions among ordinary villagers (the vast majority of people) concerning matters such as land, moveable property, loans, marriage, on the other hand, were apparently conducted mainly by oral declaration and/or ceremonial action involving oaths and witnesses, judging from references in both the Mishnah and the Talmud Yerushalmi (Hezser: 111–13). Ordinary people could not afford to hire scribes. Like everyone in antiquity, they placed more trust in the personal presence of living witnesses than in documents that could easily be forged, changed, destroyed, or lost (117). Moreover, since writing was often used by the wealthy as an instrument of power over them, in records of loans drawn up by the rich creditors, marginal peasants and artisans were understandably suspicious of written documents. One of the first acts of the Jerusalem crowd in the summer of 66 was to burn the archives, "to destroy the money-lenders' bonds and prevent the recovery of debts" (Josephus, *J.W.* 2.426–427).

In her search through the evidence, Hezser finds a general lack of scribes in small towns and villages (118–26). Tannaitic literature lacks references to scribes outside of Jerusalem. She concludes that they were rare in rural areas until the third century. Talmud Yerushalmi refers to what are apparently town-based scribes in the formulaic "X the scribe of Y" (e.g., in Magdala; Hezser: 123–24). The indications are, however, that they were trained only in the techniques of preparing writing materials and the formats and formulaic language of documents, and not the general education that might have prepared them for literary composition (124–25). The rare scribe who lived in a Galilean village in late antiquity could apparently copy but not compose.

The resulting picture of the limited function of literacy, documents, and local scribes in Galilee corresponds to what Harris and others found in the Roman Empire generally, what Thomas found earlier in Greece, and what Clanchy and others found later in medieval Europe. By the first century B.C.E. the Roman aristocracy had written contracts drawn up, particularly for large-scale loans and other transactions. Peasants and artisans, however, had little use for writing, conducting most of their dealings orally, face to face (Harris: 198–200). Little in Roman times had changed since classical Greece, where even most legal practice was conducted orally. While the wealthy had contracts written for large-scale loans and leases, sales and contacts among ordinary people were confirmed by live witnesses. Even receipts were still unknown (Thomas 1989:41–43; Harris: 68–72). Similarly in the Middle Ages, whereas the higher and lower nobility used documented transactions in writing, among the peasantry and artisans transactions were conducted by the transfer of symbolic objects and by oral agreements and personal statements, confirmed by oaths and witnesses (Clanchy: 232). As Greg Woolf concludes in his recent survey of literacy in the Roman Empire, "Where writing was used in the countryside ... it was the product of the power of the classical city and of the Roman empire over the rural hinterland. No separate rural writing practices can be attested for the early Roman Empire and writing always remained a component of either the urban or the military versions of Roman civilization" (2001:877).

Closer examination of evidence for local administrators such as "village scribes" in Egypt, finally, indicates that they would not have been capable of literary composition. Continuing analysis of the relatively abundant supply of papyri preserved in Egypt concludes not only that records survived better but also that writing was more prevalent and important in management of the economy there than elsewhere in the Roman Empire.[1] The Ptolemaic regime administered a census of all adults, a com-

---

1. While the use of writing in private economic and marriage transactions, for example, increased during the Ptolemaic and Roman times, it still did not dramatically exceed such usage elsewhere (e.g., Harris: 118, 203). As elsewhere, wealthy and high-ranking Greeks in Egypt used some documentation, while carrying out

plete land survey, and an inventory of seeds and crops (Thompson: 79). For such purposes they developed a new administrative class of scribes and bureaucrats with technical training including a complex vocabulary and syntax, a legal and bureaucratic jargon, unusual vocabulary, and abstract nouns, which served to complicate and even to mystify (Thompson: 77; Kelly: 174–75). The marked increase in the extent to which writing was used under the Romans focused also in the economic administration of the province (Hopkins: 1991). The documents include receipts for a variety of taxes and customs payments. The Romans ordered censuses carried out in all villages. Generally, large numbers of documents flowed up and down the administrative hierarchy from Alexandria to the nome offices to the village administrators (Woolf 2000:892).[2] "The very high degree of formulaic character found among declarations from a particular area and period would have been impossible without the dissemination of officially sanctioned standard forms, and it is unlikely that anyone except a professional would have had any means of learning these standard document types" (Bagnall and Frier: 18).

Evidence for *komogrammateis* in Egypt, however, suggests that their training fell considerably short of that necessary for such professionals. One of the papyri finds in Egypt provides a window onto the role and (lack of) abilities of the *komogrammateis* in Egypt, as analyzed by the papyrologist, Herbert Youtie (1971a; 1971b; 1975). It is common in Roman-period papyri from Egypt that a person who is minimally literate (a professional scribe, a secretary of a farmers' or artisans' guild, a clerk in a government office) writes on behalf of another who is *agrammatos* (unable to write Greek). In one such papyrus a certain Theon writes for his brother Petaus. But this is

---

most of their lives without "paperwork." Despite the bureaucratic environment in Egypt, ordinary Greeks and Egyptians, like their counterparts elsewhere in the Roman Empire, had little use for documents (Harris: 119, 200–201). And, as elsewhere, the wealthy and powerful used writing to take advantage of marginal peasants and artisans. The non-literate (at least in Greek) appear as lessees and borrowers in contracts that must have been written at the behest of the lessors and lenders (Youtie 1971a:173; his "middle class" categories are anachronistic).

2. The administration of large estates was closely related to the Ptolemaic and later Roman administration of the economy of Egypt as a whole. "Egyptian evidence leaves no doubt that written records were extensively used in the running of large estates" (Woolf 2002.883–84). The numerous papyrus documents pertaining to the high-ranking Ptolemaic administrator Apollonius and his agent Zeno, recording his own (private?) operation of vast estates as well as official matters, must be considered exceptional (Harris: 119). Similarly unusual, numerous documents survive from the administration of a third-century C.E. estate owned by Appianus, member of the council in Alexandria. A central office in the nome capital communicated primarily by letters with the local managers in more than thirty local village offices (Turner, E. G., 1978, "Writing Materials for Businessmen," *BASP* 15:163–69; Rathbone).

the same Petaus, son of Petaus, who from 184–87 C.E. was *komogrammateus* of a district consisting of at least five villages, including Ptolemais Hormu. As representative of the Roman government in Alexandria, Petaus had broad responsibilities for record-keeping in his district. But Petaus himself could not write. He could only sign his name to documents with difficulty by following a model—and in practicing his signature he often omitted a letter from the model (Youtie 1971a:172–73). Nor was Petaus alone among *komogrammateis* in being illiterate, as Youtie illustrates with other examples.[3] It seems clear from these cases that the *komogrammateis* in Egypt were the central government's appointees and representatives at the local level for the collection of taxes and management of the economy, but had little or no particular education for their responsibilities that would have enabled them to compose literature.

"Village scribes" seem even less likely as candidates for authorship of Q as written literature insofar as we have no evidence for *komogrammateis* in Galilee. Documents for the Ptolemaic administration of Palestine mention imperial officers such as *strategos* (military governors) and *oikonomos* (economic manager) and administrative or taxation units such as the *hyparchia* (Bagnall 1976:11–24). In some areas the Ptolemaic administration simply appointed local rulers or strongmen as tax-farmers to guarantee the state revenues. A decree of Ptolemy II (261 B.C.E.) requires parallel sets of declarations about taxes from the *komarchoi* and from the *memisthomenoi tas komas* (those buying the tax contracts for the villages). This indicates that the Ptolemaic administration imposed its own structure of royal officers to manage and enforce tax collection down to the village level, but did not tamper with the indigenous patterns in village communities. There is to date no evidence that suggests the presence of royal officers called *komogrammateis* in Galilee. Herod the Great and Antipas—and presumably the Hasmoneans before them, considering the cost of their wars of expansion—exploited the lands and people under their control to the maximum extent. But their limited territory hardly required the extensive administration necessary to exploit the Nile valley.

The only occurrence of the term *komogrammateis* in Judean sources comes in a caustic threat by two of Herod's younger sons that when they came to power they would make "village scribes" out of the sons born to

---

3. When a "village scribe" in a nearby village named Ischyrion was denounced to the chief financial officer of Egypt as burdened with debt (hence unable to meet the property requirement for the office) and illiterate to boot, Petaus defended him: after all, he had signed all the documents (i.e., he was really literate, at least in meeting the minimal requirement for a *komogrammateus*, i.e., signing his name). Similarly a certain Aurelius Isodorus, previously a *komarch*, had served for twenty years, several times as a collector of taxes and as a supervisor of the state granary—without ever having written a word (Youtie 1971a:172; 1971b:260).

Herod by his other wives, sarcastically referring to the elaborate Hellenistic-Roman education they had received (*War* 1.479; *Ant.* 16.203). We are left to speculate whether it was Herod's imperially educated younger sons or the Flavian client Josephus himself (or both) who had such knowledge of the administrative system used in the economic exploitation of the principal breadbasket of the empire. But these parallel passages in Josephus certainly do not supply evidence for the presence of *komogrammateis* in Galilee.

In the context of this volume it is not important to resolve the issue of whether Q was composed in writing. The essays in part I below focus rather on how we can imagine the oral performance of Q speeches, for even after an ancient text existed in writing, it was still recited orally to a group of people, as is increasingly being recognized. If we believe that Q was available to Matthew and Luke in written form, however, then someone with writing skills must have been involved at some point in its cultivation. And in that connection we might look to dissident scribes, former intellectual "retainers" who had joined the movement or communities of "Q people." There are several intriguing references to people who may well have been literate as involved in communities of Jesus followers at a relatively early date. The book of Acts touts not only that "a great many of the priests became obedient to the faith" (6:7), but also that when Paul and Barnabas went up to Jerusalem from Antioch less than two decades after the crucifixion, the Jerusalem community included "some believers who belonged to the faction of the Pharisees" (15:5). And the Gospel of Matthew makes reference to "every scribe w ho has been trained for the kingdom of heaven" as if there were several such intellectuals involved in the movement by around 80 or 90 C.E. (Matt 13:52). The role of such scribes in Matthew's reference, moreover, is to cultivate and interpret Jesus' teachings such as parables.

The Oral Performance of Texts

Recent studies in the limited extent and functions of literacy in Palestine, Egypt, and the Roman Empire generally, which call into question the likelihood of "village scribes" and the possibility of their written composition in the genre of instruction, lead to a far more serious question: that of the assumptions and procedures of modern biblical studies on texts such as Q. Recent wide-ranging comparative studies, in a variety of academic fields, of the interrelations of orality and literacy and of oral performance of texts (composition as well as recitation or "reading") in that context exacerbate such a basic question. Some key facets of the question have been explored in previous issues of *Semeia* and provide a convenient opening to further exploration.

Werner Kelber has been perhaps the most persistent voice insisting that biblical studies examine its basis in and commitments to the assumptions of typographic culture.

> Print is the medium in which modern biblical scholarship was born and raised, and from which it has acquired its formative methodological habits.... It is eminently reasonable ... to conduct the search for the historical Jesus, itself a product of logic's intellectual history, in keeping with the laws of logical consistency and by application of a logically-devised classificatory apparatus.... It makes sense in typographic culture to visualize texts as palimpsests, with layer superimposed upon layer, and stratum superseding stratum, building up to layered edifices.... (1994:140)

Many scholarly studies of Q—and not just the hypothesis of strata—illustrate Kelber's observations even better perhaps than the closely related approach to sources for the historical Jesus by Crossan and others in the Jesus Seminar.

> Ordering, the methodical arrangement of items, is a favorite child of logic. Confronted with a multiplicity and multiformity of phenomena, logic administers the implementation of organizing principles. Words are sequestered and regrouped by virtue of resemblances or successiveness. In order to be arranged systematically, items need first to be indexed. Words must, therefore, be categorized so as to be apportioned to divisions of classification. Stratification is one form of classification. (1994:144)

The fundamental question, however, says Kelber, is "whether Jesus and the early tradition that delivered him unto writing have played by our rules.... Were they committed, as we are, to the ethos of pure formality, compartmentalization of language, [and] stratigraphic causality?" (1994:145). And once we recognize that communication of all kinds was predominantly oral in antiquity, it seems clear by contrast that the way biblical studies reconstructs and construes texts "runs counter to speech, to interpersonal communication" (149). This has obvious implications for working on the further assumption at home in modern typographic culture of written composition of literature by individual intellectual authors (155).

Since in the ancient "biblical" world texts operated in a context of communication which was predominantly oral, it makes sense to examine the practices of "reading." To dramatize the stark contrast between ancient and medieval reading practices and the private silent reading assumed in modern Western (typographic) culture, Daniel Boyarin focuses attention on key biblical passages using the term qr', which is usually misleadingly translated "read."

> And he took the Book of the Covenant, and he qr' [proclaimed] it in the ears of the people, and they said, "All that the Lord has spoken, we will do and we will obey." (Exod 24:7)

> When all of Israel come to appear before the Lord ..., qr' [recite/proclaim] this Torah in the presence of all of Israel, in their ears ... in order that they hear and ... that they learn and they fear the Lord ... and perform all of the words of this Torah. (Deut 31:11)

And you shall come and *qr'* [recite/proclaim] the scroll [of the prophetic oracles of Jeremiah] which you have written in accord with my dictation. (Jer 36:3).

In every example the usage of *qr'* indicates "an act of the speaking that is virtually identical to that when there is no written text present," says Boyarin (13). Moreover, "all of these acts of speaking (*qr'*) are immediately followed by the desired or actual result of the performance of the speech act in the performance of the listener." Such recitation or proclamation, as that of the Torah, functions as the speech-act whose intended perlocutionary effect is obedience—as opposed, for example, to an illocutionary act of exhortation whose intended effect would be persuasion (15). As indicated further on in the story of Baruch, moreover, the term *qr'* can cover what we would call dictation from memory or a process of oral-performative recomposition as well as an act of proclaiming unrelated to any written text.

Furthermore, as Baruch explains to his audience, "He [Jeremiah] called out" (*qara'*) all of the words, and I wrote them on this scroll" (Jer 36:16–18; Boyarin: 15). What Baruch recited/proclaimed (*qr'*) before the king and his court was what Jeremiah had dictated (*qara'*) from memory for him to write down on the scroll. As Boyarin suggests, it is not that much of a jump from the communication between Jeremiah and Baruch and the royal audience in Jerusalem to later rabbinic and synagogue "reading" of the text of the Torah, in which a clear distinction was made between "the written" and "the read" (17). As William Scott Green explains (14–15), "The writing of the *sefer Torah* was mute. . . . Scripture" was conceived by rabbinic culture as "a holy object, a thing to be venerated, . . . with its holy and allegedly unchanged and changeless writing. . . . Because it had no vowels, and hence contained no discourse, in another way the Torah-writing was also meaning-less—evocative but profoundly inarticulate. . . . To transform that script into a text, to make it readable, necessarily meant imposing a determinate discourse on it." The tradition of *qere'* ("what is read"), including the essential vowels, accents, stresses, and pauses, along with euphemisms and the customary melody in which the text was chanted, which were not properties of the script, was different from *ketiv* ("what is written"; b. Berakhot 62a; Megillah 32a). In rabbinic circles "reading the *sefer Torah* was less a matter of deciphering an inscription than of reciting a previously known discourse and applying it to the writing" (Green: 14–15).

Martin Jaffee has generalized from such oral recitation of Torah in rabbinic circles and synagogues to the relation of written texts and oral recitation/performance generally. Fully aware of how cumbersome and costly scrolls were in antiquity, as emphasized by studies of ancient literacy, he points out that "a scroll was virtually useless as a handy source of information." But that was no obstacle since the text that was inscribed on the scroll "was as much a fact of their memory as it was a physical object. . . . 'reading' was the activity of declaiming a text before an audience in a social performance approaching the gravity of ceremonial ritual" (Jaffee 2001:16). The text was accessed through memory, not by consulting a written copy (Jaffee 1998:53). A telling illustration of his point is the procedure for a meeting of ten "recorded" in the "Community Rule" handbook from Qumran:

> And the congregation shall watch in community for a third of every night of the year, to recite the book (*sepher*) and to search the ruling (*mishpat*) and to bless in common. (1QS 6:6–8, my translation)

Assuming that "the book" refers to the Torah and "the ruling" to the community's own ordinances, the Qumranites were regularly engaging in ritual oral recitation of both scripture and their own legal rulings that were also inscribed on scrolls possessed by the community (as in 1QS itself). (The standard translations of "read the Book" and "study the Law" are potentially misleading, insofar as those terms have distinctive connotations in modern typographic culture, particularly in academic circles.) Thus it was standard practice even in literate scribal circles that possessed written scrolls for texts to be recited orally from memory.

Composition, Oral Performance, and Writing

While the articles in Part One below do not focus on whether Q was composed in writing, the recent research into orality-literacy and oral performance of texts just summarized does have implications for how we imagine composition of texts such as Q. The relationship between texts available in memory (and, in certain circumstances, also in written form) and their recitation before an assembled group suggests that the relation between the composition and the writing of texts may be different from what is assumed in modern print culture—and, as Kelber points out, what is standardly projected onto ancient texts by biblical and other scholars. As we are learning from recent studies of ancient Greek, Roman, and Jewish antiquity and the testimonies of ancient writers themselves, not only was the "reading" of texts carried out orally, but composition of texts was closely related to their recitation. Jocelyn Penny Small has pulled together an abundance of evidence regarding the remarkable mnemonic techniques developed by ancient intellectuals to store vast amounts of material in memory. She also cites many telling passages in which writers reflect on their own compositional practices. Even highly discursive texts were worked out in the writer's head prior to dictation to a scribe. Pliny the Elder offers a relatively full account of his own practice of composition:

> [When I wake] If I have anything on hand I work it out in my head, choosing and correcting the wording, and the amount I achieve depends on the ease or difficulty with which my thoughts can be marshaled and kept in my head. Then I call my secretary, the shutters are opened, and I dictate what I have put into shape; he goes out, is recalled, and again

dismissed. Three or four hours after I first wake I betake myself according to the weather either to the terrace or the covered arcade, work out the rest of my subject, and dictate it. (*Letters* 9.36).

As Small comments, "Incidentally, the English word 'dictate' and its relatives go directly back to the Latin '*dicto*' which meant either our 'dictate' or—and this is significant—'compose', because the common way of composing something was through dictation. In the Middle Ages the meaning 'compose' was the more common usage" (Small: 185).

To illustrate from ancient Greek and Latin composition closer to the speeches that comprise Q, orators composed their speeches, in general structure and words, relying on the resourcefulness of memory, and "without any recourse to writing," as Quintilian explains (10.6.1; Small: 182). For exhortative and prophetic material such as the speeches in Q the case of Jeremiah may be particularly suggestive. First, he dictated all the oracles that Yahweh had spoken to him for over a decade to Baruch, who wrote on the scroll and then proclaimed the oracles to the audience in the Lord's house. Then, when the outraged king burned the scroll, Jeremiah again recited all those oracles/speeches while Baruch wrote them on another scroll (Jer 36:2–6, 16–18, 21–26, 32). That is, Jeremiah retained in memory all the speeches God had spoken to him and could recite them together. Prophets and disciples of prophets would have continued such abilities and practices. The prophetic spokespersons who continued the prophetic speeches of Jesus appear to stand in just such a tradition, as suggested at points in Q speeches themselves (Q 6:20–26; 7:18–35; 11:39–52; 13:34–35). Thus even if we continue to imagine that the Q speeches evident in parallel passages in Matthew and Luke were in some way composed in writing, it is necessary to work toward a sensitivity and an approach that enables us to appreciate how their composition was embedded in oral communication, emerged from periodic oral performance, and "worked" in oral performance.

Assessment of Our Sources and Their Circumstances: Hidden Transcripts?

As long as Q was understood in terms of individual sayings carried by itinerant radicals who had abandoned normal social life to pursue a "counter-cultural" lifestyle, the ways in which it arose from and addressed people embedded in ongoing political-economic-religious life was not an issue. Somewhat of a consensus is emerging recently, however, at least among North American interpreters, that Q arose from and was addressed to a movement in Galilee in mid–first century C.E. (Arnal, Horsley, and Draper, Kloppenborg 2000). Further critical analysis of the interrelation of Q and its political-economic circumstances, drawing on a wide range of comparative and theoretical studies along with all available textual and material evidence, is of crucial importance for fuller appreciation of the message it delivers.

In this connection the work of James C. Scott offers considerable stimulation and assistance to interpreters of Q. Scott's first book, *The Moral Economy of the Peasant* (1976), presents highly suggestive comparative material and a theoretical framework for understanding Q discourses in the inseparably political-economic and cultural-moral dynamics of peasantries subject to the disintegrative impact of outside forces. His second major book, *Weapons of the Weak: Everyday Forms of Peasant Resistance* (1985), pioneers exploration of the more subtle and hidden ways in which peasants resist the various forms of domination that their landlords and rulers impose. Two of the essays in part two below (Horsley and Moreland) offer a summary of Scott's reflections on the "moral economy" of various peasantries and an application in analysis of Q materials.

Of considerable general importance in the way we assess and use our sources in historical reconstruction and textual interpretation—including the social location and social stance of Q itself—is Scott's *Domination and the Arts of Resistance: Hidden Transcripts* (1990), in which many of the implications of his earlier research and reflection come together. In this book Scott lays out a probing analysis of communication amid the structural conflict characteristic of power relations in which "those subject to elaborate and systematic forms of social subordination" (the worker to the boss, the serf to the lord, the slave to the master, etc.) are forced into a public performance of subordination (e.g., out of fear, prudence, the desire to curry favor, etc.). The "open interaction between subordinates and those who dominate" he labeled the "public transcript" (2). The latter, however, tells only part of the story of such power relations. For "every subordinate group creates, out of its ordeal, a 'hidden transcript' that represents a critique of power spoken behind the back of the dominant," usually in sequestered sites (xii). Behind a few anti-elite actions lies "a far more elaborate hidden transcript, an entire discourse, linked to ... culture, religion, and the experience of colonial rule" (15). "The powerful, for their part, also develop a hidden transcript representing the practices and claims of their rule that cannot be openly avowed" (xii). Moreover, "the frontier between the public and the hidden transcripts is a zone of constant struggle between the dominant and the subordinate" (14). Scott's purpose was to explore how we can "study power relations when the powerless are often obliged to adopt a strategic pose in the presence of the powerful and when the powerful may have an interest in overdramatizing their reputation and mastery" (xii).

As should be immediately evident, recognition of the existence of these "hidden transcripts" creates serious problems for historians and interpreters of literature. Most ancient literature, which comprises the bulk of our historical sources, derives from and articulates the public transcript. But "the public transcript, where it is not positively misleading, is unlikely to tell the whole story about power relations. It is frequently in the interest of both parties to tacitly conspire in misrepresentation" (2). Reliance mainly or exclusively on the public transcript in scholarly studies of the subordinate and their resistance is particularly problematic, for the public transcript is "systematically skewed" in the direction of the discourse of the dominant. "History and social science, because they are written by an intelligentsia using written records . . . are simply not well equipped to uncover the silent and anonymous forms of class struggle that typify the peasantry" (1985:36–37). Scott suggests that "a comparison of the hidden transcript of the weak with that of the powerful and of both hidden transcripts to the public transcript of power relations offers a substantially new way of understanding resistance to domination" (1990:xii, 15).

If only we had access to the hidden transcript of the subordinated! The subordinated almost never leave records, since generally they have been illiterate. Not surprisingly, Scott must depend heavily on American slave narratives, other oral history, and the literary characters rooted in modern novelists' astute observations of power relations. Scott's further analysis, however, may be particularly useful to biblical scholars—and in potential repayment of the debt, certain "overwritten" biblical materials may be of interest to Scott. Hidden transcripts must of necessity be cultivated in safe sites such as the slave house or the peasant village. Scott suggests that these carefully cultivated hidden transcripts provide the basis of the ability of subordinated peoples to endure, to engage fairly regularly in hidden forms of resistance, and, on rare occasions, to mount organized collective forms of resistance and even revolts. Of particular interest are those rare occasions in which a spokesperson for the subordinate "breaches" the divide, declaring in public the true views—and powerful resentment—of the subordinate, which typically leads to swift repression and/or further words and acts of resistance.

This rupture of the political *cordon sanitaire*, making public the previously hidden transcript of the subordinate, may be particularly interesting to students of Jesus and the Gospels. In New Testament studies we tend to deal with texts as texts, with at most minor distinctions between literature from the scribal elite, such as Ben Sira or the rabbis, and literature that derives from lower on the social scale, such as Mark or Q. And we treat our texts as if they were, in Scott's terms, all part of the "public transcript." But once we read Scott, it is difficult to classify Mark's narrative or the Q discourses as "public transcript," since even "Jesus'" prophetic statements against the Pharisees or the Jerusalem ruling house are really addressed to the "in-group" of the movement. Yet Q is not simply a "hidden transcript" of Galilean villagers. Insofar as a new movement has arisen, something that goes beyond life as usual in the sequestered site of the hidden transcript has happened. Q represents "Jesus" as having boldly declared the hidden transcript in the face of the power holders, in pronouncing woes against the Pharisees and prophetic condemnation of the Jerusalem rulers (see also Herzog 2004; Horsley 2004a; 2004b; 2005).

Older studies of politics in general and of Jesus and his movement(s) in particular were focused on what were probably command performances of acquiescence in the face of power, on the one hand, or on open rebellion against it, on the other. Such studies are too limited, and inadequate to unrecorded realities. Instead, Q—if it is no longer simply taken as a collection of Jesus' sayings carried by a few countercultural itinerants—can be viewed as representing and reflecting a no-longer-so-hidden mobilization of the subordinate into a village-based movement on the basis of the hidden transcript long cultivated in the Galilean villages. In Scott's terms, moreover, Q represents relatively more "cooked" rather than "raw" forms of the (ostensible) bold declaration of the hidden transcript in the public arena. "Cooked declarations are likely to be nuanced and elaborate because they arise under circumstances of offstage freedom among subordinate groups, allowing them to share a rich and deep hidden transcript" (216–17). Such, apparently, were the circumstances in Galilee where Q materials developed.

Many of Scott's observations about how the hidden transcript is cultivated in safe sites such as peasant villages can illuminate how the Jesus movement connected with Q could arise and spread in precisely such places, away from the direct surveillance of rulers and their representatives (assuming we do not take Mark's pronouncement stories involving the Pharisees' surveillance at face value!). If we are to pursue the potentially illuminating implications of Scott's insights regarding hidden and official transcripts, however, then we may need to make adjustments in our overall approach to Q and other Gospel materials. Recent scholarship on Q has sought to control the document with ever more sophisticated and finely grained analysis of genre, rhetorical forms (following Hellenistic-Roman models), literary development, redaction, and compositional criticism. Work such as Scott's pushes us, if anything, to "loosen up" in order to appreciate the integral relationship between particular cultural expressions such as Q discourses and the social forms and power relations that they presuppose, the better to investigate how those discourses arise from and address people in particular historical circumstances.

Part One

Oral Performance and Popular Tradition in Q

Essays

The Verbal Art in Q and *Thomas*
A QUESTION OF EPISTEMOLOGY

Werner H. Kelber

Texts may hypnotize us into thinking that the oral poetry they encode is static, but it isn't. (John M. Foley)

With respect to documents . . . as those of Q and the Gospel of Thomas, it is misleading to classify both under the rubric of logoi sophon. *Indeed . . . that rubric is appropriate to neither.* (Richard A. Horsley)

Q lässt sich nicht auf eine Spruchsammlung reduzieren, ebensowenig wie sich mehrere Schichten dieses hypothetischen Dokumentes nachweisen lassen. (Jens Schröter)

Many and manifold are the reasons for the steadily intensifying critical efforts devoted to Q in twentieth-century biblical scholarship. One factor undoubtedly was the identification of a linguistically and thematically independent profile of Q which was demonstrated shortly after the turn of the century by Adolf v. Harnack ([1907] 1908). But Harnack was ahead of his time. Subsequent New Testament scholarship was slow in confirming the principal correctness of Harnack's insight. Contributing toward an appreciation of his study on Q was the scholarly determination, characteristic of the historical, critical approach to the Bible, to cross canonical boundaries and to comprehend and reconstruct Christian origins with a sense of historical inclusiveness. As scholars came to encounter plural Christian genres, manifestations, life styles and experiences, and to cultivate sensitivities toward them, the existence of Q as a document of intrinsic hermeneutical and religious integrity increasingly appeared to be a plausible proposition.

Yet another reason for the revival of Q studies was the prospect it seemed to hold for a retrieval of the message of the historical Jesus. The gradual delineation of the linguistic and religious profile of Q furnished a major inducement for one of New Testament scholarship's principal projects: the search for the Jesus of history. Widely perceived to be an ancient

25

sayings collection, Q seemed eminently serviceable for a retrieval of "authentic" Jesus materials. The project of focusing on Q as source for Jesus' historical message seemed all the more tempting as twentieth-century gospel research increasingly problematized the historicity of the Jesus portrayed in Mark and the other narrative Gospels. There was, therefore, an inclination to refocus the search for the historical Jesus from the Gospels to Q (Robinson 2000:lxvi–lxviii).

Perhaps the major incentive to renewed explorations of Q was the discovery of the Nag Hammadi documents in 1945, and among them especially the so-called *Gospel of Thomas* (GT). The latter, a collection of Jesus sayings, seemed to represent a genre not unlike what Q had been imagined to be. Now even those scholars who had expressed doubts about the admittedly hypothetical nature of Q had to concede that the case of Q had received a strong endorsement, albeit from entirely unexpected quarters. Indeed, not only was the case for Q substantially strengthened, but Q scholarship was channeled into new directions. Thus, far more was happening than a revitalization of Q and Q research. With the *Gospel of Thomas* (GT) as a critical point of orientation, a new range of perspectives was opening up to scholars. Comparisons between Q and GT, detailing similarities and dissimilarities, were an obvious option that was pursued in the hope of obtaining a more accurate sense of the generic identity of the two. Comparative work of this kind suggested to some scholars the possibility of tracing a path back to a primitive sayings precursor antedating both Q and the GT. Others used GT in conjunction with Q to postulate an early bifurcation in the Christian tradition, inclining in Q's case toward an apocalypticizing direction, and in GT's case toward a gnosticizing one. In short, scholarship of this kind was working toward a new paradigm of Christian origins, and Q and Thomas were playing a major role in it.

The Form-, Source-, and Genre-Critical Approach to Q

From the perspective of the history of scholarship, the prime period of twentieth-century Q research coincided with the rise and flourishing of form and source criticism. And it is the methods and assumptions of these two approaches that have decisively shaped Q scholarship. Fundamental to form and source critical approaches to Q is the focus on isolated sayings, sources and layers. The arrival of GT and an energetic scholarly activity evaluating GT's sayings in light of Q, and vice versa, further compounded fixation on single sayings units. The best known modern example of illuminating Q in terms of sources and layers is Kloppenborg's stratigraphic model which divides Q into an early compositional layer of sapiential speeches and a chronologically secondary layer of apocalyptically inclined announcements of judgment (1987). In sum, what gave life to Q research, and what dictated many of its results, was the fourfold canon of form critical maxims: (*a*) Q is divisible into small, discrete units; (*b*) these units had a life prior to their integration into final Q; (c) they are usable for a reconstruction of the compositional history of Q; and (d) Q's history of the tradition serves as principal explanatory vehicle for an understanding of final Q.

It is reasonable to argue that Q research, focused as it was, and is, on Q's component parts and their pre-Q history, has deprived us of an understanding of the form and function of Q in its full and final integrity. But proponents and practitioners of form and source criticism by and large might well register their disagreement. From their perspective, the history of the tradition is both assumed to be retrievable and, crucially important, a key to comprehending the final product of the text. To no small degree, therefore, reconstruction of Q's composition history is designed to make sense of its final form. And yet, it is precisely over the issue of the retrievability of tradition and its role in understanding Q that form criticism has stumbled. These are propositions, quintessential to form and source criticism, that are now open to questioning, and their critical appraisal is bound to problematize vital parts of Q research.

By way of analogy, students of Q will do well to contemplate recent developments in gospel studies. Beginning in the 1960s and originating primarily in the U.S., scholars set about uncovering a forgotten dimension of the Gospels, namely their literary, narratological profile. At this stage, it is clearly verifiable that all four canonical gospels are governed by distinct narrative points of view, and that rhetorical, thematic and literary devices shaped them into narrative plots. Best known among those devices are particular arrangements of episodes, distinct plot causalities, the casting and typecasting of characters, framing devices of various kinds, multiple uses of repetition and duality, ring compositions and intercalations, strategies of misunderstanding and role reversal, pointedly executed polemics, topological and geographical configurations, and many more. The incontestable lesson we have learned is that each gospel is the result of compositional strategies aimed at a distinctly focused rhetorical outreach.

The implications these findings have for historical, form and source criticism are consequential and as yet by no means sufficiently evaluated. But one of the most significant conclusions to be drawn from the discovery of the literarily plotted gospels is that the final stage of gospel constructions is energized and designed by clearly discernible features of compositional activity. If this is conceded, the intelligibility of the gospel narratives can no longer predominantly be derived from sources, component parts or layers that are assumed to constitute their compositional history. If the Gospels are not merely the product of traditional forces, but in the end the outcome of a selective bundling of tradition into new configurations, it is imperative to pay singular attention to the texts in their present form. This is not denying that the gospels represent literary compositions with deep and tangled diachronic roots in oral and written traditions. But the point the narratological explication of the gospels is making is that there are overarching plot constructions, numerous subplots, thematically inspired figurations and compositional arrangements of various kinds that effect a reconfiguring of the traditional legacy.

If we take the final literary gospel form seriously, we will be compelled to take yet another, crucial hermeneutical step. Not only will our interpretive focus rest on the text in its present form, but the plotted nature of this final text demands that we abstain—at least for the time being—from assumptions regarding antecedent sources, stages or layers before and until we have comprehended the present text's narrative construction. In sum, gospel studies ought to emancipate themselves from the hegemony of form criticism which in its preoccupation with the gospels' component parts and their assumed pre-gospel history, had at best belittled, and at worst denied the narratological integrity of the gospels.

Now if Q exhibits a thematically coherent profile, as is almost universally acknowledged, ought one not to ask whether Q studies, in analogy to gospel studies, should likewise seek to come to terms with the final form of this document before and until consideration is given to individual component parts and their presumed compositional history. This is precisely what Schröter in his magisterial study on Mark, Q and Thomas has suggested. What has proven correct with regard to Mark, he proposes, is analogously valid for Q, "dass nämlich die Konzeption einer Schrift zunächst einmal aus deren Endgestalt heraus zu erheben ist, bevor Aussagen bezüglich früherer Stadien einzelner Texte oder gar der gesamten Schrift getroffen werden können" (1997:103). The partitioning of Q into sources and layers obstructs our vision of its genre and thematic coherence.

The work of Koester provides a notable lesson of the epistemological consequences flowing from a single-minded application of form and source criticism to both gospel and Q. His influential contributions both to the canonical and to the apocryphal gospels were first and foremost intended "to yield insights into the earliest stages of the development of the gospel tradition" (1990b:xxxi). From his perspective, form and source criticism constitute the appropriate scholarly approach to an understanding of the gospels. So confident was he of the priority, indeed superiority, of the historical, compositional analysis of the gospels that as late as 1990 he took issue with those who pursued the literary, narratological course, relegating their contributions to second place at best: "I wish that those who want to discuss the historical Jesus and the literary dimension of gospel writing would pay more attention to the transmission of traditions about Jesus and to the process of the collection of materials in ancient books" (1990b: xxxii). Accordingly, the history of the tradition constitutes the royal route to grasping the literary dimension of the gospels.

Characteristically, Koester's form and source critical work is grounded in a dual conviction. One, existing gospel texts yield traditional materials which were determinative in shaping the final textual configuration. To understand a gospel therefore requires knowing its compositional history. Two, because the truly generative work is presumed to have taken place in tradition, the final gospel text cannot be assumed to be a productive composition in the sense literary criticism has postulated. "Mark is primarily a faithful collector," Koester stated in his impressive study on *Ancient Christian Gospels* (1990b:289). It is fair to say that the results that have been forthcoming for about half a century from literary, narratological studies of the gospels emphatically challenge this assessment. The price one pays for a single-minded application of form and source criticism is thus a very steep one.

Very similar form and source critical convictions have guided Koester's equally influential work on Q. In his latest, most comprehensive study on this subject, the methodological focus is once again predominantly on composition and redaction (1990b). To be sure, he did aim at the overall purpose of Q, identifying seven clusters of sayings, ranging from "John the Baptist and the Temptation of Jesus" to "The Coming of the Son of Man." But the explication of these clusters is contingent on an analysis of individual "sayings belonging to the original document and materials added by the redactor" (135). The analysis of the sayings and their assignment to different compositional layers is executed largely by a comparison with sayings in Thomas, John, Paul, Didache, the First Epistle to Clement, and other documents. Additionally, wisdom, eschatology and apocalypticism, designations that have been current in Q research for some time, serve as criteria that help define and differentiate "the original version of Q" (150) and subsequent redactional revisions.

In part based on his own research and in part on Kloppenborg's work, Koester operated on the assumption that it was possible to move via a series of inferences backwards from the hypothetical text of Q through compositional processes to the chronological *arche* of "the original document" (Koester 1971a, 1971b, 1990b; Kloppenborg 1987). Along with many Q scholars, he employed form and source criticism not merely in the interest of analyzing isolated sayings and clusters of sayings, but also from text-driven assumptions with a view toward constructing a stemma model that postulates Q's genealogical history. But is the stemma model appropriate to an understanding of Q, or, for that matter, of the gospels? How useful is the genealogical history of a text for comprehending its function, purpose and meaning? Can one say we understand a text if we unravel the prior meaning of its constituent parts and antecedent sources or layers? How much does Q's presumed diachronic history tell us about this document's synchronic unity and outreach? These are questions that go far beyond method and model. Both in theory and in practice, the stemma model and its reliance on form and source criticism raises deep epistemological questions. How do we understand Q and the gospels? How do we know?

There was one facet of Q research that did address the final identity of Q in a way quite different from form and source criticism. It was genre criticism or *Gattungsgeschichte* which made the generic profile of Q its principal focus of scholarly attention. In the history of Q research genre criticism was coordinated with the trajectory approach initiated by Robinson and Koester (1971), and jointly these two approaches produced results that have constructed the conceptual framework within which many scholars have chosen to locate Q to this day.

The modern breakthrough for the genre critical study of Q came with Robinson's essay "*Logoi Sophon*: On the Gattung of Q" (1971). In Q research it is frequently referred to as a seminal essay. Indeed, few essays in twentieth-century New Testament scholarship, have proven as influential, especially in the United States, as "Logoi Sophon." Its significance, one should add, extends beyond Q studies into other principal areas of New Testament studies. It is one of those contributions whose impact on the discipline can hardly be overstated.

Taking up a number of hints by Bultmann concerning affinities between wisdom and Jesus sayings, and also between sayings and the designation of "Jesus as Teacher of Wisdom," Robinson proceeded to trace *logoi/logia* and sayings collections through a vast span of history, ranging from Jewish wisdom to Hellenistic gnosticism. The documents he presented as evidence for this sayings trajectory are numerous and varied, including the book of Proverbs, early Christian sayings collections, the *Gospel of Thomas*, Thomas the Contender, Pistis Sophia, the Didache, the Testament of the Twelve Patriarchs, Pirke Aboth, and others. While conceding that "designations for gattungen are less precisely and consistently used as technical terms in the sources themselves than in modern scholarship" (1971:111), Robinson nonetheless postulated the existence of a cross-cultural genre or Gattung which he called *logoi sophon* (sayings of the sages, or words of the wise). Both Thomas and Q are comprehensible by their location on this sayings trajectory. "The Gospel of Thomas indicates the gnosticizing distortion of sayings that took place readily within this gattung" (113), showing "the way in which the Sophia tradition used in Q ends in Gnosticism" (104). Both Q and GT are thereby defined as belonging to the genre of *logoi sophon*, or collection of wisdom sayings.

Robinson's formal designation of the generic concept of *logoi sophon* and its application to Q and GT had far-reaching consequences. It has given us, especially in the United States, directives on how to approach and think of Q. It has reinforced the form critical focus on the *logoi*, the smallest units of the tradition, confirming habitual thinking that in the beginning was the individual, isolated saying. It helped shore up the theoretical base for the premise regarding Q's stratification and the relegation of wisdom to the oldest stratum thereof. Last but not least, Q's genre identification lent further support to speculations about Jesus as teacher of wisdom.

It is, of course, theoretically conceivable that Q and GT represent two manifestations of a distinct genre whose progressive development is traceable over the span of centuries. But theoretical considerations aside, there are some deeply disquieting aspects about the execution of Robinson's thesis. Schröter and Horsley (1991; Horsley and Draper: 75–82) in particular, but also Tuckett and others, have subjected *logoi sophon* to scrutiny, and their cumulative criticism has disclosed rather serious defects. Briefly, we enumerate five major objections. One, the documents Robinson has summoned as evidence for his *logoi sophon* thesis belong to a great variety of texts, linguistic forms and social functions. Their disparate nature makes the reduction to a single genre problematic. Two, both within and without the Christian tradition, *logoi* is not confined to wisdom sayings, but representative of a broadly inclusive range of sayings materials. Whether under such circumstances *logoi* can serve as a genre designation at all is truly questionable. Third, by no means do all the documents cited carry the designation *logoi*, and only one (Prov 22:17–24:22) is named *logoi sophon*. From this perspective, the crucial affiliation of *logoi* with *sophon* remains inexplicable, and the generic postulation of *logoi sophon* unverifiable. Four, in form, function and social impact, Q and Thomas are so different as to disallow identification with a single genre. Indeed, the premise of *logoi sophon* has been a major force in obstructing recognition of the different identities and functions of these two texts. (Schröter 1997:93–98, passim; Horsley and Draper: 75–82, passim; Tuckett, 1996:337–54, passim). To these four objections we add a fifth one. Robinson's thesis concerning the *logoi sophon* genre of Q has entered the discipline in a programmatic essay that—in spite of its subtitle—has next to nothing to say about Q itself. Surely, any genre designation of Q must remain unconvincing unless it is demonstrated by intense analysis of the present text of Q. In sum, if a credible existence cannot be ascribed to a genre of *logoi* any more than to a genre of *logoi sophon*, and if Q and Thomas will not allow themselves to be reduced to a single genre, then Robinson's thesis seems flawed beyond repair.

An Integrative Approach to Q

The deficiencies we have observed with regard to both the form/source critical and the genre critical approach make it imperative that new ways be found to come to an understanding of Q that matches more closely the historical, thematic and linguistic realities of the document as we have it (reconstructed). It is the preeminent virtue of Horsley (and Jonathan Draper) to have placed Q research onto a new plane, and to have done so in recognition of some of the major deficits of Q studies and by giving careful attention to the text in its present, undivided form. *Whoever Hears You Hears Me* (1999) is the product of a multilateral study integrating historical, sociological, theological, linguistic, and orality-literacy studies into a model of considerable explanatory persuasiveness. It may be said that at this point in Q scholarship a dynamic interfacing of multiple disciplinary perspectives holds greater promise than any single-minded pursuit, however rigorously executed. In its integrative approach, this book makes important contributions to our understanding of the historical context, the linguistic form, the principal message, and the performative character of Q.

Postulating an indebtedness of principal aspects of Q studies to the conceptual legacy of anachronistically academic and theological premises, Horsley made a special effort to return Q to its historical matrix. To understand Q we need to understand its historical context. To that end, the work took advantage of a series of historical and sociological studies on Israel in late antiquity while paying special attention to the decades preceding the Jewish revolt and leading up to the Roman-Jewish War of 66–70 C.E. (Theissen 1973, 1978; Freyne 1980; Horsley 1989, 1995, 1996; Richardson 1996). Following what by now can be taken as a consensus in Q studies, Horsley assumed a Galilean provenance for the document. But Galilean culture, as Horsley described it, was by and large neither excessively parochial nor dominantly Hellenized. "The vast majority of Galileans were villagers" whose lives "were embedded in the traditional social forms of family and village community" (1999:59; Horsley 1995: chs. 8–10). In this situation, the imposition of Hellenistic culture by such Roman client kings as Antipas evoked hostility among the populace at large while at the same time deepening its commitment to Israelite heritage.

The historical model Horsley introduced is predicated less on ethnic categories, and more on the sociological forces of power relations, social manifestations, class differences, and political and economic relations. A fundamental social dynamic governing Israel in late antiquity was the conflict between the rulers and the ruled. Roman-appointed Jerusalem and Galilean rulers, in particular the high priestly establishment and the Herodians, lived at the top, and the majority of Galileans and Judeans at the bottom, with scribes and Pharisees, interpreters of the Torah, by and large representing the interests of the Jerusalem temple establishment. An equally important social dynamic was that between Jerusalem and the Galilean cities of Sepphoris and Tiberias on one hand and the village communities on the other. While the urban population was more directly subject to the processes of Hellenization, the rural population tended to live in faithful adherence to Israelite tradition.

Rooted in and nourished by this social, political conflict was an ideological bifurcation into what has been called the "great [or "official"] tradition" and the "little [or "popular"] tradition" (1999:98–104; Scott 1977). The former was representative of and cultivated by the urban elite, and often designed to legitimize the second temple and the interests of its priestly aristocracy. The latter, not infrequently feeding on prophetic and messianic popular movements, was upheld and valued above all by the struggling peasantry. These two traditions were not hard and fast entities any more than they were fully unitary in themselves. They interacted in many ways. Obviously, Exodus and Sinai were formative experiences for all Israelites, and both traditions grounded their identity in remembrance of these same foundational events. And yet, the two traditions were more than merely variations on common themes. Each had its own distinct profile, mode of remembering and interpretive preferences.

In what is Horsley's first principal thesis he stated that these sociocultural dynamics that pervaded Israel's history and tradition furnished the socio-cultural context for Q: "[W]e should be prepared to recognize in the very existence of Q the production of a movement mobilized on the basis of the Israelite popular tradition long operative in Galilee" (Horsley and Draper: 103). While sharing roots and key experiences of the official Jerusalem tradition, Q does represent a viewpoint sufficiently distinct to justify its designation as little, or popular tradition. In short, Q is both thoroughly Israelite in its commitment to generally held concepts and experiences, and often in conflict with established powers and traditions.

Two major consequences derive from this specific cultural localization of Q. One, when Q is read in the context of a social dynamic that pits the "little tradition" against the "great tradition" there is no reason to construe crucial Q issues such as the lament over Jerusalem (Q 13:34–35), the woes against Pharisees and scribes (Q 11:39–52), and the condemnations of "this generation" (Q 7:31, 11:29–32, 50–51) as a Christian repudiation of Israel or as a denunciation of Jews who do not support the Christian cause, interpretive versions thoroughly conventional in Q studies. As Horsley sees it, the situation of conflict in Q is not one between Christians versus Jews, but rather between the Q people who aspire to the redemption of Israel and those in positions of power. These latter ones stand under God's condemnation not for rejecting Jesus, but because they exploited the people and killed the prophetic messengers.

Two, the recovery of a Jewish matrix for Q deserves our keen attention in view of well-known tendencies in current Q studies to dissociate Jesus from Judaism (Downing 1994; Vaage 1994). Frequently these studies are based on the historically untenable and ethically dubious criterion of dissimilarity and/or problematic stratification theories. Their fundamental claim is that Cynic themes, images and attitudes pervade Q in its early stage(s), leading some scholars to postulate the Cynic identity of Jesus as popular sage. In this mode of Q studies, the notorious defamiliarization of Jesus from Judaism is raising its ugly head once again in New Testament scholarship. When, for example, the assertion is made that the "Cynic analogy repositions the historical Jesus away from a specifically Jewish sectarian milieu and toward the Hellenistic ethos known to have prevailed in Galilee" (Mack: 73), one must wonder whether in some quarters the stratigraphic analysis of the synoptic sayings tradition has become a last refuge for scholars who seek to de-Judaize Jesus. Both in view of these problematic scholarly tendencies and on the strength of its own historical persuasiveness Horsley's socio-cultural contextualization of Q should be taken very seriously.

Having examined the larger cultural forces that contributed to Q's cultural environment, Horsley next turned to an analysis of the linguistic form and thematic content of the document. In his second principal thesis Horsley stated that the text of Q is constituted not by isolated sayings but rather by blocks or clusters of closely connected sayings materials. By and large using the Critical Edition of Q, issued by James Robinson, Paul Hoffmann and John Kloppenborg, he came to the conclusion that Q, far from being a sayings collection, must be viewed as a collection of discourses or speeches each of which is addressed to a distinct thematic issue. A major difference between Q and Thomas is now in evidence: "In Q the sayings are formed into larger clusters or discourses. In Thomas . . . the vast majority of the material . . . stands in fragmentary units of single sayings, sets of two or three parallel sayings, or short sequences of two or three sayings" (Horsley and Draper 1999:84). As mentioned above, examination of form is one of the arguments Horsley adduced in objecting to a single genre for Q and Thomas.

To be sure, the definition of the linguistic profile of Q in terms of clusters of sayings is not an entirely new idea. It was especially Kloppenborg whose compositional analysis in his groundbreaking work on *The Formation of Q* (1987) had demonstrated that the present version of Q consisted of clusters of sayings or series of discourses. But such was the pull of form criticism that the discovery of discourse complexes prompted him to refocus away from Q proper to originally independent sayings assumed to have been the starting point of Q, as well as to separate strata or layers assumed to be discernible in Q. Horsley, by contrast, argued that it was precisely the character and function of the discourse clusters that provides the key to understanding Q in its compositional integrity. It meant that individual sayings could not be properly comprehended except as components of the discourses. Once again, Q research is faced with the question of epistemology. How do we understand Q? Do we know Q by knowing its "formation," for example, its compositional history? Or do we know Q by taking its final form and function with utter seriousness?

Along with others, Horsley has expressed doubts about the feasibility of isolating Q strata according to the stated criteria of "sapiential" versus "apocalyptic" (Kloppenborg 1987:102–70, 171–245). His principal objection was that the strata as defined failed to exhibit characteristically and consistently sapiential versus apocalyptic sayings materials. The first stratum, once "purged of prophetic sayings, which are explained as later insertions . . . is not particularly sapiential," while the second stratum "is not particularly apocalyptic in form" (1999:66). Curiously, *sophia* is absent from the so-called sapiential layer, but "plays a prominent role at key points in the apocalyptic/judgmental clusters" (67). From these findings Horsley drew the conclusion that the conceptual apparatus of sapiential and apocalyptic was not merely inapplicable, but in fact obstructing more than illuminating Q and Q materials. As categories, wisdom and apocalypticism were "synthetic scholarly constructs" (69, 73, passim), burdened with a century of theological employment and imprecise in their definitional and explanatory expressiveness. What is more, stipulating a conceptual dichotomy between wisdom and apocalypticism as hermeneutical key to Q was to burden Q with an unsustainable intellectual legacy.

When thus read in their present form, Q's speeches enunciate a central experience, function with a particular objective in mind, and are empowered by a distinct hermeneutic. Thematically, the unifying topic is "the kingdom of God," understood as a renewal of Israel and featured prominently at key points (Q 6:20; 7:28; 10:9; 11; 11:2, 20; 12:31; 13:18–21, 28–29; 16:16; 22:28–30). The sayings interconnecting within each speech complex, and the speech complexes interacting among themselves produce a message which proclaims/performs the Mosaic covenant renewal of Israel. By way of example, discourse Q 3:7–9, 16–17, and 21–22 announces the coming of the Prophet, Q 6:20–49 constitutes a covenantal renewal discourse (including blessings and curses [Q 6:20b–26], teaching on economic relations [Q 6:27–36] and on social relations [Q 6:37–42]), discourse Q 9:57–10:16 articulates the sending and instruction of envoys, Q 11:39–52 continues the tradition of woes of the earlier Israelite prophets, and so forth. In this way, the sequence of speeches institute consolidation of social (not individual!) identity and communal (not individual!) solidarity in the face of opposition. In short, the Q speeches seek to activate renewal with positive results for those who respond and negative results for those who do not. Q 10:16, located at the close of the mission of the envoys, functions as a formula of legitimization authorizing the Q envoys as spokespersons of Jesus: "Whoever hears you hears me, and whoever rejects you rejects me; but whoever rejects me rejects him who sent me." This constitutes the hermeneutical, or perhaps better the oral-performative key for Q.

In what is Horsley's and Draper's third principal thesis it is stated that Q (and by implication GT) is an oral-derived text, a document that was composed and performed orally. This thesis is no less consequential than Horsley's other two contributions: Q's historical contextualization and the characterization of its speech complexes. As students of a print based education and as scholars actively participating in print culture, we operate largely within the framework of typographical conventions that have dominated Western civilization roughly from the fifteenth century to the present. The invention of the letterpress, e.g., the high-tech of the fifteenth century, has structured our scholarly consciousness and created the media conditions in which biblical scholars have analyzed, dissected and interpreted texts. Horsley's work on Q contributes toward a deconstruction of our print-based hermeneutics and launches a re-imagining of Christian origins in their historically appropriate medium environment.

Very few biblical scholars have ever demonstrated what it might be like listening, rather than reading, an oral-derived text. Taking leave of the form critical premise that isolated sayings constituted the basic unit of speech, Horsley and Draper made us receptive toward appreciating Q's discourses as basic intelligible units of composition and communication. As soon as we learn to refocus from saying to discourse, the latter displays interconnecting features that appeal to the ear more than to the eye: composition in stanzas, parataxis, uses of the additive *kai* instead of subordinate clauses, linkages of various kinds, repetition of words, phrases, themes, and many more. In light of oral aesthetics, the Q discourses now appear to be the result not of a cumulative build-up of discrete sayings, and not of an imposition of textual layer upon layer, but rather of oral composition in which the discourse was itself the basic unit of communication. In following Horsley's and Draper's argumentation one is tempted to speculate that the discourse formations in Q represent a mode of communication more closely allied with speech than Thomas' isolated sayings which, it could be argued, represented a more textually manipulated mediation of speech.

As stated above, it had been Horsley's first principle that to understand Q we need to understand its historical context. Stepping back from the textual perspective, he likewise suggested that to understand Q we need to understand its oral context. And one is not the same as the other.

Reading Q as an oral-derived text revises our literary notion of text and challenges our literary conventions of reading it. In the oral context, Q ceases to be literary in the sense of being the product of a single, sterling author. In the oral context, Q ceases to be literary in the sense of being the final outcome of a series of redactional processes. In the oral process, Q ceases to be literary in the sense of disclosing its full meaning in a systematic reading from beginning to end. Nor is Q literary in the sense that all its signifying powers reside in the textual configurations. Understood orally, the speeches in Q encapsulate a world of words, phrases, ideas, images that resonate with a map of experiences and associations shared by speakers and hearers. In short, Q as an oral-derived text relies heavily on extra-textual factors, shifting meaning from production to performance.

Utilizing the work of John M. Foley on ancient Greek and Anglo-Saxon oral-derived literature (1991; 1995), Horsley and Draper introduced a conceptual apparatus appropriate to a reading of Q as oral performance. Three closely interrelated concepts illuminate the oral art and operation of Q. One, the notion of "register" connotes configurations of language that are associated with particular types of situations, forms of activities, and modes of communication. Each Q discourse reaches beyond the confines of the text and has to be comprehended in its own register. Two, the notion of tradition as "the enabling referent" takes leave of an understanding of tradition as that which preceded Q in a textually reconstructable form, and instead envisions tradition as the communications context within which Q comes into play and is ratified. Three and most importantly, the notion of "metonymic referentiality" commands a field of references where meaning is evoked in a *pars pro toto* fashion. Significant terms in Q such as *wilderness, forty days, lambs among wolves, harvest, judgment, peace, sword, Pharisees, kingdom of God,* and so on tap traditional reservoirs that dwarf Q itself in depth and breadth and uncover their connotative significance. The operations of Q's "register," of its "enabling referent," and of its "metonymic referentiality" conspire in the creation of an invisible nexus of references and identities—called up by Q's discourse performance—in which people live, from which they draw sustenance, and in relation of which Q makes sense to them.

To be sure, the modern reader may be haunted by feelings of anxiety about the sense of instability an oral-derived text brings to hermeneutics. Indeed, Q's meaning in oral performance is not quite the measurable quantity that is being postured by print culture. And yet, from the perspective of oral aesthetics, the designation of Q as a single text with a single meaning may well appear to be a grave misunderstanding.

As far as the genre question is concerned we face the problem that Q's formal opening and possibly its formal closing, frequently helpful genre indicators, may not be available to us. Horsley viewed the genre along the lines of a community manual analogous to the speeches in Matthew and the Didache, while fully recognizing that the Q discourses function so as to perpetuate the prophetic authority and proclamation of Jesus (and John) (90–93). Schröter, on the other hand, taking full account of Q's biographical sections in its genre definition, suggested an interface of "Spruchsammlung" and "Biographie:" "Eine derartige Partizipation an zwei Gattungen ist durchaus nichts Ungewöhnliches" (1997:461). Perhaps we should think of Q in its final form as a generic hybrid, participating both in biography and in manual.

Undoubtedly, Horsley's (and Draper's) proposal will be debated, challenged, modified, and even rejected. But we are now in possession of an encompassing theory about Q that merits careful scholarly attention. Horsley and Draper's *Whoever Hears You Hears Me* cannot be relegated to a footnote in the history of Q research any more than Schröter's magisterial *Erinnerung an Jesu Worte: Studien zur Rezeption der Logienüberlieferung in Markus, Q und Thomas* (cf. Robinson 2000: lxvi n. 155). These works point in the direction Q research ought to move if it is to overcome its present methodological impasse.

The *Gospel of Thomas*'s Structural Affinity with List

It has not been possible to detect consistent organizational devices by which the entries of the *Gospel of Thomas* (GT) were arranged into an intelligible sequential order. The majority of the 114 sayings and parables in the GT stand as isolated units, with only some of them constituting brief clusters of sayings. This lack of an overall thematic arrangement weighs all the more heavily since, as we have seen, Q is organized into larger clusters or discourses. The GT has placed all information units one next to the other with only minimal linking strategies and devoid of subordinate devices.

GT's layout of materials by simple coordination brings it into close affinity with the ancient genre of list. I made this suggestion first at a conference on "Transformations of the Word" at Vassar College in May/June of 1987 (Kelber 1989). Subsequently, the proposal was reiterated by John Dominic Crossan (1991). He arrived at the thesis of linking GT with the genre of list independently from my earlier article, but we both had benefited from Jonathan Smith's important essay "Sacred Persistence: Toward a Redescription of Canon" (1982). The list, "perhaps the most archaic and pervasive of genres" (Smith: 44), displays a facility of retention that ranges from vocabularies in cuneiform characters to Sumerian enumeration of trees, reeds and birds, and from administrative tallies in ancient Mesopotamia to inventories of proverbial and wisdom sayings in ancient and Talmudic Judaism, and from the famous catalogue of contingents, leaders, towns, men and ships in the Iliad (Homer, *Iliad* 2.494–759) all the way to canon, "a subtype of the genre list" (Smith: 44). There does not seem to be a limit to what is being stored. Kings and animals, plants and proverbs, oracles and legal rulings—all are subject to enrollment in lists. Typically, lists often give preference to entries of like kind. Knowledge is managed on the principle of clustering whereby like data tend to attract those of their own likeness. Basically, lists function as technological mechanisms suited for the storing of data which are deemed worthy of preservation. Their primary compositional rationale derives not from hermeneutical impulse, but rather from functional needs.

Often, although not always, devoid of organizational devices, lists have neither a beginning nor an end. While they tend to draw items of like kind, they are as a rule uninterested in arranging them in a rationally intelligible sequence. For this reason, lists often appear to the modern mind as arbitrary or unsystematic assortments of materials. Hugh Kenner, one of the few contemporary literary critics interested in the genre of list, described it as a "fragmentation of all that we know into little pieces," because it makes continuous reading from one item to the next "sublimely nonsensical" (3). Hayden White, on the other hand, in discussing medieval annals, for example, the itemization of dates, battles, crops, deaths, floods, and so forth, cautioned that "the annalist would have felt little of the anxiety which the modern scholar feels when confronted with what appear to be 'gaps', 'discontinuities', and lack of causal connections between the events recorded in the text" (13). Indeed, the modern reader who is nurtured on the masterpieces of the eighteenth and nineteenth century realistic novel, may find it difficult to appreciate the itemizing conventions exhibited in lists. Our cultural bias makes us look for meaning in connections. Haunted by the horror vacui, we tend to fill in what we perceive to be gaps, over-interpreting and misinterpreting in the interest of production of meaning. Generally subscribing to the principle of truth as logical coherence, we look for connections that add up to meaningful patterns.

Yet the GT does not present us with the plausibility structure of compositional and thematic coherence. Least of all does it enlist its sundry items into the service of a narrative organization. When taken as a genre in its own right, the GT might well consider narrative coherence as an interference with the itemization of its plural pieces. What obviously matters is the placement of saying and parable one next to the other, so as to allow each item its own say. The listing of discrete materials, e.g., this hoarding of oral treasures and speech events, may thus be understood not as a fragmentation of meaning, but as a distinctly authentic approach to reality.

To claim that the GT shares close affinity with the ancient genre of list is not the same as to say that in its present form GT functions as a list. Here I register disagreement with Crossan who unequivocally states: "The *Gospel of Thomas* is a perfect example of a list" (237). It is not. While the bulk of the materials in the GT display their origin in the genre of list, the text has been provided with a formal introduction and conclusion. Both exercise a transforming impact on GT' generic indebtedness to the list. At the outset, Jesus is introduced as the "living Jesus" who functions as the speaker of the sayings and parables. At the end, the colophon, possibly the result of later scribal activity, sums up the 114 sayings and parables in terms of *The Gospel according to Thomas*. By its own definition, therefore, Thomas is a gospel, and not, or no longer, a list.

No mere inventory of items, the GT carries materials that are perceived to proceed from the mouth of the "living Jesus," and to carry his authority in the act of speaking: "Jesus said," "therefore I say," "he said to them," and so on. There exists an unmistakable connection between the absence of a narrative syntax and the authoritatively speaking "living Jesus." Narrative as a rule constructs a spatio-temporal framework which serves to historicize every single character, including that of Jesus. In the absence of a constructed time sequence, the GT lacks a sense of history and historical identity that Western culture has progressively been able to evoke. Hence the "living Jesus" is staged in a manner that allows him to retain his present, speaking authority. This is the case despite the fact that the GT is a writing project, and "writing puts everything in the past" (Tyler: 135). But the combined effect of promoting the "living Jesus" and the absence of a narrative syntax can be viewed as GT's attempt to escape a sense of pastness that is inevitably created by a written narrative. Unencumbered by a narrative construction of space and time, the "living Jesus" claims present authority, eluding, or rather seeking to elude, entrapment in the past. Clearly, there are hermeneutical complications built into the GT that transform its indebtedness to the genre of list.

As is well known, the GT "lacks" any religious consideration of Jesus' death. In view of GT's strategy to extend the present authority of Jesus as speaker of sayings and parables, its nonexistent treatment of Jesus' death seems perfectly sensible. Indeed, what may be perceived to be a deficiency from the perspective of the narrative gospels could be entirely in keeping with GT's strategy of re-presenting Jesus, speaker of sayings and parables. Advocacy of Jesus' authority in and through death could well conflict with a text whose emphasis lies on the protagonist's present. A genre that seeks to authorize the "living Jesus" cannot simultaneously attribute meaning to his death, promote life through mediation of his death, or espouse his godforsakenness, let alone absence, through death in crucifixion. It is, therefore, by no means implausible that sayings dealing with Jesus' death are absent on intrinsic hermeneutical, theological grounds. Again, in its present form, the GT is not entirely a random collection of materials.

The first saying, moreover, issues a programmatic directive for all subsequent sayings and parables: "Whoever finds the explanation (hermeneia) of these sayings, will not taste death." This declaration has been installed at the outset so as to subordinate all other sayings and parables under a single, controlling directive. Most importantly, this is an injunction that issues a call for interpretation, and not a thematic directive that subsumes all materials under a leading motif. At this point, the functional needs for preservation have been overridden by the hermeneutical task of interpretation.

What may come as a surprise is that interpretation is perceived to be so weighty a matter as to concern life and death: finding explanation generates deliverance from death. It may not be farfetched, however, to discern in the life-giving power of the sayings and parables the activist potential of words which, when voiced and sounded forth, takes effect in believers, creating life for some and destruction for others. And yet what is particularly notable in GT is that life is not to be conferred in the enabling act of performance in and of itself, any more than it is to be found ready-made inside the margins of the text. The specific hermeneutical challenge Thomas poses to hearers and readers lies in the claim, in the promise even, that life is to be found in the act of interpretation.

Although Thomas' shuns the notion of direct oral efficaciousness of its speech materials in the act of proclamation itself, its hermeneutical roots are nonetheless sunk deeply in oral sensibilities. "Finding the explanation" must not necessarily invoke the posture of individual readers silently pondering the texts in front of them. Granted that the verbal arts in late antiquity exhibited vast media complexities, a privatized reading of and meditation on Thomas, the very scenario that may come most readily to the mind of text-driven readers in modernity, may well be the least likely scenario. Invoking explanation and interpretation suggests, first and foremost, that sayings and parables bear more (and different) meanings than a literal reading would dictate, and that they are, therefore, not directly accessible. This is strongly suggested by GT's reminder that hearers are being confronted with the "secret words," spoken by the living Jesus and written down by Didymos Judas Thomas. Given the words' secret status, it is most unlikely that the act of "finding" the explanation has recourse to the orderly world of lexical classifications, be they ancient or modern, or that interpretation is fixated on the single, authorial meaning. Demanding search for the explanation of secret words suggests, secondly, that hearers and readers are asked to open up the potential resources these words are perceived to carry within themselves. This may, thirdly, mean to hear them idiomatically in the cultural register shared by speaker and hearers alike, or, what is but a variation of the former, metaphorically or metonymically as powerful signs that resonate (or are made to resonate) with traditional connotations. At any rate, a cooperative enterprise appears to be envisioned involving delivery and interpreting reception.

From the perspective of performance theory, Jesus' sayings and parables may well be orally delivered with the aid of verbal cues and signals that assist audiences in how to hear and "read" the message. It follows that in Thomas, as in all oral poetics, we will have to envision alternate performances of the same sayings and parables. Likewise, Thomas' sayings and parables, as all oral poetics, will be voiced in alternate performance contexts, each one yielding more or less diverse results. If the literary-minded readers wish to hold each saying and parable to one single meaning, they would betray the verbal dynamics of the "living Jesus" who purports to keep his message in the present and alive. Despite its chirographic form, Thomas does not wish to be understood as a product. As all oral poetry, it seeks to remain a process.

We need to return to GT's structural affinity with the genre of list. Although provided with a formal opening that articulates the hermeneutical program of the "secret words," and equipped as well with a formal ending that defines the text as Gospel, GT appears to have modified a sense of its genetic history of clustering and itemization. But it owes too much to its compositional background as list to have been able to efface it altogether. Following the introductory saying all the way down to the colophon, Thomas still has retained all, or most of, the appearances of a list. Horsley rightly suggested that "perhaps Thomas can be appropriately characterized as a collection of sayings" (85). Taking the references to "secret words" at the outset and to Gospel at the end in full seriousness, Thomas may, therefore, most suitably be called a Sayings Gospel.

The question this definition raises is whether GT's final designation of

Gospel predominates over its initial self-characterization of "sayings," or vice versa, or whether Gospel and "sayings" are to be taken as co-equals, jointly constituting its genre identification. Is GT the Gospel to be intellectually defined and understood concretely in the sense that all sayings and parables are unifiable under a single proposition? Does the GT as Sayings Gospel project a sense of unity that is made up of the sum total of its 114 parts?

In answer to these questions it is once again worth remembering GT's unambiguous opening statement: finding explanation constitutes the key to the whole. Clearly, what matters is not the finding and application of a single thematic topos to Jesus' sayings and parables. While kingdom materials are present in GT, "they do not play the same role in providing a unifying theme" (Horsley and Draper: 87), as they do, for example, in Q. GT cannot, therefore, be intellectually defined in terms of a single thematic proposition, let alone be reduced to a dominantly stable message. The unifying aspect of this Gospel is its demand for interpretation. It is, therefore, a genre that, in spite of its invocation of 'Gospel' requires patient hearing of each of its sayings and parables. It is, and will always be plural. As such, the Sayings Gospel represents a genre that has remained beholden to the itemization of sayings characteristic of list, while at the same time claiming a sense of the integrity of the whole (Gospel). It is a generic hybrid that aspires to have the best of both worlds.

Performance and Tradition
THE COVENANT SPEECH IN Q

Richard A. Horsley

Some student friends recently commented to me, after reading one of the most widely marketed books on the historical Jesus, that modern Gospel scholarship appears to be laboring under a double disability. Gospel scholars and Jesus interpreters, they said, seem to have an extremely limited attention span, often focusing on no more than a single verse at a time. This limited attention span then becomes a contributing factor in the second disability. In addition they focus only on the printed text, without considering how gospel materials or a complete Gospel story might have come alive in oral recitation. I attempted to explain how biblical studies arose from a tradition of reading the Bible verse by verse, often as prooftexts for theological and ethical doctrine, from the King James Bible, where it was all codified by chapter and verse for easy referencing. One of the students, a performing musician, responded by drawing an analogy from music. It seemed to her like Gospel scholars tend to focus on one or two measures of a score at a time, but never realize that the notes on that score are merely symbols for parts of larger melodies, fugues, and movements or of whole choruses and arias, cantatas and operas. They have not yet discovered the work as a whole, much less considered what it would be like in performance.

Approaching Q as Oral Performance

Recent studies of the media of communication in the ancient Mediterranean world have made unavoidably clear that Gospel materials and the complete Gospels as texts were produced in a predominantly oral communication environment. Even if a text such as Q existed in writing, it was recited orally in a group setting. So we interpreters of Gospels and Gospel materials need help. Having been focused so heavily on analysis of written texts and so deeply immersed in the assumptions of print culture, we are left singularly unprepared to appreciate oral communication and performance. Other academic fields with somewhat similar materials and issues, fortunately, have gained new perspectives and explored new approaches that may be helpful for Gospel materials. A few pioneers have shown the way toward appreciation of orality and oral performance. For the last two decades Werner Kelber has been calling Gospel studies to move beyond anachronistic assumptions and models based on modern print culture, and to learn from historical and theoretical studies of the relation of orality and literacy (1983; 1994). Paul Achtemeier (1990) and Pieter Botha (1992) along with Kelber called the field to recognize the predominantly oral communication environment in antiquity. Kelber (1983) explained that Q materials present themselves as the oral performance of Jesus' words and that their survival depended on their social relevancy. Joanna Dewey (1989; 1992; 1994) and Botha (1991), drawing on oral studies and oral-formulaic theory, then demonstrated the oral features of Mark's narrative. In the meantime, anthropologists, ethnographers, folklorists, medievalists, and classics scholars were carrying out ever more innovative and sophisticated analyses of oral performances and of written texts that derived from originating oral performances.

Of particular importance for Gospel studies, John Miles Foley, the leading theorist of "verbal art," has brought together insights from oral-formulaic theory and other studies of oral-derived classical and medieval literature, on the one side, and sociolinguistics, ethnopoetics, and the ethnography of performance, on the other, into highly suggestive theorizing of "immanent art" and oral performance (Foley 1991; 1995; 2002). It is that interplay and combination of historical investigation, ethnography, experimentation, comparative reflection, and theory that Jonathan Draper and I attempted to adapt for exploration of the speeches in Q as oral performance (Horsley and Draper 1999). We have each continued to read and adapt other studies since, partly following the lead of Foley's ongoing work.

The following exploration represents an attempt to further adapt this developing mix of comparative studies and theory in application to Q speeches, in order to present an alternative but compatible and overlapping approach to a closely related "performance" of the (same or) similar text dealt with by Draper in this volume. The focus is not on the issue of whether Q was "originally" composed in writing or orally. We know of Q, of course, only because parallel speech materials of Jesus were transmitted in writing in the Gospels of Matthew and Luke. Gospel texts such as Q speeches or Markan narrative continued to be recited orally however widely distributed they may have become in written manuscripts. In fact, interaction between manuscripts, memory, and oral recitation apparently continued into late antiquity, as some text critics are beginning to recognize (Parker). Because Matthew and Luke reproduced speech material of Jesus in parallel form with many marks of oral performance we have access to what Foley calls an "oral-derived text" or a "voice from the past" (1995;

2002). Composition may have involved an interaction between the oral and the written; and repeated performance may have involved such interaction. The Jesus-speeches that can be reconstructed from the parallels in the written manuscripts of Matthew and Luke (that we call "Q") thus offer an unusual opportunity to appreciate how they may have "worked" in oral performance.

Outline of an Approach

In approaching Q as oral performance we can no longer ask what individual sayings in themselves mean. That might be appropriate for the separate logia of the Gospel of Thomas as object of reflection or contemplation, given the hermeneutical principle in its first logion. But individual sayings are and were not the basic units of communication. To find units of communication we must focus rather on the speeches or discourses constituted by the clusters of sayings still evident in the parallel materials in Matthew and Luke. Since Q consisted not of individual sayings but of Jesus-speeches that were performed orally before a group, we should ask rather how the speeches communicated to their listeners. For the speeches in Q, as in any acts of communication, it is necessary to consider the interaction between speaker and hearers as they live out of their cultural tradition in a particular context. That in Q we are dealing with what Foley (2002) would call a "voice from the past" means that to hear this historical oral communication appropriately we must listen, insofar as possible, in a historical cultural and social context. To simplify our analysis to four interrelated aspects, to hear Q discourses/speeches as oral performance, we must determine the contours of the "*text*," attend to the performance *context* in which the speaker addresses the hearers, sense the *register* of the speech appropriate to that context, and cultivate knowledge of the cultural *tradition* out of which the speech resonates with the hearers (Foley 1995; Horsley and Draper: 160–74).

This approach to Q speeches as communication moves beyond the standard approach developed in Gospel studies and complicates the theory of "verbal art" developed by Foley in a number of respects. Two in particular require special critical attention, in connection with *context* and *tradition*.

"Text"

The first step is to figure out what the *text* or message communicated is/was. For an orally-derived text for which we are dependent on a "transcript" of the performance, we have little more than the "libretto" before us in chirographic or printed form. Given the previous habit of treating Q as a collection of separate sayings, it will be particularly important to "listen" for what may be the complete units of communication. Individual sayings or verses were not intelligible units of communication, but merely fragments thereof. To work from analogies with other performances, we want to consider not just a few isolated lines but whole arias or speeches in the larger context of the complete libretto of an opera or the complete script of a play. In Q the intelligible units of communication would presumably be particular speeches or discourses focused on particular issues (Kirk; Horsley and Draper: 83–93, 166–68). It would also help to hear those as components of the complete sequence of speeches that constituted Q.

Context

In order to understand a message or communication properly it is necessary to hear it in the appropriate *context*: wedding, funeral, political rally, intimate embrace. Context determines the expectation and the appropriate hearing of the message. We would not expect to hear the aria by the Queen of the Night from Mozart's "Zauberfloete" at the Grand Ol' Opry. Often to tune into a message we adjust to particular contexts within a general context of communication. In the general context of a Christian church service, for example, we shift from one particular context to another, for example, from adoration and praise to prayer to scripture reading to sermon to offering.

Attempting to appreciate Q speeches as message(s) communicated by a speaker to a collective audience thus requires the interpreter to combine critical attention to the context with critical attention to the text. "Text" cannot be considered apart from context. The grandfathers of form-criticism (Bultmann and Dibelius) said something similar: that form could not be considered apart from social function—which the next generation of Gospel interpreters tended to forget in their focus on form abstracted from social function. Similarly, some recent interpreters of Q assumed that they could establish the meaning of sayings considered separate from consideration of the context (and cultural tradition), and then on that basis deduce the social context. Texts in performance, however, like any messages in communication, are always already in a relational context. Just as the performance context of the liturgy of the mass is presumably a congregation gathered for worship, so the performance context of Q speeches was presumably a community gathering of participants in a Jesus movement (168–70).

Consideration of the context of Q speeches in recitation, however, is more complicated than that of other types of "oral poems" and the performance of epic poems such as the *Iliad* or *Beowulf,* key "texts" on which the theory of verbal art has been developed. The performance context of the Q speeches was not one standardized over many generations of repeated performances. It was rather a gathering of community in a newly developed movement apparently among the peasantry in Galilee and beyond. If we are to attempt to hear Q speeches in the concrete historical context of their more narrowly considered performance context, therefore, the historical context must be considered with as much precision as possible.

Recent researches have made accessible the multiple political-economic-religious conflicts that characterized Roman Palestine at the time of the early Jesus movements. Modern essentialist constructs such as "Judaism" and "apocalypticism" and other anachronistic concepts block rather than facilitate access to historical context.

Register

The message must then match, or be in the appropriate *register* for the context. A funeral dirge would not go over very well at a wedding, or the Hallelujah Chorus at a rock concert. The appropriate register depends on three factors: the subject matter being communicated, who is participating in the communication, and the mode of communication. The language-of-love would thus be the appropriate register for the expression of love between partners whispering sweet nothings into each others' ears. Often a certain discourse, including body language and paralinguistic gestures, is "dedicated" to a certain communication context, as in the case of weddings or funerals or the introduction of distinguished professors to deliver endowed lectures at an august institution of higher learning. A certain register of language is often activated by sounds or phrases that set up expectations in the listeners, signaling the communication context and the register of discourse about to be heard. If we are in the right context and clued into the register for a regularly repeated performance, we already know the message being communicated. "Dearly beloved, We are gathered here together . . ." "The Lord be with you . . ." One Q speech offers an example of the failure to appreciate the register and context of Jesus' and John's prophetic performances in their program of renewal of Israel:

> We played the flute for you, and you did not dance;
> We wailed, and you did not weep. (Q 7:32)

Often the performer is assuming a certain role appropriate to the communication. Funerals are usually conducted by clergy. In political rallies candidates and other speakers address followers or concerned citizens. In ancient scribal circles instruction involved a teacher addressing his students: "Oh my children, . . ." (Sir 2:1; 3:1; 4:1; 6:18; etc.). At the popular level, a prophet, such as Yeshua ben Hananiah, repeatedly pronounced a lament over the imminent fate of the ruling city Jerusalem (Josephus, *War* 6.300–309), a message in a prophetic register heard by crowds and overheard by an anxious aristocracy. The clues or cues to the register (and context) of the message being communicated is often indicated in the way it references the cultural tradition shared by speaker and listeners—which makes knowledge of the tradition all the more important for us modern interpreters.

Tradition and Metonymic Referencing

When the audience hears the message in the register appropriate to the communication context, they then resonate to the message out of the cultural *tradition* in which they and the performer are grounded. In every one of the communication contexts and registers offered as illustrations above, there is a cultural tradition out of which the hearers resonate with the message, whether at weddings, political rallies, or the Grand Ol' Opry. The cultural tradition, however, is far more important for communication through oral performance of texts in a traditional society where oral communication is far more dominant than in a highly literate modern society or postmodern multimedia society. It is particularly important for biblical scholars still striving to cut through the assumptions of print culture in which we are so deeply embedded to recognize this. And since recent literary analysis of biblical narrative, while helpful in many ways, may have perpetuated those assumptions, it may be appropriate to illustrate from the difference between a modern novelist's communication with a silent reader and an ancient performance of the Iliad or Beowulf or the Gospel of Mark (Foley 1991; 1995; Horsley and Draper: 170–74, Horsley 2001: ch. 3).

A modern novelist individually manipulates inherited or idiosyncratic materials in a new direction or from a new perspective, thus *conferring* meaning on her fresh new literary creation (that is then read privately by a silent reader). The traditional oral performer, on the other hand, depending on standard strategies long familiar to his collective audience, summons conventional connotations of conventional structures evoking a meaning that is *inherent*. Communication through a performance or recitation, therefore, depends much more heavily on extra-textual factors as meaning is evoked *metonymically* from the tradition with which the listeners are familiar. In contrast to the originality of conferred meaning in modern literary texts, traditional oral performance cannot depart from, because it depends upon, traditional references of symbols, phrases, and formulas. Each performance causes what is immanent to come to life in the present; it recreates the networks of inherent meaning. The what and how of communication in the performance of a text such as the Iliad or the Gospel of Mark depends on a whole range of cultural memory in which the social identity and self-image of a people or community is embedded. In emphasizing the crucial importance of cultural tradition or memory for the communication happening in Gospel materials such as Mark and Q, Kelber has compared it to a biosphere in which a people's whole life is encompassed and nurtured (1994: esp. 152–59).

While cultural tradition is far less significant for us post-moderns, we also experience how metonymic referencing works in experiences that may enable us better to appreciate how it worked in oral performance of texts in societies more embedded in their cultural traditions. Whenever I hear on the radio, say around mid-January, the voice of Martin Luther

King saying "I have a dream . . . ," then simply that brief phrase spoken in King's inimitable cadence resonates deeply within my memory in metonymic referencing that evokes a whole movement, a whole period of my life and the life of American society. It evokes intense feelings of eager hopes, vivid experiences, outrage, and deep sorrow. When that happens, moreover, I cannot help but renew my own personal commitment to certain values and causes.

As interpreters who stand at a considerable distance from the original historical context of a text such as Q we are unusually dependent on the cultural tradition in our attempts to hear the message appropriately. Our only clues as to the performance context and the register in which the message should be heard may come from our acquaintance with the tradition that it references.

The Special Importance of Israelite Tradition for Hearing Q as Oral Performance

It is thus particularly important for us as "eavesdroppers" or "over-hearers" of Q speeches who stand at a distance from the original historical situation to become as thoroughly acquainted as possible with the tradition out of which the performer spoke and the hearers resonated. It seems fairly clear that the Q speeches are rooted in Israelite tradition. Despite the recently fashionable interpretation of individual Q sayings on the basis of perceived parallels to "counter-cultural" Cynic philosophical materials, there is a great deal of agreement among interpreters that Q exhibits numerous allusions to Israelite figures and motifs (Kloppenborg Verbin 2001). Recent research into the cultural life of ancient Judean and Galilean society, however, has seriously complicated how ancient Israelite cultural tradition operated and requires us to move well beyond the standard conceptual apparatus of Gospel studies.

The first problem that should be faced seriously is that Israelite tradition was not unitary and existed on different social levels. A consensus seems to have emerged, at least among American interpreters of Q, that Q materials originated in a Jesus movement based in Galilee (keying on the place-names Bethsaida, Capernaum, and Chorazin, and on the agrarian imagery), but not in elite literate circles in the newly built cities of Sepphoris and Tiberias. Four factors that have become clear from recent research on various aspects of life in first century Galilee, however, make it highly unlikely that Galileans would have known Israelite tradition in the form previously imagined in New Testament studies on the assumption of a widely-known standard version of the Hebrew Bible. First, no standardized version of "the Law and the Prophets" existed, perhaps until well after second-temple times (Ulrich). Second, scrolls of the books of the Torah and the Prophets would have been extremely costly and unwieldy; the limited number that existed belonged in the Temple and in scribal circles (Hezser). Third, it appears that few Galileans would have been literate, able to read a scroll in Hebrew (Hezser). Moreover, fourth, Galileans had come under the rule of the Jerusalem high priestly regime and "the laws of the Judeans" only about a century before the birth of Jesus, and the scribal and Pharisaic representatives of the Jerusalem regime would hardly have been able to "re-socialize" the people in the Jerusalem-based proto-biblical version of Israelite cultural tradition during that time. They certainly had no basis in the synagogues of Galilee, which in the first century were not (yet) "Jewish" religious buildings (archaeologists have not yet found such), but Galilean village assemblies which met to discuss community affairs as well as to hold prayers (Horsley 1995, 1996).

Insofar as Q speeches are rooted in Israelite tradition based in Galilee, therefore, it must have been what anthropologists would call the Israelite "little tradition" (Scott 1977 and the introduction to this volume). That is, assuming that Galileans, the vast majority of whom lived in village communities, were descendants of ancient Israelites and/or of Israelite heritage, they cultivated popular Israelite tradition orally in those village communities. Galilean Israelite popular tradition may well have come into some interaction with the Jerusalem-based "great" tradition during the first century B.C.E., but would hardly have been identical with the version we know from the Jerusalemite great tradition that formed the basis of the later-canonized Hebrew Bible. For interpreters of Q, however, the difference between the Galilean Israelite popular tradition and the Jerusalem-based "great tradition" means obvious problems of sources for the former. What scholars know as the Hebrew Bible, derived from one of the versions of the Jerusalemite great tradition (Ulrich), does not provide a direct source for the Galilean Israelite little tradition. At best it provides a window onto it. A modern scholar can only extrapolate from it, fully aware that it has been shaped and edited by Jerusalem scribal circles working for and articulating the perspective and interests of the ruling Jerusalem priestly aristocracy. Among the effects of these recent researches into the fluid condition and variety in Israelite cultural tradition is to lead scholarly interpreters of texts to recognize that we are not working with the kind of "control" over written textual sources that we may have assumed previously.

The second problem is closely related to the first. The Israelite popular tradition in Galilee would almost certainly have been cultivated orally in the dominant language among Galileans, Aramaic. But Q was in Greek. There might be two possible explanations of the relation of Q speeches in Greek to the Israelite tradition in which they were deeply rooted, each one based in a theory about how the Jesus movement that produced and used Q spread. One is that the movement had expanded into the Galilean cities Sepphoris and/or Tiberias, where more Greek was spoken than in villages, taking nascent Jesus-traditions with them. The other is that the movement had expanded into villages and towns of the surrounding countries, such as those subject to Tyre, Sidon, Caesarea Philippi, the Decapolis, etc., in which the villagers/townspeople presumably spoke more Greek than in Galilean villages (Horsley 2007). The second possibility at least appears to have a potential parallel in the Gospel of Mark, in which Jesus is portrayed as having worked in the villages or "regions" of Tyre, Caesarea Philippi, and the Decapolis (perhaps grounding the later expansion of a Jesus movement in the ministry of Jesus himself). In this second scenario, the participants in the movement who performed or heard the Q speeches need not have been descendants of Israelites, but could have been people who identified with Israelite tradition as the basis of the developing, expanding movement. People(s) who had only recently and secondarily learned and identified with Israelite tradition would have been less deeply yet intensely attached to it.

The third problem is that culture involves more than particular items such as names, place-names, and motifs, but broader patterns, connections, and "discourses," as well. The very concept of *register* implies such cultural realities as discourses devoted to certain memories and other cultural patterns. Just as the very sound of Martin Luther King's voice evokes the memory of a whole period of American history for people of my generation, so a reference to Moses would evoke a whole set of associations of exodus, wilderness wanderings, and covenant-making. Culture also involves distinctive patterns that persist over many generations. I stumbled upon some of these in gathering and examining Josephus's accounts of several movements in 4 B.C.E. and again from 66–70 led by popularly acclaimed kings and several other movements in mid-first century led by popular prophets. The distinctively Israelite similarities exhibited by these two types of popular movements, despite their differences in particulars, can only be explained by particular patterns embedded in cultural memory or earlier movements led by the young David and others (a popular "messianic script") and earlier movements led by Moses and Joshua (a popular "prophetic script"). The discovery of the Dead Sea Scrolls, and the Community Rule and the Damascus Rule in particular, enabled us to realize that Mosaic covenant patterns had persisted into late second-temple times, at least among scribal-priestly circles. As long as study of Q and other Gospel materials focused mainly on individual sayings, broader cultural patterns remained unseen partly because they were not sought. Once we recognize their persistence, however, we must be open to the possibility that Q speeches and the Markan narrative may be metonymically referencing whole cultural patterns.

Awareness of these complicating aspects of Israelite tradition should better enable interpreters to appreciate how performance of Q speeches may have referenced that tradition metonymically, in order the better to detect the context and register of the speeches and to appreciate how the speeches resonated with the hearers by such referencing. In contrast with previously standard procedure based on assumptions of print culture, in which scholars looked for "quotations of scripture" (even if only words or phrases), we can attend more sensitively and subtly to images, motifs, and patterns of cultural memory.

There is yet another aspect of the cultural tradition that Q speeches reference as they resonate with hearers. Insofar as communities of Jesus-adherents who comprised the audience of the Q speeches were part of a popular movement that had built upon a rich Israelite cultural tradition, the tradition out of which the Q speeches resonated was a double one. In addition to and building on the broader and deeper Israelite tradition, a more focused and recent tradition of Jesus-lore had developed. The broader and deeper Israelite tradition featured a long line of prophets, some of whom had pronounced God's judgment against oppressive rulers and some of whom had led the formation or renewal of the people. In the developing Jesus-tradition, Jesus was apparently understood as the fulfillment of that line of prophets. He had both pronounced God's condemnation of current rulers and led a (new) renewal of Israel. The broader and deeper Israelite tradition included an increasing longing for "the kingdom of God," when God would finally take action against oppressive human rulers to heal their suffering, relieve their indebtedness, and restore just social-economic relations. In the developing Jesus-tradition, Jesus had proclaimed, manifested, and restored practice of the kingdom of God. The Jesus tradition was the exciting and inspiring fulfillment of the old. This can be seen in several of the speeches. Q 6:20–49 is performative speech in which Jesus renews the Mosaic covenant (explored below). Q 7:18–35 proclaims that Jesus had been manifesting the kingdom of God in healings, exorcisms, and preaching. In Q 9:57–10:16, Jesus commissioned envoys to help heal, preach and organize people in the village communities (Horsley and Draper: ch. 10).

Prior to closer examination of the Q covenant speech in particular, we can note a few examples of how we may be able to detect the performance context and register of some Q speeches by closer attention to Israelite popular tradition. The speech in 7:18–35 that identifies Jesus as the coming one who is already accomplishing the prophetically articulated longings of Israel for the blind to see, the deaf to hear, and the poor to have good news preached suggests the sense of fulfillment in the prophetic mission carried out by Jesus. This further suggests that the performance context of the speech is a popular movement of renewal of Israel and the register one of fulfillment of prophetic expectations. The allusions to Elijah's commissioning of Elisha that preface the mission speech in 9:57–10:16 suggests that, by analogy, Jesus' envoys are also sent on a prophetic mission to renew Israel. Again the allusions suggest that the performance context is a popular movement of renewal and the register that of commissioning for mission. In this case the use of what appear to be a popular cycle of Elijah-Elisha stories by the Deuteronomic History in the Jerusalemite "great tradition," combined with the occurrence of (other) popular prophetic movements right around the time of Jesus, provide fairly strong indications that such a register continued in the popular memory, along with periodic prophetic movements of renewal.

The series of woes against the Pharisees in 11:39–52 take the same (oral-performative or oral-literary) form as the series of woes that appear in the books of Amos, Isaiah, and Habakkuk, and has parallels in the Epistle of Enoch. This indicates fairly clearly that Q is using standard prophetic forms still alive in the popular tradition. The performance context is, again, a prophet-led renewal or resistance movement, and the register is that of prophetic woes against rulers and their representatives for their treatment of the people. Similarly, the prophetic lament against the Jerusalem ruling house resembles earlier Israelite prophetic laments and has a striking parallel in the near contemporary prophetic lament by the peasant prophet Yeshua ben Hananiah mentioned by Josephus. Clearly the Q speeches not only refer significantly to key memories in Israelite culture, but utilize basic Israelite cultural forms, particularly prophetic forms, that were still very much alive in popular circles. And such references aid us in detecting the performance context(s) and registers of the Q speeches.

Hearing Q 6 in Oral Performance

As suggested in the theory of oral performance outlined above, the first step is to ascertain the "text" or message that was recited before a community of a Jesus movement. For modern interpreters relatively unfamiliar with the cultural tradition of the speaker and audience, the next step is to become more familiar with the Israelite tradition out of which it resonated with the hearers. That will enable us to better appreciate the way the speech "worked" as it resonated with the audience by referencing that cultural tradition.

Q 6:20–49 as a Coherent Speech

Attempting to ascertain the complete "text" or message being communicated is a departure from standard studies of Q, for which the text is an unproblematic given (once the wording of particular sayings is "reconstructed" from the parallels in Matthew and Luke). Assuming that Q was a collection of sayings, standard studies focus attention on sayings as separate entities. Since they are based on the presuppositions of print culture, standard approaches to Q and other Gospel materials are uninterested in communication (which would be difficult, if not impossible, in separate individual sayings). Rather they treat Gospel materials as discrete (written) textual artifacts to be examined and interpreted as if they contained some inherent meaning in themselves.

Representative of what has been the standard approach to Q as a collection of separate individual sayings, Tuckett treats sayings as separate abstract entities that possess meaning in themselves. Like previous Q scholars, he attends to the sequence of the sayings in Matthew and Luke, in order to establish the existence of Q. But interest in the order of Q does not carry over into consideration of possible patterns taken, for example, by the sequence of sayings in Luke 6:20–49 that is paralleled in Matthew 5–7, and the issues that such combinations of sayings might be addressing. Rather, separate sayings (or short combinations such as 6:22–23) are discussed largely according to the Christian theological issues to which they appear relevant. In his earlier compositional analysis, Kloppenborg did attend to the pattern of 6:20–49. He argues that this cluster followed the pattern found in sapiential discourses such as Prov 1 and 3:13–35. In his later study of the social context of Q and substantive issues addressed by Q, however, he does not discuss Q 6:20–49, or any of the other discourses he identified in his compositional analysis, as a complete discourse. He rather reverted to the standard practice of discussing individual sayings according to the historical or, more commonly, the Christian theological issue(s) they seem to match. Analysis of Q 6:20–49 as a complete discourse in oral performance, however, like Kloppenborg's and Kirk's compositional analysis, suggests that it displays a coherent structure as a speech.

Insofar as we have been trained, on the assumptions of print culture, to read texts silently from the print on a page, it is difficult for us even to imagine how a given text would sound. In trying to appreciate Q speeches in oral performance, I have found helpful Dell Hymes' suggestion that oral-derived texts often take the form of lines (clause), verses, stanzas, and scenes or acts. When we attend to language patterns in Q, its speeches sound like poetry, with parallel lines usually of three or four words or phrases each. The lines can then be seen to be in sets that form "verses" and "stanzas." Since Q as a whole is not a story or epic poem, the overall structure cannot be heard as a sequence of scenes and acts. It is rather a sequence of short speeches on various concerns of the audience.

Given our habituation to print, it may be helpful to see the "text" of Q 6:20–49 blocked in "measured verse" in order to begin to imagine how it might have sounded in oral performance. This is presented in transliteration to keep printing costs down and to enable those without Greek to appreciate the Greek sounds. For the latter the English translation may also help not only to render the sense but also to facilitate an indirect appreciation of the repetition of words and verb forms in parallel lines and across stanzas. While usually following the wording agreed upon by the International Q Project, I have at points been led to an alternative by poetic considerations of oral performance. Further reflection on the text-in-performance has resulted in some changes in the reconstruction of the text transliterated and translated in Horsley and Draper. Perhaps it is well to keep in mind that the "text" below is based on a reconstruction (by the International Q Project) that is also based on reconstructions (of the critical texts of Matthew and Luke) from comparison of ancient manuscripts that text critics are now recognizing involved a certain interaction with continuing influence of memory and oral performance. (See the transliterations and translations on the following pages.)

Some of the key markers of oral-derived texts are repetition of words, sounds, and verbal forms, and parallel lines and sets of lines. The speech in Q 6:20–49 is remarkably rich in these regards. As a careful overview and reading aloud of the transliteration or the translation blocked in poetic lines will indicate, the stanzas of this speech consist largely of parallel lines, even four or five, which repeat the same or similar words in the same verbal forms. Even where the form moves away from parallel poetic lines into dual prose parables, the latter are closely parallel formulations. Where the lines are not precisely parallel (about trees and fruit, good and wicked men), they feature different combinations of the same words. Even beyond the parallel lines and other formulations, there is much repetition of sounds between lines and stanzas (Horsley and Draper: 210–15). Among other features that Bauman and Hymes suggest are typical in oral performance, figurative language comes to the fore in the later stanzas.

Even short of a fuller awareness of Mosaic covenantal tradition we can discern the language patterns within the stanzas and steps, and the connections and cohesion of the various steps in the speech. In a series of parallel lines, the two stanzas in step I deliver well-balanced blessings and woes on people at the opposite ends of the economic divide.

The teaching section in step II has a well-defined argumentative structure. The first stanza gives commands in (two or more likely four) parallel lines, the first being the more general category of "loving enemies," the rest being more specific about local conflictual economic relations. In another four parallel lines, the second stanza moves the commands into mainly economic relations in the local community, focusing on borrowing and lending. The third stanza applies "the golden rule" to these relationships as both explanation and motivation. Then in three parallel lines of rhetorical questions and reply, the fourth stanza calls the hearers to a standard of economic relations higher than that displayed by outsiders and (other) categories of people who are known for having lesser standards. This section of the speech is then summarized by a recapitulation of the commands, moving from the more general to the more specifically economic, and sanctioned by a promise of great reward and a call to imitate God's generous treatment of even unkind and wicked people, presumably referring back to the enemies and those who abuse, etc.

In the third step of the speech the commands shift focus to conflictual social relations in the local community. In an argumentative pattern less elaborate than the previous section, the first stanza gives a general command and principle, the second offers two (negative) illustrations, and the third, in an elaborate play on words and three rhetorical variations on the

Q 6:20–49 blocked in measured verse for hearing

Step I.
A.1. Makarioi   hoi ptochoi,   hoti humertera estin   he basileia tou theou.
2. Makarioi   hoi peinontes,   hoti chortasthesesthe.
3. Makarioi   hoi penthountes,   hoti paraklethesesthe.
4. Makarioi   este hotan   oneidisosin   hymas
                       kai dioxosin
                       kai eiposin poneron   kath' hymon
                       heneken   tou huiou tou anthropou.
5. Chairete   hoti ho misthos hymon   polus   en to ourano.
6. Houtos gar edioxan   tous prophetas   tous pro hymon.

B.1. Ouai   hoi plousioi   hoti apechete   ten paraklesin hymon.
2. Ouai   hoi empeplesmenoi   hoti peinasete.
3. Ouai   hoi gelontes   hoti penthesete
4. Ouai   hotan hymas   kalos eiposin   pantes
5. Houtos gar edioxan   tous pseudoprophetas.

Q 6:20–49 Translation in Measured Verse Blocked for Hearing

Step I.

A.1. Blessed are	the poor	for yours is	the kingdom of God.
2. Blessed are	those who hunger,	for you shall be filled.	
3. Blessed are	those who mourn,	for you shall laugh.	
4. Blessed are	you when	they reproach	you
		and speak evil	against you
		on account of	the son of man.
5. Rejoice and	for your reward	is great	in heaven.
For so	they persecuted	the prophets	before you.
B.1. Woe	to those who are rich,	for you have received	your consolation.
2. Woe	to those who are full,	for you shall go hungry.	
3. Woe	to those who laugh,	for you shall mourn.	
4. Woe	when all people	speak well	of you.
5. For so	they did	to the false prophets.	

Step II.

A.1. Agapate   tous echthrous   hymon,
  2. kalos poieite   tois misousin   hymas.
  3. Eulogeite   tous kataromenous   hymas,
  4. proseuchesthe   peri ton epereazonton hymas.

B.1. Hostis rapizei se   eis ten siagona,   strepson   auto kai allen.
  2. kai [ ]   sou to himation   aphes auto   kai ton chitona.
  3. To aitounti   se   dos,
  4. kai apo tou danizomenou   ta sa   me apaitei.

C.1. Kai kathos thelete   hina poiosin   hymin   hoi anthropoi,
         houtos   poieite   autois.

D.1. Ei agapate   tous agapontas hymas,   tina misthon echete;
         Ouchi kai telonai   to auto   poiousin;
  2. Kai ean agathopoiete tous agathapoiountas hymas,   tina misthon echete;
         Ouchi kai hoi [hamartol]oi   to auto   poiousin;
  3. Kai ean danisete   par' hon elpizete labein,   tina misthon echete;
         ouchi kai hoi [ethnic]oi   [to auto]   [poiousin]

Step II.
A.1. Love   the enemies   of you(rs),
   2. {Do good   to those who hate   you.
   3. Bless   those who curse   you,}
   4. Pray   for those who abuse   you.

B.1. To the one who strikes you   on the cheek   turn   also the other.
   2. And [from the one who takes]   your coat   [offer]   also the tunic.
   3. To the one who asks from you   give,
   4. And from the one who borrows   do not ask back.

C.1. And as you wish   that people   would do   to you,
   2. thus   do   to them.

D.1. And if you love   those who love   you,   what credit is that to you?
        For even the toll-collectors   do the same.
   2. And if you do good to those who do good to you,   what credit is that to you?
        For even the sinners   do the same.
   3. and if you lend to those from whom you hope to receive, what credit is that to you?
        Even the [other peoples]   do [the same]

E.1. Plen agapate   tous echthrous   hymon
     kai agathopoiete   kai danizete.
     Kai estai   ho misthos   hymon   [polus].
  2. Hopos genesthe huioi tou patros   hymon,
     hoti ton helion autou   anatellei   epi ponerous   kai agathous . . .
[??] Ginesthe   oiktirmones   hos ho pater hymon oiktirmon estin.

Step III
A.1. Me krinete   [hina] me krithete.
     [En ho gar krimati   krinete   krithesesthe.]
  2. Ho gar en metro   metreite   metrethesetai hymin.

B.1. Meti dunatai   tuphlos   tuphlon   hodegein?
     Ouchi   amphoteroi   eis bothunon   pesountai?
  2. ouk estin mathetes   hyper ton didaskalon
     arketon to mathete   hina genetai hos ho didaskalos autou.

C.1. Ti de blepeis   to karphos   to en to ophthalmo   tou adelphou
                          ten de en dokon ten en to [idio] ophthalmo ou katanoeis?
  2. pos [dunatai   legein]   to adelpho sou:
     aphes ekbalo   to karphos ek tou ophthalmou sou,
     kai idou   he dokos   en to ophthalmo sou?
  3. Hypokrita.
     Ekbale proton   ten dokon   ek tou ophthalmou sou,
     Kai tote diablepseis
     ekbalein   to karphos ek tou ophthalmou   tou adelphou sou.

E.1. But love   the enemies,   of you(rs)
     and do good,   and lend,
     and will be   the reward   of you[rs]   great.
  2. And you will become   sons   of your   Father,
     for his sun   rises   on the evil   and the good.
  3. Be   merciful,   as your Father   is merciful.

Step III.
A.1. And do not judge   and you will not be judged
     [for with the judgement   you judge   you will be judged,]
  2. for with the measure   you measure   it will be measured to you.

B.1. Can a blind person   guide   a blind person?
     Will not both   fall   into a pit?
  2. A disciple   is not above   his teacher
     but everyone will trained will be like   his teacher.

C.1. Why do you see   the speck   in the eye   of your brother,
     but   the log   in your own eye   you do not notice?
  2. How [can you say] to your brother,
     "Let me remove   the speck   from your eye,"
     and behold,   there is a log   in your own eye?
  3. Hypocrite!
     Remove first   the log   from your own eye,
     and then you will see
         to cast out   the speck   from the eye   of your brother.

Step IV.
A.1. Ouk estin   dendron kalon   poioun   karpon sapron
     oude palin   dendron sapron   poioun   karpon kalon.
  2. Ek gar tou karpou to dendron   ginosketai.
     meti sullegousin   apo akanthon   suka
                     a ek tribolon   stafulas.

B.1. Ho agathos anthropos   ek tou agathou thesaurou   ekballei agatha
     kai ho poneros anthropos ek tou ponerou thesauou   ekballei ponera.
  2. Ek gar perisseumatos   kardias   lalei   to stoma.

Step V.
A.1. Ti   me kaleite   kyrie, kyrie,
     kai   ou poieite   ha lego?

B.1. Pas ho akouon   mou tous logous   kai poion autous
  2. Homoios estin   anthropo,
     hos okodomesen   autou ten oikian   epi ten petran.
  3. Kai ... hoi potamoi ... prosepesan ... te oikia ekeine,
     kai ouk epesen   tethemelioto gar   epi ten petran.

C.1. Kai pas ho akouon   mou tous logous   kai me poion autous
  2. Homoios estin   anthropo,
     hos okodomesen   authou ten oikian epi ten ammon.
  3. Kai ... hoi potamoi ... prosekopsan   te oikia ekeine,
     kai epesen   kai en he ptosis autes   megale.

Step IV.
A.1. There is no   sound tree   which bears   bad fruit,
     nor again   a bad tree   which bears   sound fruit.
  2. For from the fruit   a tree   is known:
     they do not gather   figs   from thorns,
     or   grapes   from a bramble bush.

B.1. The good man   from the good treasure   brings forth   good (things).
     The evil man   from the evil (treasure) brings forth   evil (things).
  2. For from an overflow   of the heart   speaks   the mouth.

Step V.
A.1. Why   do you call me,   "lord, lord,"
     And   not do   what I tell you?

B.1. Every one   who hears my words,   and does them
  2. is like   a man
     who build   {his} house   upon the rock.
  3. And the rain came down and the river beat upon that house,
     and it did not fall,   for it had been founded upon the rock.

C.1. And everyone   who hears my words,   and does not do them.
  2. is like   a man
     who built   {his] house   upon the sand.
  3. And the rain came down and the river beat upon that house,
     and it fell   and its [fall] was   great.

same theme and point, exhorts the listeners to tend first to the beam that is obscuring their own vision, before lashing out against their neighbors.

The final two steps in the speech focus on motivation and sanction for the commands and exhortations given in the previous two steps. The first stanza of step four, with more plays on words in parallel lines, picks up on the economic theme of the first and second steps with the image of bearing fruit. The second stanza then addresses motives of speaking good and wicked things, picking up on the commands in the third step of the speech. The final step gives a sanction on all the commands given in steps two and three with a double parable. Thus not only is there coherence within the different steps of the speech, but there is a clear cohesion across the sections that enable us to discern that a clear rhetorical structure in the speech as a whole. The *text*, the "word" that we are trying to hear through the "words" in the lines and stanzas and sections, is the overall speech of Q 6:20–49.

Even before we move more fully into the covenantal tradition that this speech references, we can detect at least a few clues as to its performance *context* and *register*. Insofar as the content of the commands given in steps two and three pertains to economic and social relations of people in regular interaction with each other, borrowing and lending, insulting and criticizing one another, the context and the register of the discourse must have some connection with local community relations (Horsley 1987: ch. 9). Further investigation and awareness of the Israelite covenantal tradition will enable us to become far more precise about the key aspects of this speech in oral performance.

Israelite Covenant Tradition

Since the Mosaic Covenant was central to Israelite tradition generally, it may not be surprising that we have several sources from the scriptural great tradition, and the scribal communities that cultivated it, that help us project likely cultivation of parallel little tradition in the villages of Galilee in connection with which Q materials originated (Horsley and Draper: ch. 9).

The Mosaic Covenant given to Israel on Sinai (Exodus 20:2–17) exhibits a distinctive structure. It opens with a brief statement of God's deliverance of the people from bondage in Egypt, then presents ten fundamental principles of social policy, four demanding exclusive loyalty to God and six concerning key aspects of social-economic relations among Israelites. Inserted into the second and perhaps the fifth principle are blessing-and-curse-like sanctions on keeping the principles (20:5b–6, 12b). The Covenant proper is then followed by a covenantal "law-code" or "ordinances" (Exod 21–23) that apply the basic principles of social policy to social-economic life. The whole is framed by covenant ceremonies (Exod 19 and 24).

The covenant renewal ceremony in Josh 24 exhibits the same structural components. Following the lengthy recitation of what Yahweh has done for Israel (24:2-13) comes a call and commitment to exclusive service to Yahweh (24:14-28) that involves obligation to observe "statutes and ordinances" (24:24-26), with the people witnessing against themselves and a large stone as witness (24:22, 26-27) and the threat of punishment for violation of the ordinances (24:19-20). The book of Deuteronomy is structured according to these same components: a recitation of God's deliverance of the people, a sustained body of covenantal laws and ordinances interspersed with covenantal exhortation, followed by a long list of blessings and curses. The book concludes with another recitation of the Mosaic covenant, with emphasis and reminder of God's deliverance and remembering the blessings and curses.

The fundamental structure in all of these covenantal materials is threefold: a pronouncement of God's deliverance, presentation of covenantal principles, laws, and/or teachings, and a promise of reward (blessing) for keeping and of punishment (curses) for not keeping the principles, laws, or teachings.

The Mosaic covenant was also simplified and continued in other forms. Already in Deuteronomy covenantal materials were couched in terms of two ways, the way of life and the way of death (30:15-20), in which the blessings and curses became the rewards or punishments that would result from the choice of way. Also as scribal circles began to cultivate mosaic covenantal materials, they identified the wisdom they had traditionally cultivated with the Torah (Prov 1-9; Sir 24). Sayings that might be formally classified as "sapiential," therefore might well be sapientially shaped covenantal teaching. For example, Sir 29:1 ("The merciful lend to their neighbors; by holding out a helping hand they keep the commandments") perpetuates the central Mosaic covenantal theme stated in Exod 22:25 of mercy manifested in local economic relations.

Because of the importance of the economic basis of life in an agrarian society, Israelite tradition included in the covenantal "statues and ordinances" and other covenantal teachings elaborate provisions for maintaining the economic viability of each family in the village community that constituted the fundamental social unit of Israel. Israelites were to give or lend to their unfortunate neighbors, and they were to lend without interest (Exod 22:25-27; Deut 15:7-11; Lev 25:35-38). For more serious difficulties of spiraling indebtedness and enslavement for debt, Israel developed the principles of the cancellation of debts and release of debt-slaves every seven years (Exod 21:2-6; Deut 15:1-5, 9, 12-18; Lev 24:39-43).

Some traditional covenantal teachings go well beyond case laws for concrete occurrences of violence and injury to address the social tensions and conflicts that fester in social relations and that might lead to violence. For example, the covenantal teaching in Lev 19 includes admonitions against holding grudges, harboring resentment, and allowing hate to simmer (19:17-18).

The discovery of texts from the Qumran community has provided a remarkable window onto the continuation of Israelite covenantal tradition, including the remarkable tenacity of the fundamental structure of the covenant (Baltzer). While heavily adapted to suit the apocalyptic perspective and rigorous discipline of the community, the Community Rule from Qumran (1QS and parallels from 4Q) not only includes basic Mosaic covenantal material, but is a renewed Mosaic covenant in form. It even includes instructions for the ceremony of covenant renewal. Remarkably, the document both follows the basic structure of the Mosaic Covenant and also adapts that traditional structure in ways that are highly suggestive for our hearing of the longest speech in Q. The key section that runs from 1QS 3:13–4:26 follows the basic three-step structure of the Mosaic covenant. But that whole section also constitutes an overview of the declaration of God's eventual deliverance as a prologue to the remainder of the Rule that lays down covenantal rules for the community, its council, and its master (5:1–11:24).

Moreover, the Damascus Rule also found at Qumran follows the same broad covenantal structure. After the opening prologue reviewing Israel's history under its God (1:1–6:11) come covenantal rulings for the community (6:11–7:4) followed by declarations of long life and salvation for those who keep the covenant and retribution for those who do not (7:4–6, 8–10; and in recension B, 2:28–36). The laws and instructions for community life in the rest of the document appear to "flesh out" the basic principles of community life, somewhat parallel to the way the covenantal law-code in Exod 21–23 does in the "original" Mosaic covenant.

Even more significant for our hearing of the speech in Q 6:20–49 are the adaptations made to the covenant components at Qumran. First, in the opening section of instructions for covenant renewal ceremonies, the blessings and curses component has shifted function. While these are still, in effect, sanctions on keeping the covenant laws, the blessings and curses now reassure the members of the community of their own redemption by God. In the longer covenantal instruction that follows, the blessings and curses no longer function as closing sanctions, but have been taken up into the declaration of God's deliverance. Thus a declaration of God's deliverance in the present and/or future complements or replaces that of God's deliverance in the past as the basis of the people's obligation and motivation to keep the covenantal laws and teachings.

Second, the Scrolls retain the "sanction" component. The Damascus Rule declares salvation for covenant keepers and destruction for covenant violators, only now without the explicit language of blessings and curses (see further the parallel in Barnabas 21:1).

Third, the Community Rule indicates clearly that renewal of the Mosaic covenant was ceremonially enacted (1QS 5:6–11; 6:14–16). The master and/or priests and Levites delivered covenantal instruction to the covenantal community. They were literally "blessing the men of the lot of God" and pronouncing "curses on all the men of the lot of Belial." The renewal of the covenant was an annual performance (1QS 2:19–22). Members of the Qumran community, which was literate, wrote this down (with serious variations from manuscript to manuscript). But the written form of covenant renewal was incidental or merely instrumental to oral performance or enactment of covenantal renewal.

Fourth, a number of themes and particular features of covenantal teaching at Qumran may be significant windows onto what other communities might also be doing. The prologue proclaims "an end of injustice" (1QS 4:18–24; cf. Q 6:20–21). The community that holds fast to the renewed covenant "shall practice . . . justice and uprightness and charity and modesty, . . . [and] no stubbornness of heart" (1QS 5:4–6), and the community members "shall love each man his brother as himself; they shall succor the poor, the needy, and the stranger" (CD 6:20–21; cf. Q 6:27–39). No one is to "address a companion with anger or ill-temper . . ." or "hate him, . . . but [is to] rebuke him . . . [and] admonish him in the presence of witnesses (1QS 5:25–6:1; paralleled in CD 7:2–3; 9:2–5; cf. Q 6:37–38; and the closely related Q 17:1–4).

Hearing Q 6:20–49 as a Covenantal Renewal Speech

Once we have refreshed our own cultural memory of what were the likely contents of ancient Israelite tradition, the number of allusions that the speech in Q 6:20–49 makes to Israelite covenantal laws and teaching is striking. Insofar as the Israelite tradition in which Q speeches were grounded was unwritten popular tradition, it is inappropriate to look for "scriptural quotations." Yet insofar as Israelite popular tradition was paralleled in the Jerusalem-based great tradition, one version of which lies behind what we know as the Hebrew Bible, we can catch many of the allusions to Mosaic covenantal tradition from our familiarity with written texts such as Exod 20–23, Deuteronomy, and Leviticus 19 and 25. "Be merciful, just as your Father is merciful" clearly alludes to or even recites a covenantal principle, such as the one found in Lev 19:2. The commands and exhortations in Q 6:27–36 remind us of traditional covenantal teaching such as seen in Lev 19:17–18, which concludes with the injunction to "love your neighbor." To love your *enemy* is reminiscent of traditional covenantal teaching such as found in Exod 23:4–5 and Deut 22:1–4. The reference to the "cloak" in the Q commands is clearly an allusion to the garment taken in pledge, dealt with in Exod 22:25–26 and Deut 24:10–13 (cf. Amos 2:8). Jesus' command to lend freely is surely a reference to the covenantal command to lend freely, as in Exod 22:25 and 25:35–38.

These multiple references in the exhortations of 6:27–36 to covenantal commands, laws, and ordinances should be sufficient to lead us to listen for other covenantal components in the speech. Matthew's expansion and reshaping of this Q speech, "the Sermon on the Mount," has long been recognized as a covenantal discourse. What about the Q speech Matthew used? In fact, if we simply attend to the structuring elements in Matthew 5–7, which he apparently derived directly from Q, we can recognize the fundamental covenantal components as the structuring elements in Q as well.

To take the more obvious ending of the speech first, "hearing my words and (not) acting upon them" (6:47–49) performs the same function in the Q speech as did the "blessings and curses" in the early versions of Mosaic covenant (as evident in Deut 27–28). Heard in isolation, the double parable of the houses built on the rock and the sand sounds simply like just another piece of wisdom. In this speech, however, it is framed as a simile to "keeping my words," a term used traditionally for the basic covenantal commands, and it is located structurally as the concluding sanction on covenantal teaching (in the tradition of Exod 21–23; Deut 15; Lev 19). The Damascus Rule and the Epistle of Barnabas (and Deut 30:15–20) provide other examples of the sanction component pronouncing salvation and punishment without the explicit language of "blessings and curses."

"Blessings and curses," of course, are prominently present in the Q covenant speech. But what formed the closing sanctioning component in the early Mosaic covenantal texts has been transformed in the Q speech into the opening declaration of new deliverance. Even Q interpreters who are convinced that Q 6 is comprised almost exclusively of sapiential instruction admit that the beatitudes are not typical sapiential macarisms. And the Community Rule from Qumran provides a clear example of how the "blessings and curses" component of the Covenant could be relocated and transformed into (part of) the prologue as a declaration of God's deliverance expected in the imminent future.

Even from this brief survey it is possible to recognize that the speech in Q 6:20–49 not only makes numerous references to covenantal teaching, but that structurally and substantively the speech constitutes a covenantal discourse standing in a long tradition of covenantal teaching. This also enables us to "catch" certain indications of the text, context, and register of the speech. The *text* being performed is the whole speech, not the separate sayings or sections. "Blessed are you who . . ." signals God's new action of deliverance on which the renewal of covenant commands and commitment can be based. And the covenant renewal is not complete until the closing sanctions are delivered in the double parable motivating the hearers to "keep my words." While the speech seems to have five "steps" or "sections" when heard somewhat like Hymes hears stories as a series of "scenes," the overall structure of this covenantal speech has three parts:

- declaration of God's deliverance: "blessed are the poor/ woe to the rich," 6:20–26
- covenantal teaching/admonitions: "love your enemies; do not judge," 6:27–36, 37–42
- motivation and sanction: "from the fruit a tree is known; houses built," 6:43–45, 46–49

Matthew's "Sermon on the Mount" has the same three-part overall structure: blessings and so on (5:3–16); covenant law and teaching (5:17–7:12); and sanctions (7:13–27).

Within the more general context of the assembly of a movement or community, the particular performance *context* of this speech is the community's celebration of covenant renewal. In a new movement it is conceivable that this might have been on a weekly basis. The speech, moreover, is clearly in the covenant *register*. This is evident both in the structural framing components, the blessings and the "keep my words," and in the many covenantal commands and exhortations that allude to traditional covenantal teachings.

What makes the whole speech "work" is that it references the Israelite covenantal *tradition* in multiple ways, one after another, on basic economic issues and on troublesome social conflicts that would have been dividing and weakening the village communities. Hearing pronouncement of God's new act of deliverance gives the hearers "a new lease on life," renewed hope that their lives will indeed be blessed. And that enables them to then hear the admonitions to "get their act together" on the basis of the deeply-rooted traditional Israelite covenantal values of mutual sharing and solidarity over against the difficult political-economic circumstances they all have to deal with. It is also important to recognize that the referencing of Israelite covenantal tradition lies not only in all the particular allusions to familiar customary covenantal laws and teachings such as that about a garment taken in pledge, but in the structural components and the very action that is taking place in the performance of the speech. The hearers are invited to resonate with the whole tradition of covenant making and covenant renewal in their culture, from Moses and Joshua to John the Baptist's preaching that preceded Jesus' own. To play with our analytical categories, the communication context and register both reference the tradition and thereby resonate with the hearers in the community that identifies with and lives in and on the basis of that tradition.

In considering the ways in which the hearers would likely have resonated with this speech as it metonymically referenced the popular Israelite covenantal tradition, we may focus on possibilities not evident from other modes of appropriating Q materials. The opening declaration of blessings and woes, for example, would have resonated with people who believed their situation hopeless because they were suffering under the implementation precisely of the covenantal curses. To those who believed themselves unworthy and perhaps even cursed, the speaker proclaimed "yours is the kingdom of God" and then, correspondingly declared that it is the rich who stand under the curses for having violated the covenant.

A major factor in the way that the covenantal speech in Q resonated with its hearers as it referenced covenantal tradition would have been its relevance to their concrete life-situation. As noted above, the exhortative content of the speech pertained to local economic and social interaction, evidently in circumstances of poverty, hunger, debt, and multiple social conflicts, that is, to village communities. Villagers, who comprised the vast majority of any traditional agrarian society such as in ancient Palestine and Syria, are always marginal economically, under pressure to render up their produce to multiple layers of rulers, leaving insufficient resources for family and community life. That scarcity—hunger and debt ("Our Father, . . . give us bread . . . and cancel our debts")—leads to internal social tensions and conflicts. The covenantal speech in Q begins with the assurance of God's action in addressing precisely such economic and social distress. The covenantal teachings that reference covenantal tradition through focal instances, such as the "garment taken in pledge" and generous lending, then challenge and empower the people to renew their own commitments to the communal sharing and mutual support that stood at the basis of traditional Israelite community life. But that tradition and references to it would also have resonated with other, non-Israelite villagers as well. As we can explore in a related essay in Part Two below, comparative studies of other peasantries make clear that the Israelite covenant tradition addressed some of the most fundamental issues faced by villagers nearly anywhere, regardless of their particular cultural-ethnic heritage and language. The covenantal speech in Q and the Mosaic covenantal tradition in which it was rooted and which it referenced would have been easy to identify with and to appropriate by other ancient peoples. And that enables us to understand also how a movement sustained by repeated performance of speeches such as Q 6:20–49 could easily spread from Aramaic-speaking Galilean villages to Greek-speaking villages in southern Syria and beyond.

Jesus' "Covenantal Discourse" on the Plain (Luke 6:12–7:17) as Oral Performance
POINTERS TO "Q" AS MULTIPLE ORAL PERFORMANCE

Jonathan A. Draper

1. Introduction

The popularity of the new quest for the historical Jesus has given the question of sources for the Jesus tradition a new urgency. Central to the reconstruction offered by many scholars is the twin assumption that Q is a written source, which can be analysed like other literary sources, and that it is the earliest and therefore the most authoritative source for the quest. A further assumption is that the material in Q originated as isolated or "floating" sayings unconnected with each other until they were put together in written form. The result of these assumptions has been a flood of publications about Q and its redaction, in which its existence as a document is hardly even questioned any more. Scholars live in a world dominated by print, by books, by personal libraries, desks and paper, and today, of course, the computer. This tends to colour our perceptions of the way traditions develop. Yet William V. Harris (1989) has shown that the ancient world was predominantly an oral culture also, with less than ten percent of any ancient community, namely the elite and its retainer class, likely to be able to read, let alone write. Whether Jesus himself was able to read and write must remain an open question (one would have to ask *how* a peasant from a village of a few hundred people without public buildings could have been literate), but clearly the majority of his followers would have been illiterate. There is thus some advantage in approaching the question of Q and the earliest Jesus tradition from the vantage point of the third world, where orality often remains the dominant cultural practice–often to the dismay of theological educators seeking to teach within the paradigm of Western "essay-text literacy" (Gee 1996; cf. Draper 1997).

Southern Africa before the arrival of the missionaries was a world without text or writing, dominated completely by oral tradition. The arrival of literacy was closely associated with the arrival of the Bible. Most South

Africans are at least functionally literate today, but the underlying cultural practice remains, in many ways, oral, even with respect to the Bible (Draper 1996). The oral forms and traditions remain operative, even in writing, as Jeff Opland's excellent study of Xhosa *izibongo* has shown (1983; cf. Gunner 1984; Brown 1998), and many subsequent studies have confirmed the resilience and flexibility of various South African oral traditions (for instance, the various essays in Sienaert et al. 1991; Brown 1999). Embedded oral forms and traditions allow people to remember astonishing amounts of material, while at the same time ensuring that the material is to some extent always fluid and adaptable. For instance, the praise poems of the Zulu kings, collected by Trevor Cope (1968), show both stability and partial verbatim agreement from one performance to another, but also considerable variety in the ordering and choice of the possible components to suit the occasion. The choice of material points the message of the performer on a particular occasion and often implies criticism or flattery of the person being praised relating to some current affair by means of the reference of the tradition (e.g., Opland 1983:7–9, 99–103; Vansina 1985:100–114). Partial citation of the tradition depends on the community's familiarity with the whole tradition. The performance can begin and end at any point without losing the concentration and appreciation of the hearers. There is no "original performance" or "original text." There are only particular performances, varying according to circumstances.

Studies of orality in relationship to text made by anthropologists have made significant progress in recent years (excellent survey in Botha, 2003). The early studies of Parry (collected in Parry 1971) and Lord (1960) have given place to those of Walter Ong (1967, 1982) and Jack Goody (1977), and their initial theories have, in their turn, been partly challenged and partly developed by Ruth Finnegan (1970, 1977, 1988), Dennis Tedlock (1971, 1985), Dell Hymes (1981), Jeff Opland (1983), Jan Vansina (1985), Jack Goody (revised position, 1986), and John Miles Foley (1985, 1988, 1991, 1995), to name but a few. Scholars of Q are not unaware of the importance of the question of oral tradition for the mediation of the sayings of Jesus. Yet their conception of oral tradition, and its relationship with text, in the field of New Testament studies is still dominated by form criticism, which emerged in Germany in the 1920s on the basis of late nineteenth Century theories of folk tradition (Horsley and Draper).

While other issues have long since been resolved, the question of the relationship been oral tradition and written text remains open. The idea propounded by Ong and Goody, based on the theory of Vygotsky and Luria, that literacy re-structures consciousness and that there is a "great divide" between orality and literacy as a result, has been largely abandoned (even by Ong and Goody) after the research of Scribner and Cole. A more balanced viewpoint today sees a continuum between "primary orality" and textual "literacy," in which oral forms and traditions persist even after a person may become literate (see especially Opland 1983).

Secondly, even in "literate" societies in the ancient world, texts were largely performed aloud and received orally, rather than read individually in silence (Achtemeier 1990; Dewey 1989, 1991; Botha 1991, 1993). Consequently, even after an oral tradition is written down, it may continue to function almost entirely in oral performance and produce new forms and versions which may get written down again. It is thus more appropriate to speak of oral-derived texts for texts like Q in Matthew and Luke, and to reserve the expression "oral tradition" strictly for oral performances where no written texts exist in the society (i.e., primary orality).

Thirdly, it is now recognized that few could read in the ancient world, so that even members of the ruling elite may have required a scribe to read and write for them as an *emanuensis*. Less than ten percent would have been literate and, while most people in the ancient world would have been aware of texts and their function, they would have been acquainted with texts exclusively through oral performances.

This lack of awareness of developments in the study of orality-literacy have distorted the study of Q. John Kloppenborg, for instance, in his seminal work, *The Formation of Q*, specifically addresses whether Q is oral material or a written composition, since "the understanding of the genre of a text is always constitutive to the act of understanding" (1987:2). He concludes that Q was a literary production in the nature of a *chriae* collection of sayings of divine wisdom attributed to Jesus (and John), analogous to Cynic *chriae* (324). Consequently, narrative parts of Q such as the temptation of Jesus or the healing of the Centurion's servant are seen as late additions at a time when the literary tendency was towards *bios* or a life of Jesus as hero (261). However, Kloppenborg bases his understanding of oral tradition on models which stress the "great divide" between oral and written tradition too strongly. Galilee was not a truly oral culture, since writing was known and used even if the majority of the members of that culture were illiterate. The existence of a written tradition extends the possibilities of transmission, continuity and composition of oral tradition even where it is not directly utilized (Goody 1987:91–100). Oral tradition continues to be performed even where it exists already in written form as an *aide memoire*. The kind of individual silent reading and writing of texts in isolation from a community was unknown in the ancient world, and indeed unknown until the advent of widespread literacy and mass print culture associated with the twentieth century (Cf. Ong 1982:156–60). Thus multiple forms of an oral tradition could co-exist side by side with a written text of the same tradition, and emerge in rival texts as well (e.g., the different versions of the orally performed hymns and stories of Isaiah Shembe in the rival communities headed by rival successors; see Hexham 1994, as against Muller 1996, Gunner 2002). I suspect that the relationship between oral and written tradition is just as complex and problematic in the case of Cynic *chriae* as it is with the Jesus tradition, so that the analogy is more apparent than real. This would be the subject of a separate study. Oral texts written down do not lose their most characteristic features, although clearly the paralinguistic features will be lost—gesture, intonation, pause, pitch and so on. Anthropologists have recently been forced more and more to find ways of recovering oral performances frozen in text by transcription (e.g., Hymes 1981; Tedlock 1971; 1985). The nature and context of the performance have to be identified from the "textual rhetoric" which encodes the "tradition of reception" (Foley 1995:148). Treating such a "frozen oral text" as if it were a literary or scribal composition distorts interpretation. Nevertheless, it comes to us today via a written text, so that it can no longer be termed "oral tradition" in the undifferentiated sense that we have used of southern African oral tradition before the arrival of the missionaries. Hence, in this paper, we will refer to such "frozen oral text" in the gospel tradition as "oral-derived text" rather than the older expression "oral tradition." Oral performance operates in a different register (particularly in terms of code and mode) from literary composition, and it produces a different discourse (Horsley and Draper).

These observations are particularly important in any attempt to approach the Covenantal Discourse[1] of Jesus in Q. Kloppenborg seems to assume that an oral performance means "simply a set of folk sayings of a pre-literate group" (1987:90). Study of oral-derived text, however, shows that it can have a high level of sophistication and most characteristically is performed in coherent discourses associated with particular contexts. He assumes that the Christian movement was largely a "middle class" phenomenon (ibid.), whereas this terminology is inaccurate and misleading in ancient societies, which were based not primarily on wealth and control of the means of production but on inherited status and the land (Rohrbaugh 1984:519–46; cf. Ste. Croix 1981; Alföldy 1985). There was no "middle class" in the ancient Mediterranean world, and modern anthropological studies of peasant societies, ancient and modern, offer more appropriate models (e.g., Wolf 1966; Sjoberg 1960; Lenski 1966; Lenski and Lenski 1985). We have to think of a simple opposition between the ruling elite (including their retainer class), and the peasants (including carpenters, fishermen etc.). So in the case of Q, we would have to ask starkly: was it the production of the ruling elite or of peasant society in the first instance. Peasants were virtually certain to be illiterate in the ancient Greco-Roman world, where no more than ten percent of any region were likely to have been literate (and mostly from the ruling elite, naturally, with some overflow into urban traders on the fringe of the retainer class: Harris 1989:329). In this literate group, the majority would be able to read and fewer to write,

---

1. The term "covenantal discourse" is preferred to "sermon" here, since it emphasizes the communal, performed nature of the material. Besides this, the word "sermon" is filled with later Christian content inappropriate to the analysis of a first century oral-derived text.

although they may have had some vicarious access to texts. For the vast illiterate majority, their culture was mediated through oral performance, since even the written texts were performed aloud by specialists and remembered orally rather than read in isolation (*contra* Kloppenborg 1987:7, "a text is meant to be read, not performed"). Even the literate would be used to *hearing* texts recited rather than reading them alone.

While it is not a direct parallel, in the early colonial period in southern Africa, local literate entrepreneurs in the "corner shops" in small rural towns provided their skill in reading aloud and writing from dictation to the illiterate majority, so that letters flowed to and fro from the mines and cities to the rural areas. Of course, cheap writing material and postal services have no real parallel in the ancient world and schooled people from local communities would also have been much scarcer. Still, the reading of letters or scrolls over and over again would have made the written text into living word, as the Zulu, Sambana Mtimkulu, responding to a letter from his brother, Zatshuke Mtimkulu, on 12 October 1884, wrote, "we have heard your words my brother just as if it were a person speaking them to us here" (Khumalo 2003).

Kloppenborg gives four reasons against a consideration of Q as oral tradition: "the presence of strong verbal agreements of Matthew and Luke, the use of peculiar or unusual phrases by both evangelists, agreements in the order of Q pericopae and the phenomenon of doublets" (1987:42). These assumptions need to be closely examined in the light of new evidence concerning oral-derived text.

Firstly, he is right in rejecting the idea of a school memorization program lying behind the Jesus tradition (as in Gerhardsson 1961), for which there is no evidence in a considerable body of recorded material. In Luke the narrative framework of the covenantal discourse is freely composed, while ritually performed, mnemonically structured or proverbial material is more fixed in form. The narrative preserves elements of setting and story necessary for the proper understanding of the latter. Hence it is necessary to distinguish between material structured for memorization and narrative or philosophical material (Goody 1987). This can be illustrated from the transcribed reminiscences of the illiterate Zulu woman, Patricia Nomguqo Dlamini (Draper 2002; Filter and Bourquin 1986), at the age of about sixty seven, who had been a member of King Ceteshwayo's *isiGodlo* (something like a harem) in her youth and became a key Christian evangelist in Zululand after the king's defeat and her conversion. Her reminiscences contain verbatim recitals of *iziBongo*, dance songs and spells, together with accounts of the actual occasions on which they were performed, even in the case of the war song sung by Dingaan's warriors in the massacre of Piet Retief and his men at the royal kraal, which she learnt from her father (Ibid.: 13–14). The highly structured nature of the poems and songs results in their preservation with a high degree of accuracy, while the surrounding narrative is ad lib. The same result can be found in the Zulu oral material collected by James Stuart from multiple sources (translated in Cope 1968; cf. Opland 1983, Gunner 1984).

Secondly, the use of peculiar phrases by both Matthew and Luke is not an argument against oral-derived text, since the use of metonymic markers is characteristic of its function. John Miles Foley has demonstrated that peculiar words such as archaisms and lexically opaque words in Serbian oral charms are really metonymic: they "embody a semantically unencumbered species of coding in which the concrete integer... can stand for a complex and richly nuanced traditional idea under the aegis of the performance event" (1995:114–15). These words are retained by the oral-derived text precisely because of their peculiarity, because they mark out a particular discourse unequivocally. This is particularly clear in the Zulu *iziBongo* praise poems, where epithets associated with particular historical figures are no longer understood but continue to be passed on verbatim because of their metonymic associations, i.e. the mere mention of the praise name conjures up the person even if its reference is not understood (Cope 1968:35; Gunner 1984:266–69).

Thirdly, the existence of a common order for the pericopae is no argument against oral-derived text at all: it assumes that oral-derived text is passed on in small, disembodied units with no identifiable context. This was the assumption of the form critics, but it does not hold up in the face of recent studies of oral-derived text. In fact, the reverse is true: oral-derived text is transmitted in coherent discourses and has no meaning outside of specific contexts of performance (Foley 1995:47–49). Even a proverb, which comes closest to disembodied currency, depends for its meaning on a specific cultural context since it is "tied to its interactional setting" (Penfield 1983:2), and often depends on an underlying assumed narrative. The extended covenantal discourse of Jesus, which is extant in various performances of Q, demonstrates a certain coherence in overall structure and content with considerable variety in particulars. Luke 6:12–7:17 seems to be presenting the covenantal discourse in its simplest form, in contrast to the much expanded and developed performances of Matthew 5–7 and the *Didache* 1–6.

Fourthly, the relevance of the phenomenon of doublets is ambivalent as a basis for testing the presence of oral tradition. Repetition or redundancy is a common feature of oral performance, since it aids memory and fluency in reception of the tradition: "the mind must move ahead more slowly, keeping close to the focus of attention much of what it has already dealt with. Redundancy, repetition of the just-said, keeps both speaker and hearer surely on the track" (Ong 1982:40). The argument, in my opinion, runs the other way, in favour of oral-derived text, with respect to doublets.

Finally, Kloppenborg argues that there are no signs of oral character in formulaic diction, mnemonics, and balanced units. Part of the task of this chapter will be to demonstrate that, on the contrary, the units of the covenantal discourse of Jesus in Q show a clear oral patterning and structure, which will have aided performance and remembrance of the tradition.

To compare the covenantal discourse on the plain in Luke's performance and the covenantal discourse on the mount in Matthew's performance, together with the same material in the *Didache*, would be an impossible task for this essay. So we focus on the covenantal discourse in Luke and finish with some observations on the way it relates to the other performances of the same oral tradition. Our assumption is that the search for an original text of oral-derived text is an illusion that indeed results in neutering the tradition and systematically *mis*-understanding its performative significance. This is because the coherent *discourse* of oral-derived text depends, like all communication, in fact, though more intensively, on discerning the discourse *register*. Words do not mean in and of themselves, but only in combination with other words in particular communicative events, in particular communicative contexts, between particular senders and receivers, and in particular communicative genres.

2. Discourse Register

Without wishing to belabor the point, we need to remember that words have meaning only in context, since there is no neutral or absolute meaning of a text. As the sociolinguist M. A. K. Halliday makes clear:

> Now one important fact about speaking and understanding language is that it always takes place in a context. We do not simply 'know' our mother tongue as an abstract system of vocal signals, or as if it was some sort of grammar book with a dictionary attached. We know it in the sense of knowing how to use it; we know how to communicate with other people, how to choose forms of language that are appropriate to the type of situation we find ourselves in, and so on. (1978:13)

Words do not mean in and of themselves. They mean in relation to other words and to the guesses (usually well-founded) we make about how they relate to each other and what we take to be happening (Gee 1996:77). We can only understand what is meant in speech or writing when we know what is going on socially. There is no abstract meaning:

> Essentially what this implies is that language comes to life only when functioning in some environment. We do not experience language in isolation—if we did we would not recognize it as language—but always in relations to a scenario, some background of persons and actions and events from which the things which are said derive their meaning. This is referred to as the "situation," so language is said to function in "contexts of situation" and any account of language which fails to build in the situation as an essential ingredient is likely to be artificial and unrewarding (Halliday 1978:28–29).

We can only understand a written or spoken statement because we know what is going on. If we do not know what is going on, we are likely to systematically *mis*-understand. This is the basis on which most comic plays and films operate. Someone says and does things which are inappropriate to the situation out of ignorance, while the audience has access to the information the dramatic character does not have (e.g., Malvolio strutting about in his cross-gartered stockings in Shakespeare's *Twelfth Night*).

As a guideline, we could take Halliday's three factors which determine the register of communication: what is going on and where is it happening (*field*); who is communicating with whom, including aspects of class, gender, and power relations (*tenor*); and what method of communication has been adopted, that is, speech, song, letter (*mode*). Unless we take account of these things we will not be successful dialogue partners. These factors were developed on the basis of his research into spoken language, though they apply equally to written language. The difference is that what is written can be more discursive and explicit, since the writer and the reader have the chance to take time, to go back and forward, to reconsider what has been communicated, whereas what is communicated orally cannot be revisited. It is remembered only if it is memorable. Most of the time we are not concerned about whether people remember what we say beyond the moment, but when we are anxious for whatever reason that our words be remembered, we take particular care to structure our communication for memory. For this reason, mnemonic clues become particularly important: repetition, inclusio, formula, sound patterning, rhythm, balance and verbal signals to mark the divisions in thought. In performance we use silence, volume control, bodily signals and eye contact also, which are lost, of course, when an oral performance is transcribed.

3. Luke's Performance in the "Covenantal Discourse on the Plain"

Like Brandon Scott and Margaret Dean in their innovative "sound mapping" of Matthew's Covenantal Discourse on the Mount (1993), I have been attempting to "hear" the sound of the Greek text. However, my approach differs in two significant respects.

In the first place, I believe that their analysis mistakenly ignores the aspect of discourse register, which is the key to understanding an oral performance. I argue that an oral performance, even one frozen by being transcribed in text, will signal its register rhetorically, as John Miles Foley has rightly pointed out (1995:60–98; cf. Horsley and Draper: 175–94, 250–59). In the case of Jesus' covenantal discourse in all its forms, this will involve taking the narrative framework of the covenantal discourse seriously. The narrative framework signals the register, and stripping it off, on the assumption that it is redactional, seriously prejudices any attempt to understand the oral performance. In the case of Luke's performance, this means that the discourse consists of 6:12–7:17. Yet, the narrative framework is more freely composed in the style of Luke's narration elsewhere. This suggests that *narrative* performance is not rhetorically encoded in the same way as the discourse of Jesus and cannot be set out satisfactorily in models of sound patterning.

Secondly, since I find it very difficult to *hear* a Greek text, I prefer to work with the concept of sound balance, and to see alliteration and assonance as supportive of sound balance. Finally, I want to explore the way the sound balance interacts with binary oppositions, where these emerge from the text. I am not a structuralist, but I am intrigued at the way binary oppositions seem to emerge in oral texts, in a way they do not necessarily seem to in written texts. I agree with Dell Hymes that our "sound map" should not follow mechanical rules slavishly, but should allow an interaction of syntactic, sound and sense markers to determine our oral reconstruction. I will provide two different analyses of the oral-performative features of the whole passage.

The first will follow Hymes' model of "measured verse," which stresses the narrative flow of the whole, and is based on finite verbs and connectives. Hymes shows especially well how an oral performance tends to use couplets and triplets, and to fall naturally into larger balanced units (Horsley and Draper). I will use the English text for this, to aid speed of our comprehension and perception of the flow of the performance.

The second will follow Marcel Jousse's model of "rhythmography," which stresses the performative balance of small units within the overall structure. Again, there will be little time to analyze my decisions in detail, but at least I can give an overall impression, which can be justified in detail elsewhere. Edgard Sienaert, Jousse's translator and exponent (1990; 1999; Sienaert and Conolly), interpreting the work of Marcel Jousse (1990; 1997), has argued that oral performance is marked by careful structuring of "units of sound and sense uttered or chanted in a single breath." These are rhythmically balanced in terms of "cradling" and "lifting":

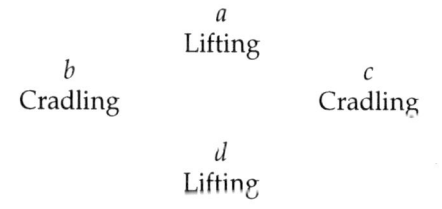

```
                    a
                 Lifting
        b                      c
     Cradling                Cradling
                    d
                 Lifting
```

This rhythmic balancing implies the bodily movement of alternatively rocking back and forward or side to side, which characterizes the memorization and performance of oral tradition in primary oral communities. The alternating movements mark and coordinate the units of material. Jousse claims that these characteristics of oral performance, which he himself learnt as a French peasant child, chanting and singing oral tradition under the instruction of his illiterate mother (Sienaert and Conolly: 66), are universal and relate to the physical nature of a human being and the spoken language:

> As Man is situated in time and in space, all his re-play will necessarily be distributed and sequenced—in other words, it is rhythmed. This rhythm in turn is governed by Man's bodily structure. While the Universe is neither left nor right, neither up nor down, neither back nor front, Man is bilateral. To be efficient therefore, storage or memorisation will have to be mimismic, rhythmic and bilateral. And with repetition, patterns or formulas take shape which make further storage and classification of mimemes, and hence their retrieval, easier. (Sienaert and Conolly: 69)

Jousse's understanding is also supported by the research of Chafe (1980, 1994; cf. supported also by Gee 1996:103) which finds that all speech is formed in short rhythmic blocks or "idea units" often alternating with short pauses. It could even be that this characteristic of oral speech (which can be blocked out by reflective literacy) relates to the neurological process of passing signals from the left front lobe of the brain, which controls speech, to the right front lobe, which provides integration and logical structuring.

On the other hand, important acts of oral re-membering, where content is especially significant, will be ritualized (i.e., what Jousse calls *geste*). The physical balance of the performance is expressed in the dense balanced structuring of the oral-derived text. Jousse's rhythmographic presentation of this system of balance provides a useful test of our contention that this is oral-derived text, against Kloppenborg's contention that Q has no "balanced units." If the text of Q we are examining is presented in this way, then it again displays a clear oral patterning, which is related to the "measured verse" presentation. I have put the number of accented syllables in the Greek text, followed by the number of syllables, in each sound box, to give an idea of the relative length of units and their balance, even though we know little or nothing about the relation of Greek accents to the way it was spoken in first century Koine.

3.1 The Covenantal Discourse on the Plain in Measured Verse

And it came to pass in those days

He went out into the mountain to pray and he was spending the night in prayer to God.

And when it was day he called his disciples to him and [was] choosing from them twelve whom he also named apostles

> Simon whom he also named Rock and Andrew his brother
> and James and John
> and Philip and Bartholomew
> and Matthew and Thomas
> and James son of Alphaeus and Simon called Zealot

and Judas son of James and Judas Iscariot who became a betrayer.
And going down with them he stood on a level place
and a great crowd of his disciples
and a great multitude of the people
from all Judea and Jerusalem
and from the vicinity of Tyre and Sidon
who came to hear him and to be healed from their diseases.
And those who were afflicted by impure spirits were healed and the whole crowd tried to touch him because power went out from him and healed all.

And lifting up his eyes to his disciples he said

A   1a Blessed are you poor
      b   because yours is the kingdom of God
     2a blessed are you who hunger now
      b   because you shall be filled
     3a blessed are you who weep now
      b   because you shall laugh.

B   1a Blessed are you
      b   when people hate you
      c   and when they cast you out
      d   and despise you
      e   and cast out your name as evil
            for the sake of the Son of Man
     2a rejoice on that day
      b   and jump for joy
     3a for look your reward is great in heaven
      b   for their fathers did the same things to the prophets.
C   1a But woe to you rich
      b   because you have your consolation
     2a woe to you who are filled now
      b   because you shall hunger
     3a woe to you who laugh now
      b   because you shall grieve and cry

D   1a Woe [to you]
      b   when all people speak well of you
     2a for their fathers did the same things to the false prophets.

But to you who hear I say

A   1a Love your enemies
      b   do well to those who hate you
     2a bless those who curse you
      b   pray for those who abuse you.

B   1a To the one who strikes you on the cheek turn also the other

	b	and from the one who takes your garment do not withhold your cloak
	2a	to everyone who asks you give
	b	and from the person who takes what belongs to you do not ask back
	3a	and as you wish that people do to you
	b	do the same to them.

C	1a	And if you love those who love you
	b	what grace is that to you?
	c	for even the sinners love those who love them
	2a	for also if you do good to those who do good to you
	b	what grace is that to you?
	c	even the sinners do the same thing
	3a	and if you lend to those from whom you hope to receive
	b	what grace [is] that to you?
	c	even sinners lend to sinners to receive the same back.

D	1a	But you love your enemies
	b	and do good
	c	and lend without hoping for anything back
	2a	and your reward will be great
	b	and you will be sons of the Most High
	c	because he is kind to the ungracious and evil.

E	1a	Be merciful
	b	as also your Father is merciful
	2a	and do not judge and you will not be judged
	b	and do not condemn and you will not be condemned
	c	forgive and you will be forgiven
	3a	give and it will be given to you
	b	good measure pressed and shaken and overflowing will be given into your lap
	c	for with what measure you measure it will be measured back to you.

But he spoke to them also a parable

A	1a	Surely a blind person is not able to lead a blind person?
	b	will they not both fall into a ditch?
	2a	A disciple is not above the teacher
	b	but when finished everyone will be as his/her teacher.
	3a	But why do you see the fleck in your brother/sister's eye
	b	but do not notice the plank in your own eye?
	4a	How can you say to your brother/sister "Brother/sister let me take out the fleck which is in your eye"
	b	when you yourself do not see the plank which is in your own eye?
	5a	Hypocrite, first take out the plank from you own eye

| | | b | and then you will see clearly to take out the fleck which is in your brother/sister's eye. |

B   1a   For a good tree does not produce bad fruit
      b   and again a bad tree does not produce good fruit
   2a   For each tree is known by its own fruit
      b   for they do not gather figs from thorns
      c   and they do not pick grapes from a bramble bush
   3a   The good person brings good out of the good treasure of the heart
      b   and the evil brings evil out of evil
      c   for the person's mouth speaks out of the fullness of the heart

C   1a   And why do your call me, "Lord, Lord"
      b   and you do not do what I say?
   2a   Everyone who comes to me and hears my words and does them
      b   I will show you what s/he is like
   3a   s/he is like a person who built a house
      b   who dug and delved and laid the foundation upon the rock
   4a   and when the flood came the water beat against that house
      b   and it could not shake it because it was built well

D   1a   But the one who hears and does not do
      b   is like a person who built a house upon ground without a foundation
      c   against which the water beat
   2a   And immediately it fell.
      b   and great was the fall of that house.

When all his words were completed in the hearing of the people

He entered into Capernaum and the slave of a certain centurion was sick and about to die who was honoured by him and hearing about Jesus he sent to him elders of the Jews asking him to come and save his slave and those who came to Jesus urged him earnestly saying, "He is worthy for you to do this for he loves our nation and he built the synagogue for us." And Jesus went with them but when he was already not far from the house the centurion sent friends saying to him, "Lord, do not trouble yourself for I am not worthy for you to come under my roof and therefore I did not presume to come to you but say the word and my servant will be healed for I also am a person under authority having soldiers under my authority and I say

> to this one, "Go" and he goes
> and to another "Come" and he comes
> and to my slave "Do this" and he does."

And hearing these things Jesus was amazed at him and turning to the crowd who were following him he said, "I say to you not even in Israel have I found such faith." And returning to the house the messengers found the slave healed.

And it came to pass next he entered into a city called Nain and his disciples went with him and a great crowd and as he drew near the gate of the city and look a dead man was carried out only son to his mother and she was a widow and quite a large crowd from the city was with her.

And seeing her the Lord had compassion on her and said to her, "Do not weep" and coming he touched the coffin and those who carried it stood still and he said, "Young man I say to you get up" and the dead man sat up and began to speak and he gave him to his mother. And all were afraid and gave glory to God saying,

> "A great prophet has arisen among us"
> and, "God has watched over his people."

And this word went out in all Judea and the surrounding region concerning him.

Luke's performance of the Covenantal Discourse is very coherently structured, with intratextual signals to mark out the movement. Using Hymes's dramatic terminology, Luke's version is structured as an act within his overall narrative into five scenes.

The first scene, which provides the opening frame for the discourse, is signaled by the vague general storytelling opening "and it came to pass in those days," which is common in the Hebrew Scriptures (*wayehi*) and Septuagint (*egeneto de*). It introduces narrative, which sets the register for the performance of the Jesus tradition. The central reference point is Sinai and Moses.

The next three scenes comprise the covenantal discourse itself and are signaled by formulae referring to Jesus speaking: *elegen* (6:20), *lego* (6:27), *eipen de* (6:39). A minor difference of focus may be signaled in Luke's performance in each of the three scenes by the mode of address: "you," addressed by Jesus in the third person, perhaps with an eye on the disciples; "you who hear," addressed by Jesus in the first person, perhaps with an eye on the crowds; "them," addressed by Jesus in the third person, perhaps with an eye on corrupt community leadership or opponents.

The final scene provides the concluding frame and is signaled by a backward reference to his speaking, "And when all his words were completed in the hearing of the people": *epeide eplerosen panta ta remata autou*, which also have a story telling ring to them, as well as a concrete cultural reference to Moses speaking to the people of Israel (7:1; cf. Deut 32:45 "and when Moses had finished all these words to all Israel," *wykl mshh `t kl hdbrym h`lh `l kl ysr`l*). It concludes with two legitimating miracles and an epilogue (scene v B3), confirming that Jesus is the prophet whom God promised to raise.

The validity of these performance markers is confirmed by the coherence of the content and structure of each of the acts. In particular, the three central scenes of the covenantal discourse consist of two scenes arranged in four stanzas framing one scene of five stanzas. Internally, these stanzas are mostly structured into couplets and triplets.

The frames at the beginning and the end are connected in an *inclusio* by the reference to healing alongside teaching, as its fulfilment and legitimation. They are both "performed" in Luke's characteristic narrative style, although heavily influenced by the Septuagint Sinai narrative on which they are based. The reference to Jesus going up the mountain to pray to God and the call of the twelve and the address to the crowds of the people after he goes down to the plain below the mountain, are metonymic references to the Sinai tradition. Moses goes up the mountain to talk with God, while the people wait below. Moses takes a select few representatives of the twelve tribes up the mountain with him. Moses goes down the mountain to address the people waiting on the plain. Jesus fulfils the Deuteronomic tradition's expectation that "a prophet like unto Moses" will arise to lead the people in the future (Deut 18:18–22), as we shall see. The call of the Jewish authorities for a sign is refused by Jesus according to the Markan tradition, but here a sign is given to support the authority of Jesus' words in the Covenantal Discourse, namely two miracles. The miracles lead the people to say that, "A great prophet has arisen among us" (Luke 7:16). His prophetic words in the "covenantal discourse on the plain" are authenticated by the power which flows from him (6:19). The power flows from the one who has spent time in God's presence, just as Moses has to put a veil over his face after spending time on Sinai with God (Exod 34:29–35). God has visited his people (*epeskepsato o theos ton laon autou*), who are groaning under the affliction of foreign domination and injustice (just as he did through Moses, Exod 3:16, 4:31, 13:19; 32:34; 39:2: the word *epeskepsato* is a rare one, especially in this sense. It is used elsewhere only in Numbers, with a different sense). The reference to the crowds from Judea and Jerusalem and the vicinity of Tyre and Sidon in 6:17 is matched by the reference to Judea and "the whole surrounding area" in 7:17). In the narrative scenes in Scene I and Scene V the narrative is arranged in a twofold sequence.

The final narrative frame section in Luke 7:1–17 consists of two linked miracles of healing: the covenant duty to care for the foreigner in the midst (*ger*) and the widows and orphans is reaffirmed by the healing of the Centurion's Servant and the raising to life of the Widow's Son. This last scene provides an inclusio with the opening narrative in 6:12–19, in the acclamation of the people, that God has visited and redeemed his people, in raising up for them a prophet like Moses. In addition, the "word" goes out about Jesus' "deed" into "the whole of Judaea and all the region surrounding," which echoes the response to Jesus' word and deed by the disciples and crowds in 6:17–19.

A characteristic of Luke's performance of the covenantal discourse of Jesus is that he uses repetition, usually fourfold or threefold, in balanced couplets, to signal perlocutionary emphasis, for example:

> When people hate you
> and when they cast you out

and despise you
and cast your name out as evil.
Or again, the promised reward is:
Good
and pressed
and shaken
and overflowing.
Or a man building a house:
Who dug
and delved
and laid the foundation.

This is rather like a pause for effect at a particularly important juncture in an oral performance. Another technique seems to be a careful balancing of the stanzas in the central acts, so that for instance the two stanzas on blessings in the first scene of the covenantal discourse are balanced by two stanzas on curses. The first two stanzas in the second scene of the covenantal discourse balance the last two, both sets beginning "love your enemies." The first two stanzas on blind/sighted and good/bad fruit balance the building on rock and on sand. These features, together with the balanced parallelism of couplets and even within couplets, indicate an oral *mode* of performance. The brevity and allusiveness of the sayings confirm the oral register, in that they depend on metonymic reference to the wider culture for their interpretation. It is part of the received opinion concerning the "Sermon on the Mount" or the "Sermon on the Plain," with which most of us grew up, that it contains "an exalted ethic" which no-one can ever hope to fulfil. This reflects more on our distance from the culture and register of Jesus' covenantal discourse than any inherent truth (and also absolves us of the necessity for putting it into practice).

3.2 The Covenantal Discourse on the Plain in Rhythmographic Representation

We have already seen that the narrative introduction and conclusion to the Covenantal Discourse on the Plain in Luke are rather freely formulated. They do not fit into a rhythmographic structure. However, the teaching itself illustrates Jousse's belief in the balanced structure of ritual oral performance or *geste*. It also shows that the teaching material is structured into three units of four components, each introduced by a narrative reference to Jesus which stands outside of the covenantal discourse and gives the clue to the reference of each section. These three units are then in turn framed by the narrative introduction and conclusion. In the schematic representation given below, "cradling" is represented by units set out side by side, while "lifting" is represented by units set out in the middle of the page. The usual motion for the process of remembering which accompanies speech is "cradling," rocking from one side of the brain to the other.

Jesus' "Covenantal Discourse" on the Plain

The motion of "lifting," then, represents a break in the rhythm either for emphasis or to interrupt and so frame one unit from another.

And lifting up his eyes to his disciples he said

Blessed are you poor	because yours is the kingdom of God
blessed are you who hunger now	because you shall be filled
blessed are you who weep now	because you shall laugh

Blessed are you
when people hate you and when they cast you out
and despise you and cast out your name as evil
for the sake of the Son of Man

Rejoice on that day and jump for joy
for look your reward is great in heaven for their fathers did the same to the prophets

But woe to you rich because you have your consolation
woe to you who are filled now because you shall hunger
woe to you who laugh now because you shall grieve and cry

Woe [to you] when all people speak well of you
for their fathers did the same things to the false prophets

But to you who hear I say

Love your enemies do well to those who hate you
bless those who curse you pray for those who abuse you

To the one who strikes you on the cheek turn also the other

and from the one who takes your garment do not withhold your cloak

to everyone who asks you give

and from the one who takes what is yours do not ask back

and as you wish that people do to you do the same to them
And if you love those who love you what grace is that to you?
for even the sinners love those who love them

for also if you do good to those who do good to you what grace is that to you?
even the sinners do the same thing

and if you lend to those from whom   what grace [is] that to you?
         you hope to receive
   even sinners lend to sinners to receive the same back

      But you love your enemies   and do good
                       and lend   without hoping for anything back
         and your reward will be great and you will be sons of the Most High
          because he is kind to the ungracious and evil

                   Be merciful   as also your Father is merciful
               and do not judge   and you will not be judged
             and do not condemn   and you will not be condemned
                       forgive   and you will be forgiven
                          give   and it will be given to you
                    good measure
                    Pressed   And shaken
                 and overflowing
                 will be given into your lap
   for with what measure you measure   it will be measured back to you

              But he spoke to them also a parable

      Surely a blind person is not able   will they not both fall into a ditch?
          to lead a blind person?

      A disciple is not above the teacher but when finished everyone
                                           will be as his/her teacher

      But why do you see the fleck in   but do not notice the plank in your
            your brother/sister's eye   own eye?
                How can you say to your brother/sister
   "Brother/sister let me take out the fleck   when you yourself do not see the
                 which is in your eye"   plank which is in your own eye?
                          Hypocrite
   first take out the plank from you own eye   and then you will see clearly
           to take out the fleck which is in your brother/sister's eye

      For a good tree does not produce   and again a bad tree does not produce
                         bad fruit   good fruit
                  For each tree is known by its own fruit
   for they do not gather figs from thorns   and they do not pick grapes from a
                                             bramble bush

      The good person brings good out of   and the evil brings evil out of evil
              the good treasure of the heart
          for the person's mouth speaks out of the fullness of the heart

And why do you call me, "Lord, Lord" and you do not do what I say?
    Everyone who comes to me
    and hears my words and does them
I will show you what s/he is like s/he is like a person who built a house
    who dug and delved
    and laid the foundation upon the rock
    and when the flood came the water beat against that house
    and it could not shake it because it was built well
    But the one who hears and does not do
    is like a person who built a house
upon ground without a foundation against which the water beat
    and immediately it fell and great was the fall of that house

A rhythmographic presentation of the text confirms most of the features highlighted by the measured verse presentation. However, it shows much more clearly the feature of balance and parallelism. The balance extends not just to the structure of individual units within each scene, but also to the relation between the units. It seems that the performer's favourite technique is to provide a theme in the first section, develop it in the second section, restate it in the third section and then develop it again in the third. The theme of the scene runs through all four sections, often in the form of a binary opposition.

For instance, in the blessings and curses scene at the beginning of the first part of the covenant discourse, it is obvious: the overall theme is reward (*misthos*) and this is played out in terms of blessings for the needy and curses for the wealthy. The *misthos* is a reversal of normal expectations of reward and punishment. But in the second and fourth sections of the blessings and curses, this is developed in terms of the response to Jesus as the *prophetic Son of Man*, who suffers persecution with his followers. The performer varies the use of the formula, privileging blessings over curses, which is not surprising given the fact that the disciples are being addressed. The fourfold repetition of the obloquy to be expected by the follower of Jesus is balanced by the twofold repetition of joy, and an emphasis on the great reward. The curses, on the other hand, are barely stated, presumably since the rich people addressed are inside the community and the goal is conscientization to sharing (a big carrot and a little stick). In this respect, the greatest warning to the rich concerns "laughing," which merits a couplet suggesting a double threat, "because you will grieve and weep."

Likewise, the theme of reward (*misthos*) and punishment is taken up again in the second part of the covenant discourse, concerning love of enemies, in almost the same words used in the first part. Within this overall theme, the performer takes up a threefold pattern, revolving around the key words "love," "do (good)" and "lend (give)." At the heart of it is the idea that one should love, do good, and lend to human beings who cannot reciprocate, with the promise that this makes them sons of God and that he will reward them. The desirability of the reward, wildly beyond what is given up now, is emphasized with a series of balanced set of couplets, alternately lifting and cradling, "good measure, pressed and shaken, and overflowing," which balance the loss to be accepted by the follower of Jesus, set out at the beginning of the second part, but contrast the cruelty of human behavior with the goodness of God. The four epithets, mostly redoubled in the perfect participial form, heighten the sense of the superabundance of the reward.

The third part of the covenant discourse is also dominated by the theme of reward and punishment. This is couched in terms of survival or destruction of the house built. However, judgment is implied in the first two sections also, since the implication is given that judgment is based on the works/ fruits. Within this framework, the opposition which dominates is the opposition between hearing/saying/seeing and doing/bearing fruit. Again, there is an inclusio binding the whole scene together, namely the idea of falling down: of the blind person and of the unfounded house.

Often there is a balance between a positive and a negative statement of the same theme. This is obvious in the blessings and curses, but it operates even at the micro level, e.g., in "To the one who strikes you on the cheek turn the other also/ and from the one who takes your garment do not prevent even the cloak. To everyone who asks you give/ and from the one who takes what is yours do not ask back." So too in the series of four negatives (in couplets) followed by four positives (in couplets): "And do not judge and you will not be judged/ and do not condemn and you will not be condemned/ release (debt)/ and you will be released (your debt)/ give and it will be given to you."

Clearly, the whole performance is constructed in a formulaic manner, even though not in the rigid kind of way that Serbian epic singers perform! The blessings and curses follow a form established in the Hebrew Scriptures, as part of the covenant formula. The form is elaborated in the first part in the first two units and then varied/ abbreviated in the third and fourth.

The second part brings together a variety of forms. First, unexpectedly generous (inappropriate and potentially shameful) action is demanded of the hearers. The demands are given in strikingly memorable couplets, and then summed up in the Golden Rule. Second, there follows a series of three rhetorical questions, which repeat the same theme, that even sinners know how to do what is in their own interest, while the hearers are challenged to go beyond sensible self-interest. Third, there is a repetition of the first two sections in brief, but it brings in the concept of the heavenly reward due to those who show the nature of the Father in their actions. Fourth, there is a repetition in the new form of repeated balanced couplets the idea that one should do to others what one wishes done to oneself, this time motivated by the reciprocity of God in judgment and in giving.

The third part utilizes the form of parables, which are explicitly signaled in the introductory formula, "But he said to them in parables." Three parables explore sight and blindness/ obstructed vision; teacher and pupil (lodged between two parables on vision, so that vision is equated with teaching); two parables explore trees/ plants bearing fruit commensurate with their nature; two parallel parables follow about building a house with or without foundations.

In terms of sound patterns, the rhythmographic presentation shows clearly the way in which parallel units are balanced in terms of sound, and re-inforced by alliteration and assonance.

4. Field

We have already noted the importance of the reference to the mountain. Jesus goes up to talk to God and to choose the leaders among his followers. The metonymic reference is clearly to the Sinai tradition. Moses goes up the mountain to talk with God, while the people wait below to receive God's word and make a covenant with him. The particular occasion in the tradition to which Luke's performance relates is the ascent of Moses with Aaron, Nadab and Abihu, together with seventy of the elders of Israel, to see the God of Israel. At the foot of the mountain, Moses summons all the people and enacts a covenant with Yahweh sealed with blood (Exod 24:1–18). The tradition differentiates between leaders and all the people (*cwl ysrael*). In the same way, Luke's performance distinguishes between the disciples and the crowds.

This metonymic reference to the Sinai tradition points to the *field* of the discourse: what is taking place and where. What is taking place is a renewal of God's covenant with Israel enacted by Jesus as a prophet like Moses. This is confirmed at the conclusion of the Covenantal Discourse, "And when all his words were completed in the hearing of the people": *epeide eplerosen panta ta remata autou* (7:1), which is reminiscent of Deut 32:45, "and when Moses had finished all these words to all Israel" (*wykl mshh `t kl hdbrym h`lh `l kl ysr`l*). Likewise Exod 24:7, in which Moses reads the words of the covenant aloud before sprinkling the people with the blood of the covenant. In the face of social and economic collapse in Israel, which is interpreted as the consequence of Israel's failure to keep the covenant–thus activating the curses of the covenant–Jesus renews the covenant with Yahweh and promises that the curses will be replaced by blessings in response to the obedience of the people (Horsley and Draper: 195–227).

The context *field* of covenant renewal is not a mere hypothetical or theological category, but is a well-known communicative event in first century Palestine. We are fortunate to have the testimony of the *Manual of Discipline* (1QS) from Qumran, which is roughly contemporary with Luke's performance.[2] The community of the *Manual* enacted a covenant renewal ceremony every year. While the specific content of their performance is likely to have been influenced by the specific theological understanding of the sect and its priestly-scribal class location, its effectiveness clearly depends on the existence of the covenant renewal as a continuing tradition in Palestine. The covenant renewal ceremonies which are recorded in the Israelite tradition (e.g., Josh 23, Neh 9, Dan 9:4–19, 2 Kgs 22–23, Jer 34:3–22, 1QS 2–4) all require the public recital before the people of the covenant stipulations and the blessings and curses. While peasant communities in the small villages would not have had the possibility of reading from texts, we can assume that they would have continued the tradition of public recital of the covenant with Yahweh, with its blessings and curses.

The occasion for the performance of covenant renewal was provided by a consciousness of breaking the covenant, which required the partner in breach of the covenant to throw him/herself on the mercy of the other partner in confession, seeking pardon. The Dead Sea Scrolls, as well as a host of other texts of the period from the first century B.C.E. to the first century C.E., reveal an acute consciousness of dis-ease in the social body of Israel. Roman occupation and the imposition of the Herodian ruling class in addition to the Temple aristocracy created an economic crisis for the peasantry which has been frequently documented (e.g., Grant 1926; Horsley 1987; Crossan 1991). The greed of the ruling class is attacked by the retainer class, as in the Psalms of Solomon and the *pesherim* from Qumran. In other words, the consciousness that Israel stood in breach of the covenant in the time of Jesus was linked to social and economic crisis. The preaching of John the Baptist in Q 3:7–10 already prepares the way for this consciousness, and Luke's Jesus begins his ministry with a proclamation of social and economic good news for the poor (4:16–21).

To return to the question of oral performance, we can affirm here that the context *field* is one of covenant renewal. The shape of the performance follows in a general way the form of the covenant renewal, though not precisely. Luke's performance begins with the blessings and curses of the covenant, indicating that absolute commitment is required. In terms of the covenant renewal pattern, the blessings and curses imply a historical reversal, which is stated as accomplished. Hence it legitimately takes the place of the historical section of the covenant treaty, even though formally the blessings and curses belong at the end of the treaty as part of the sanctions.

The second part consists of the stipulations of the covenant and relates to concrete social and economic behavior. They are required of "all Israel":

---

2. The difficulty of dating the Dead Sea Scrolls is well known, and it would be fruitless to try to address it here. However, few date these documents outside of the range of the beginning of the first century B.C.E. to the end of the first century C.E. This is sufficient to establish the connection we are making here.

"to you who hear." The key metonymic reference in the stipulations is provided by the command to love. Although the following references are taken from the scribal production of the ruling elite, they come from particular sections of Leviticus and Deuteronomy, which seem to derive in part from oral tradition incorporated into the codified law of the Temple state. Apart from the normal use of the word to refer to family relationships in the Hebrew Scriptures, the word `hbh is prominent in the passages which set out the conditions of the covenant and possession of the land in Lev 18–20 (the so-called Holiness Code) and Deuteronomy. In Lev 19:18, the word occurs in the context of a series of stipulations relating to social and economic justice: the law on gleaning to provide food for the poor and the alien (19:9–10); the law on theft and fraud (19:11); the law on false swearing (19:12); the laws on oppression and failure to pay the hired man on time (19:13); the law on just treatment of the physically impaired (19:14); the law against favoritism in judgment (19:15); the laws against slander and perverting the course of justice (19:16). Finally there is the provision against hatred and revenge seeking (19:17–18). Central is the stipulation that, "Never seek revenge or cherish a grudge towards your kinsfolk; you must love your neighbor as yourself, I am the Lord." In Leviticus 19:34, the rule on "loving the other as oneself" is extended also to "the stranger who sojourns with you." The use of "love" in Deuteronomy is somewhat different, namely that God loves his people and requires them to love him in return and keep his statutes (e.g., 7:9; 10:12; 11:1, 13). However, it is clear there also that God especially loves the poor and the sojourner (10:18–19). In other words, the stipulations of the covenant in Deuteronomy connect the requirement to love God, to love the poor and the sojourner with the love God shows to those within the covenant in a reciprocal manner.

The difficulty in the requirement to love the neighbor is the question of defining the neighbor. The Levitical Code and Deuteronomy connect the command to love the neighbor with the prohibition of revenge, but it was clearly a contentious issue (which Luke addresses elsewhere in the Parable of the Good Samaritan, 10:25–37). In a time of social disintegration and economic pressure, the question must have become urgent. The stipulations of the covenant renewal set out in Luke's performance of the Covenantal Discourse stand in this tradition of Leviticus and Deuteronomy. Enemies who hate, curse and abuse must not draw out reciprocal hatred, but love. Specific instances of social injustice are treated: physical violence, enforcement of debt pledges (removal of the garment), and lending when there is little prospect of repayment. Instead of an ethic of revenge, the Covenantal Discourse advocates an ethic of generosity and shame. To turn the other cheek when struck turns an insult back to shame the violator without giving fresh cause for revenge. To give the person one's inner garment when the outer one is seized for debt is to shame the debt collector with nakedness and place an obligation on him to clothe the naked, since there are no less than thirty prohibitions against uncovering the nakedness of others in the covenant stipulations of Lev 18–20. To refuse to ask back from another what has been borrowed places that person under obligation and shame in terms of future transactions and is a more effective deterrent than trying to seek revenge. Hence the stipulations of the covenant renewal in the Covenantal Discourse both stand in the tradition of Leviticus and develop it to relate to the specific conditions of social and economic collapse in the first century C.E. The principle goes beyond a "tit-for-tat" revenge and a "you scratch my back I'll scratch yours" reserve. The generosity of the creator and sustainer God turns this around and calls the member to seek to reverse what Richard Horsley has called the "downward spiral of violence" in the community by active participation: "Love your enemies and do good and lend without hoping for anything back." Luke's performance of the Covenantal Discourse bases this principle of generosity firmly on God's nature and on the promise of the super-abundant blessings which will flow back to the generous person (6:36–38).

The third part contains the sanctions of the covenant renewal formula. We have already noted that it is addressed to the anonymous "them," which suggests a certain distancing from the people addressed (perhaps corrupt leaders or opponents of Luke's community in his performance). It is also told in the form of parables, which is an effective form of attack, since it can take the form of "if the cap fits wear it" without providing specific instances. The first two stanzas relate strongly to questions of leadership: blind leaders, disciples of Jesus who do not live like him, those who discipline others when they are guilty themselves. The second two stanzas relate to the importance of fulfilling the stipulations and remind the hearers of the blessings and curses with which the Covenantal Discourse began. The parable of the houses built on the rock and the sand provides an alternative form of the blessings and curses.

We have seen that the narrative marker, "When all his words were completed in the hearing of the people," refers metonymically to the words of Moses on the plain before Sinai or before Nebo (at the end of Deuteronomy). The covenant renewal is ratified now not by blood, however, but by miraculous healing. But the healing of the centurion's slave introduces a startling new element: this is a Gentile who shows faith greater than Israel and who receives the healing! Then the one who receives the second healing is a widow whose son is restored to life. The references we have noted to the requirement of the covenant stipulations to love the stranger and the widow in particular are activated. The scope of the renewal is widened without further explanation at this point. The ambiguous reference to "the vicinity of Tyre and Sidon" and "Judea and the surrounding region" opens up the possibility that the covenant might extend beyond the confines of Israel.

5. Tenor

The tenor is signaled by the metonymic references to Moses and covenant. As in the Deuteronomic tradition, Jesus speaks as "a prophet like unto Moses" who has arisen to lead the people (Deut 18:18-22). The whole five-scene performance (frame at the beginning and end, bracketing the three parts of the Covenant Discourse) is concluded by the declaration of the crowds that "A great prophet has arisen among us" and "God has watched over his people" (7:16). Hence the tenor of the covenantal discourse is not that of a wisdom teacher giving gnomic wisdom, as has often been supposed in recent writings, but that of a prophet speaking the judgments or oracles of God into a particular situation. In this case, the field of covenant renewal implies that the covenant people have sinned and broken the covenant. In renewing the covenant, the prophet sets out again the stipulations of the covenant with all the authority of Yahweh. This accounts for the solemnity of the speech: "And lifting up his eyes to his disciples he said."

The tenor is influenced not just by the nature of the speaker—a prophet delivering oracles or Yahweh—but by to whom he is speaking. We have indicated in our analysis of the structure that the addressees change in the course of the covenantal discourse. The address of the prophet calls the covenant people to repentance and renewal, warning them of the dangers of breaking the covenant in terms of social and economic justice, but also promising them blessings for living according to the terms of the covenant.

The tenor of this communicative event is not limited to pronouncing the terms of the covenant renewal, but includes deeds of power. This is signaled in both Scenes I and V. So the words are perceived as words of authority, heralded and confirmed by miracles. Just as Moses is able to back up his words with miracles and plagues when he speaks to Pharaoh, by parting the Red Sea, and with manna and meat as well as water from the rock, so Jesus as the prophet like to Moses enacts his words with power. The whole of Luke's performance of the covenantal discourse fits coherently in the context of covenant renewal enacted by the "prophet like Moses." Social collapse and disease signals that the people have broken the covenant with Yahweh; he sends a prophet to call them back in repentance and confession to renew the covenant, and to pronounce the promise of a renewal of blessing and restoration. The call of twelve disciples also signals the renewal of Israel, as Sanders (1985) has convincingly argued, and the power to heal which flows from Jesus both confirms the authority of the covenant renewal and provides evidence of the restoration of shalom.

The only unexpected element here is that the miraculous healing is given to the slave of a Roman officer. The blessing flows beyond the boundaries of the covenant people to encompass even the gentile who demonstrates faith. The same extraordinary characteristic of this covenant renewal is heralded by the vagueness of "the vicinity of Tyre and Sidon" and "the surrounding region."

6. Implied and Real Communicative Event

In Luke's performance, the tradition has a strong cohesion and structure. It could stand on its own. It seems to have retained the simplicity of an oral performance, as if Luke is deliberately encoding it the way it should be used in the context of a community covenantal renewal discourse. He seems to have considerable sensitivity as a performer to the nature of the sources he weaves into his narrative, as we see also with the hymns of the birth narratives. We can never know for certain whether or not he was utilizing a written source Q or whether he was drawing on his own memorized knowledge of the covenant tradition. Nevertheless, I believe that there are strong grounds for arguing that the oral features of the covenantal discourse are entrenched in his performance. What needs to be researched in more detail is the variety and evolution of the performances of the covenantal discourse tradition over time, across the work of Luke, Matthew, Thomas, the *Didache* and perhaps even 1 Clement, paying due attention to the changes in field, tenor and mode.

While such an investigation is clearly beyond the scope of this paper, a cursory examination indicates that all these writings show clear signs of communication in the oral *mode*. With the partial exception of the Gospel of Thomas, they utilize mnemonic arrangements in couplets and triplets within coherent stanzas arranged in consistent patterns of three or five. Often these larger clusters, or scenes, are arranged in similarly patterned sequences within larger units, or acts. We have also noted the paratactic construction, parallelism, repetition and linkage typical of oral performance. Much of this survives even the scissors and paste method of the International Q Project Text.

Utilizing the model we have developed, it becomes clear that another consistent aspect of the register across the three performances is that of *field*. The covenant renewal tradition deriving from the Deuteronomic tradition remains constant, even though different strands within it are stressed. The blessings and curses of the covenant are found in all the performances, as are the stipulations as to the kind of life required in the land of promise. The performances differ in the extent to which they provide a preamble or antecedent history. Luke is most specific in relating the performance to Moses talking with God on Sinai and coming down to give the law to the people, which relates to his understanding of Jesus as the "prophet like to Moses." Matthew is more guarded about Jesus as a new lawgiver, since his performance stresses that the law abides for ever, while Jesus is an interpreter and fulfiller of the law by means of the "greater righteousness." Jesus is seen by Matthew primarily as Davidic messiah and Isaianic Suffering Servant. Yet his performance is arranged in a manner very reminiscent of the Mosaic covenant and his provision of three miraculous signs and the inclusion of the healing of a leper also suggests the example of Moses, as we have seen. The *Didache* lacks the narrative frame of Matthew and Luke, and the blessings and curses remain only in vestigial form. Nevertheless, it emphasizes the element of choice posed by the Deuteronomic tradition with the way of life and the way of death. In Thomas only fragments of this tradition remain, and the gospel uses the tradition more as the starting point for the creation of existential reflection to destabilize the world of the individual and lead on to *gnosis*. While the fundamental covenantal register remains constant, the beginnings of divergence can also be seen, relating to the different contexts of the various performances.

The emergence of the Gentiles as significant members of the emerging Christian communities has naturally had an effect on the *tenor* of the performances. Matthew's performance affirms the unaltered significance of the law and moves in the direction of legal disputation. Jesus appears not as lawgiver but as Christ and legal interpreter. Luke's performance plays down the position of the law in his performance and stresses healing, compassion and economic justice. Jesus appears as a new lawgiver, building on the tradition of the prophet like Moses. The *Didache* reduces the context of Israel's history to a minimum and specifically applies the legal provisions of the covenant to a Gentile situation. The Covenantal Renewal Discourse has moved in the direction of catechesis of Gentiles. Nevertheless, the general covenantal field remains the context for the communicative event in each of their performances.

An analysis of the covenant discourse material which proceeds on the assumption that the clue to understanding lies in reconstructing a prior source by means of a *textual* relationship will distort the interpretation. A focus on exact verbal correspondence results in a textual abstraction, which blurs the essential signals of field and tenor that vary from performance to performance, depending on the audience and the occasion. It removes nearly all of the signals for the *tenor* of the performance. This is hardly surprising, since the question of "who is speaking to whom" is the most specific aspect of the performance context. The leadership are addressed by Luke, himself a church leader, and are particularly challenged about questions of wealth and socio-economic justice. In Matthew, an educated retainer class scribe, who is a skilled interpreter of the law, is debating with other legal interpreters, both inside the Christian movement (those who regard the law as superseded by the advent of the Messiah) and those outside the Christian movement (the Pharisees), about the position and interpretation of the law. He is also very concerned about the basis on which people, and especially Gentiles, are admitted to the community. A teacher charged with the catechesis of Gentiles wishing to join the Jewish Christian community provides instruction for his catechumens in the *Didache* and speaks as an adopted father to adopted children.

If these signals of *tenor, field* and *mode* are removed altogether from the text by a process of textual abstraction, such as we see in the restriction of "Q" to what the performances have in common, then contact with the rhetorically coded oral text is lost. The *mode* markers are blurred and disguised by becoming printed in continuous and undifferentiated form. Jesus disappears into text, or an aspect of literary textual culture familiar to the researcher and open to the tools of literary criticism. Since the *field* markers, which make the performance culture specific, have been removed, then the material may be seen as timeless and universal, an abstract truth valid for all time and place. Since the *tenor* markers indicate exactly who is speaking and to whom in a specific culture and context, the modern reader becomes a performer also of timeless and universal truths.

7. Conclusion

The way the Bible has been appropriated in South Africa is profoundly oral. It is widely understood as "Word of God." But this does not necessarily have the fundamentalist overtones the expression has assumed in the West (although historical criticism is certainly experienced as alienating in the African context in my experience). The Bible is sung, performed, danced and acted. The physical presence of the Bible as book is everywhere in evidence, but the printed book often plays an iconic rather than a literary role. Several African Biblical scholars talk of the Bible as having "inculturated itself," almost as if it has a volition beyond human agency (Bediako 1990, 1992; Sanneh 1989, 1990, 1994; for a critique see Maluleke 1996, 2000). Perhaps we have here the influence of the strongly oral appropriate of the Bible, which continues to operate in Africa and which is closer to the nature of the "history of traditions" than Western concepts of literary influence.

Responses

Response to Kelber, Horsley, and Draper

Joanna Dewey

It is a pleasure to respond to part one of this Semeia Studies volume on *Oral Performance, Popular Tradition, and Hidden Transcript in Q*. In particular, my response is to Richard Horsley, "Performance and Tradition: The Covenant Speech in Q," and Jonathan A. Draper, "Jesus' 'Covenantal Discourse' on the Plain (Luke 6:12–7:17) as Oral Performance: Pointers to 'Q' as Multiple Oral Performance." In these articles, Horsley and Draper both expand on their work in *Whoever Hears You Hears Me: Prophets, Performances, and Tradition in Q* (1999), pushing further their understanding of Q—and in particular Q6—as oral-derived text reflecting oral performance. I also include discussion of Werner Kelber's article, "The Verbal Art in Q and Thomas." It raises questions about the genres of Q and Thomas, providing some helpful overview and methodological principles for appreciating Q.

All three authors roundly reject the traditional approach of viewing Q as a literary work consisting of individual sayings whose literary stages of development may be established. All three view Q as made up of discourses as the fundamental unit of meaning. (Of course, as Kelber notes, Koester and Kloppenborg both recognized that Q consisted of clusters of sayings; however, they still focused on the individual saying as the unit of meaning and of historical development.) Furthermore, Horsley, Draper, and Kelber recognize these discourses as oral-derived texts that need to be studied as oral performances. As oral performance, their situational contexts of performance and the cultural tradition(s) in which they are embedded are crucial elements for determining their sense and their impact. They are, if you will, performance texts that take their meaning from their performance contexts, their manner of performance (tone of voice, body movement, gesture, etc.) and the traditions they reference. They are not disembodied universal teachings applicable across time and place. Thus all three authors, building on Horsley's and Draper's earlier book, are proposing a new way of approaching Q based on the largely oral media world of the first century, which they deem to be Q's media world. They are surely correct in their fundamental understanding of Q as oral-derived material, and in their call for this radically different approach to Q from the norm of contemporary Q scholarship.

I shall begin with their critique of the typical approach of contemporary Q studies, turn then to Horsley's and Draper's readings of the covenantal discourse of Q6, its oral renderings and its historical context. Then I shall discuss questions concerning Q as a whole and the possible interaction of orality and literacy in its formation. For to recognize the individual discourses as the primary unit of meaning and as oral-derived texts does not address the broader question of the formation of Q as a whole, and the interactions of orality and scribality in the process of formation.

I

Their critiques of traditional Q scholarship as represented by Kloppenborg are fully convincing. Kloppenborg's (1987, 2000) and Arnal's understanding of Q as a written document of literate village scribes does not hold up. In his introduction, Horsley summarizes the current work on ancient literacy in Galilee, which indicates that there simply were not village scribes sufficiently literate in Aramaic, let alone Greek. Draper similarly disposes of Kloppenborg's four arguments that Q had to have developed as a written text (1987). Kelber presents a more fundamental critique: source and form criticism are the wrong tools for understanding Q; tradition history is not the key to comprehending the final product of a text. Applying what we have learned from gospel studies, namely "that each gospel is the result of compositional strategies aimed at a distinctly focused rhetorical outreach," Kelber argues passionately that we must understand the final text before consideration is given to individual parts and their compositional history. The procedure is not to build up from the isolated individual unit to the final composition, but first to understand the final composition. Kelber then gives an excellent summary of Horsley's and Draper's book with its use of multiple methodologies, including orality studies, suggesting that their approach is a more viable way forward in Q studies.

II

Horsley and Draper both demonstrate the success of beginning with the entire discourse, at least in regard to the covenantal discourse of Q6 as a discrete discourse. They also show clearly the discourse's roots and viability in oral discourse. They present three renditions of Q6 that highlight the verbal and thought repetitions and parallels—all three versions showing the richness of mnemonic patterns in the text. Building on the work of Dell Hymes, each author lays out the text in "measured verse" presenting similar but not identical texts. In addition, Draper lays the text out according to Marcel Jousse's model of rhythmography, in which the whole body takes part by moving backwards and forwards and from side to side as the text is recited. All three demonstrate the abundant use of sound and word repetition, although I would need a video providing sound and motion as well as text to follow Draper's rhythmographic presentation. These presentations are, I believe, all ways to enable those of us accustomed to print culture to see patterns we do not know how to hear. So also are the sound mapping of Brandon Scott and Margaret Dean and, for that matter, my surface structure presentation of Mark 2:1–3:6 (Dewey). It may not matter so much what particular system we use, as long as we use some method to slow us down so we can see/hear verbal and sound echoes. These echoes are so abundant that there are many slight and not so slight variations on how we could lay out the text, just as there certainly were many actual variations in multiple tellings of the discourse.

Horsley limits his analysis to the covenant discourse of Q6:20–49. Draper defines the extended covenantal discourse in Luke as Luke 6:12–7:17. He argues that the longer text is necessary because it is Luke's narrative framework that provides the rhetorical clue to the discourse register—to what is going on in context. His larger analysis also vividly shows the more literary, less mnemonic style of the Lukan frame. It is easy to see how the core Q6:20–49 could be orally remembered and performed, in contrast to its narrative frame.

All three authors stress other important points about the discourse as performance. First, the unit of meaning is the entire discourse, not each individual saying contained in the discourse. Each individual saying derives its meaning not in isolation but only as part of the whole speech. Second, and perhaps more important, as oral-derived discourse, the speech derives its meaning from the cultural tradition it references. Horsley describes this tradition, accurately I believe, as a double one: the broad Israelite popular or little tradition, and "a more focused and recent tradition of Jesus-lore." As is characteristic of oral literature, reference to the tradition functions metonymically, or part for the whole. Horsley adduces the helpful example of how just hearing the phrase "I have a dream" evokes the whole Civil Rights movement of the 1960s. Similarly, references in the Q6 discourse evoke the covenant and covenant renewal traditions. Finally, all three authors stress the importance of the performance event— who is addressing whom, where and on what occasion—as an important shaper of the discourse and clue to interpreting it. Of course, appreciating performances presents scholars with difficulties since we have only the textualizations as they occur in Luke, Matthew, and perhaps other early Christian writings.

I would affirm that, in these articles, Horsley, Draper, and Kelber have established the appropriate starting points for studying Q. The appropriate unit for investigation is the speech or discourse, not the individual saying. The particular speech or discourse existed in some forms orally before becoming part of a larger Q or part of Luke or Matthew—and probably continued to exist orally independent of a larger Q or gospel. They are oral-derived texts. For us, trained in print culture, it is helpful to lay out the text in clauses or phrases so that we can appreciate the oral repetitive character of the speech. As oral-derived texts, they draw on and reference metonymically the cultural traditions of the performers and audiences. If we are to advance in our understanding of Q material we need to begin here.

III

If we begin our consideration of Q with oral-derived speeches, what implications does this have for our understanding of Q? It certainly mandates that we study the cultural tradition, particularly, in so far as we can, to study the popular tradition. Part two of this volume and our increasing investigations in the field of social memory are steps in this direction. Furthermore, what does the understanding of Q as consisting of oral-derived discourses say about Q as a whole and its oral and/or scribal nature? Here the three contributors to this section diverge.

Kelber focused on the larger unit, Q as whole, asking questions of genre. He suggests that Q in its final form is a hybrid of community manual and biography. His primary (and convincing) argument is that Q and the Gospel of Thomas are different genres. As an aside, I raise the question: should John the Baptist material really be considered one of the Q clusters or should it be considered a separate entity, with its different subject matter and its high degree of verbal identity between Matthew and Luke? Perhaps, as many have suggested in regard to Luke's infancy narrative about John, this Baptist material also derives from traditions concerning John the Baptist, and should not be considered part of Q material at all. Without the Baptist material, we are left more with a community manual and as a result a more coherent whole. As a whole the collection of disparate discourses may have a common purpose.

More significantly, Kelber stresses that recognition of the oral nature of the Q material shifts how we are to understand it, in effect questioning how to interpret it:

> Reading Q as an oral-derived text . . . challenges our literary conventions of reading it. . . . In the oral process, Q ceases to be literary in the sense of disclosing its full meaning in a systematic reading from beginning to end. . . . Understood orally, the speeches in Q encapsulate a world of words, phrases, ideas, images that resonate with a map of experiences and associations shared by speakers and hearers. In short, Q as an oral-derived text relies heavily on extra-textual factors, shifting meaning from production to performance.

Kelber concludes: "from the perspective of oral aesthetics, the designation of Q as a single text with a single meaning may well appear to be a grave misunderstanding." With this argument, Kelber has moved sharply away from understanding Q a single coherent text or "Q gospel".

Draper does not address the question of Q as a whole. Rather, he draws on his own experience in the far more residually oral culture of

South Africa and his studies of orality to insist that there is no original performance or original text, only different particular performances. He focuses on one performance, Luke's; he is analyzing Luke, not Q. He includes the narrative framework in Luke on the grounds that this will help signal the register of the performance, so crucial to understanding it. Further, he does not take a stand on how the material came to Luke: "We can never know for certain whether or not he was utilizing a written source Q or whether he was drawing on his own memorized knowledge of the covenant tradition." What is necessary for Draper is the covenantal tradition, not an oral or a written Q.

Furthermore, Draper briefly contrasts Luke's performance with those found in Matthew and the *Didache*, enabling us to see the shifts in register. Luke's rendition minimizes the importance of Israel's Law while stressing healing, mercy, and economic justice. Matthew's rendition affirms the Law and Christ as interpreter of the law. In the *Didache*, the covenantal discourse has become more of an instruction manual for Gentiles. Noting how these three different extant textualizations of the covenantal tradition shift the meaning and focus should alert us to how variable and adaptable oral performances of this tradition must have been. Each of the various Q discourses would of course be subject to its own variations according to particular performance contexts. In addition, performance is influenced not only by content—the words—but also by gesture, intonation, pacing, and interactions between speaker and audience. Such multiple performance possibilities for each discourse independently of the other discourses reinforce Kelber's argument that Q may not have functioned as a single text with a single meaning.

Of the three, Horsley alone clearly posits Q as a whole as an oral composition which he believes arose within and addressed a mid-first century Galilean movement. He writes, "Insofar as (many or most of) the speeches in Q may have been performed together, the performance may have consisted of a sequence of speeches." It does not seem likely to me that the different discourses would *orally* have been gathered into one whole, to be performed on a single occasion. Horsley recognizes and deals briefly with the fact that the Q material is in Greek while the Galilean village movement would have spoken Aramaic. He does suggest a couple of ways the discourses could have come to be in Greek, but he does not adequately acknowledge the likelihood that scribes bilingually literate scribes—were likely part of that process.

A more important argument against the oral concatenation of the discourses into a whole is that oral cultures do not tend to gather oral material formally into coherent wholes. When Westerners requested the African story teller Candi Rureke to narrate all the stories of the Nyanga hero Mwindo in order, he was astonished, insisting that such a thing was never done (Ong: 146). Tellers of the Q material may well have been familiar with several or all of the discourses, and may have performed them in various combinations as appropriate on different occasions, but they are unlikely to have thought of or performed them as one whole discourse in any sort of stable order.

More typically in oral cultures, teaching is embedded in narrative for purposes of ease of memory (Havelock: 174). We see this in the Gospel of Mark, the most oral in style of the gospels. Rather than gathering teaching on fasting and prayer as it is in Matt 6, in Mark it is embedded in narrative episodes: fasting in the dispute over why Jesus' disciples do not fast (Mark 2:18–20) and prayer in the episode of the discovery of the withered fig tree (11:20–25). In fact, embedding the various Q discourses into narrative is precisely what Matthew and Luke have done in their textualizations of the Q material. It is perfectly possible that the discourses traveled independently orally and were embedded orally or textually into narratives for ease of remembering.

Yet, in the last few decades, scholars have come to view Q as a coherent whole. We have come to call it the Q gospel. As noted earlier, the discourses may have had a common purpose as a community manual. That impression of unity suggests scribal influence to me. Alan Kirk has argued convincingly for scribal influence in the evolution of Q as a series of discourses. He suggests that it consists of a series of composite speeches using standardized deliberative formats and elaborations of chreia. It is of course such similarities of structure as well as content that suggest to us that Q is a whole. But such similarity is likely the work of scribes; direct transcription of oral performances would likely result in a much greater variety of structures. Kirk concludes, "The regularity of the form of these speeches across the length and breadth of Q points toward scribal formalization" (11). As Kirk argues, Q would still be an oral-derived text displaying both oral and literate influences. He describes Q as "an artifactualization of a tradition of oral moral exhortation (13–14).

We thus have the two possibilities: *either* separate oral (or transcribed-oral) discourses embedded into the narratives of Matthew and Luke *or* a larger Q document that shows clear evidence of scribal activity. As Draper states, we will never know for a certainty how the material came to Luke and Matthew. I would suggest, however, that it is not necessarily an either/or, *either* primarily oral transmission of separate discourses *or* an orally-derived textual Q that has been substantially worked over by scribes. First century media culture is characterized by extensive interaction back and forth between oral and literate transmission (Parker). The existence of a text does not stop or even greatly influence oral transmission. It seems to me possible, even probable, that Matthew and Luke each had access to written versions of Q, which of course would have varied considerably from each other (Parker), *and* also knew some quite independent orally transmitted renditions of the discourses. This is after all how such an oral/literate culture tends to function. I expect there was both oral transmission of the various Q discourses and written (but still very flexible) transmission of a collection of Q discourses.

In sum, all three authors, Horsley, Draper, and Kelber, have forwarded our understanding of the Q material and, it is hoped, steered Q scholarship into new directions. It has been a pleasure to respond to their articles, enlarging my own understanding of Q and of the interactions of orality and literacy in the first century.

Oral Performance in Q
EPISTEMOLOGY, POLITICAL CONFLICT, AND CONTEXTUAL REGISTER

Vernon K. Robbins

The essays by Werner Kelber, Richard Horsley, and Jonathan Draper in this volume exhibit three distinctively different performances of academic discourse about oral interpretation of literature. Their essays are contributions to the movement since the last part of the twentieth century to re-introduce the study of oral tradition into interpretation of the Bible. I will address Kelber's essay first, which performs a philosophical discourse it characterizes as "epistemological"; Richard Horsley's "Introduction" and essay second, which enact a political discourse using categories that emerge out of a "conflict model" of culture that "liberation" interpreters introduced into biblical interpretation during the 1980s; and Jonathan Draper's essay third, which emerges out of a cultural and political context that experienced both positive and negative oral uses of the Bible during an era that launched the New South Africa in the 1990s. These three essays, which approach oral tradition from significantly different perspectives, bring major issues concerning the relation of oral to written literature to view in highly informative ways.

Werner H. Kelber: Hybrids in a Philosophical Mode

Werner Kelber's essay is a philosophical exploration of the relation of Q and the *Gospel of Thomas*, which he properly defines in the title as "epistemological." The categories Kelber uses emerge out of the "trajectory" mode of biblical interpretation James M. Robinson and Helmut Koester used to introduce "dynamic" strategies into biblical interpretation during the 1960s to replace what they perceived to be dominant "static" strategies (Robinson and Koester). Kelber's approach to oral and written tradition in the essay has deep roots in twentieth century *wissenschaftliche* German scholarship. This tradition of interpretation is hermeneutical rather than rhetorical (pp. 28, 37, 38; cf. Wuellner 1989; Robbins 2004). Hermeneutical interpreters ground academic discourse in theory that is both explainable and defensible through philosophical discourse. Kelber's essay constructs its philosophical position by addressing oral tradition as "verbal art" (Bauman 1977; not mentioned by Kelber). The focus is not, then, on dynamics of oral performance. Rather, a philosophical question concerning the nature of orality as "verbal art" in Q and *Thomas* drives the discourse in the essay. Kelber enacts his approach by focusing on "the final stage of gospel constructions," which produces "the outcome of a selective bundling of tradition into new configurations" and makes it "imperative to pay singular attention to the texts in their present form" (p. 28). An irony emerges in the essay when Kelber moves to Q, since Q is a "reconstructed source" rather than a "final text." Nevertheless, Kelber approaches both *Thomas* and Q as "final texts" and draws his conclusions from this perspective.

The special approach in Kelber's essay is to assert that Q and *Thomas* do not belong to the same genre. Rather, each text, in its own way, is a "generic hybrid." Kelber's strategy is to assert that the two "final texts" contain different "oral poetics," because each text has a relationship to different "genres" or "Gattungen" of literature. Kelber achieves this conclusion about *Thomas* by starting with a "certainty" he has about the *Gattung* of *Thomas*, which he has gleaned from Jonathan Z. Smith: "GT's layout of materials by simple coordination brings it into close affinity with the ancient genre of list" (p. 38).[1] In this genre, Kelber states:

> Knowledge is managed on the principle of clustering whereby like data tend to attract those of their own likeness. Basically, lists function as technological mechanisms suited for the storing of data which are deemed worthy of preservation. Their primary compositional rationale derives not from hermeneutical impulse, but rather from functional needs." (40)

At this point, then, Kelber's focus is not on the relation of *Thomas* to oral tradition, but on the "philosophical" nature of the final written text as a "storage place." Having achieved this certainty, Kelber takes a decisive turn away from list by disagreeing with Crossan's view that *Thomas* is a "pure list." The beginning and ending of *Thomas*, Kelber asserts, give this "storage place" a "hermeneutical" function as "gospel" (p. 42). Kelber does not clarify in this context what he considers "gospel" to mean, nor does he observe that the beginning and ending are "logia" (sayings) rather than a "narrative" introduction and conclusion. Kelber uses the title at the ending of the "final text" of *Thomas* to define the text in terms of a "desire" to function as a gospel. In the end, then, *Thomas* is not simply a list. Rather, it is a "Sayings Gospel" that "remained beholden to the itemization of sayings characteristic of list, while at the same time claiming a sense of the integrity of the whole (GOSPEL)" (p. 44). At the end, Kelber personifies *Thomas* as a "generic hybrid" with desires. It "aspires" to be both a "list" that stores and a "gospel." The reader is not told what its desires as "gospel" might be.

---

1. Using the view of list as "perhaps the most archaic and pervasive of genres" (Smith 1982:44).

In his discussion, Kelber never observes that a special characteristic of *Thomas* is the presence of "Jesus said," "the disciples said to Jesus," or some variation at the beginning of each of the 114 logia. In other words, Kelber overlooks the attribution of all of the logia to one special personage and this personage's conversation partners, which gives each logion the nature of an "attributed *chreia*." In other words, Kelber fails to emphasize that *Thomas* is an excellent example of a list properly called "a list of sayings of a wise man." Instead, he uses the concept of "list" to dissociate his discussion completely from Robinson's category. This is an extreme move that weakens various aspects of his argumentation. Kelber also avoids any discussion of *Thomas* as an "oral-derived text." Thus, he does not mention the substantial number of Q sayings in *Thomas*;[2] nor does he discuss clusters of sayings in *Thomas*, present analysis of various logia or clusters to exhibit this orality, or exhibit relationships between some of the sayings clusters in Q and *Thomas* (Robbins 1997:88–92). The absence of these things weakens Kelber's comparison of *Thomas* with Q in serious ways.

Once Kelber has asserted a view of the genre of *Thomas* as a list, which gives it a function as a storehouse of knowledge, and juxtaposed this observation with the aspirations of the final text to function as a gospel, Kelber turns to the nature of the "verbal art" in this "generic hybrid." The issue for him is how this "storage" text might function orally, once it was written with a "primary compositional rationale" that was "not hermeneutical." A key, for him, is the absence of any internal "thematic coherence" that a reader might be expected to "construct" as s/he hears the text read from beginning to end. In other words, the final text has no overarching rhetoric. As a "storage place," composed like a "list," it has "poetics" rather than "rhetorics." Analysis of a text's poetics rather than its rhetorics is, of course, inherent to Kelber's philosophically oriented hermeneutical approach. Rhetorics, as Wuellner explained some years ago (Wuellner 1989), became an alternative to hermeneutics in European interpretation during the twentieth century. Kelber formulates the issue concerning orality in *Thomas* in terms of whether, "as in all oral poetics, we will have to envision alternate [sic, alternative] performances of the same sayings and parables" (p. 43). Kelber concludes, then, that although *Thomas* is a "product," namely a storehouse of sayings, "it seeks to remain a process." While the reader might think this is a result of the aspirations of *Thomas* as a "gospel," Kelber says it is a characteristic of "all oral poetry" to remain a process (p. 43). A special characteristic of *Thomas* as verbal art, however, and its "unifying aspect," is present in "its demand for interpretation" in the introduction. *Thomas* "is, therefore, a genre that, in spite of its invocation of gospel, requires patient hearing of each of its sayings and parables. It is, and will always be, plural" (p. 44). Kelber appears to presuppose, then, that a gospel

---

2. "Of the seventy-nine sayings of *Thomas* with Synoptic Gospel parallels, forty-six have parallels in Q" (Koester 1990b:87).

"wants" one single interpretation. In contrast, *Thomas* presupposes plural interpretations. The "orality" of the verbal art in *Thomas* lies in its interception of any presupposition, even if it is "gospel," that there may be "one single meaning" for any of its sayings. Rather, patient hearing will continually produce plural meanings for the sayings and parables contained in it. Kelber's "hermeneutical" approach, then, presents a conclusion that there is a "hybridity" in the internal nature of *Thomas* that produces a dynamic tension between its function as a storehouse of knowledge and its function as a verbal text demanding interpretation that will always be plural. The necessity for the plurality lies in the absence of a "single thematic topos" throughout *Thomas* (p. 44), which leads us to Kelber's discussion of Q, which he presents as a major alternative to *Thomas*.

Kelber's intellectual definition of Q, for purposes of comparing it with *Thomas*, derives from a conclusion, which he asserts "is almost universally acknowledged," that "Q exhibits a thematically coherent profile" (p. 30). Kelber uses some of Horsley's insights and words to support a position that "kingdom materials" provide "a unifying theme" that can "be intellectually defined in terms of a single thematic proposition" in Q (pp. 37, 44). For Kelber, then, there is an inner "hermeneutical" coherence in Q that does not exist in *Thomas*. What, then, is the nature of this coherence, and what is its relation to orality?

Kelber asserts that "[t]he modern breakthrough for the genre critical study of Q" (p. 32) occurred with James M. Robinson's essay "Logoi Sophon: On the Gattung of Q" (1971), but this progress introduced a serious misunderstanding. Severe limitations for interpretation followed as the result of Robinson's focus on "individual sayings" rather than "clusters of sayings" in Q (p. 31). Two decades later, Helmut Koester identified "seven clusters of sayings" in Q, but his focus "on composition and redaction" (1990b) in individual sayings still prevented the analysis from moving forward in a truly productive manner. At this point, Kelber identifies the problematics of Robinson's thesis about Q and *Thomas* as "reduction to a single genre" of *logoi sophon* (p. 33). Robinson "postulated the existence of a cross-cultural genre or *Gattung* which he called logoi sophon (sayings of the sages, or words of the wise)" (p. 32). Kelber's strategy with both *Thomas* and Q, then, is to start with a "breakthrough" in the understanding of genre ("list" for *Thomas*; and "sayings of the wise" for Q). As we saw above, Kelber disqualified the genre "sayings of the wise" for *Thomas* by replacing it with "list of sayings." We will see below that Kelber replaces "sayings of the wise" for Q with the genre of "manual." For Kelber, the correct observation for each final text is that it is a "generic hybrid," and none of the strands in either hybrid is to be associated with a generic concept of "sayings of the wise." This is, one might think, a remarkable denial of the nature of sayings attributed to wise men in these texts! Here is the way Kelber enacts the analysis.

Kelber's first step is to present "five major objections" to the view that *logoi sophon* can be understood as a widespread cross-cultural genre. The fourth and fifth objections are the means by which he moves to his thesis of "hybridity." Fourth, "Q and *Thomas* are so different as to disallow identification with a single genre"; and fifth, Robinson's essay on *logoi sophon* "has next to nothing to say about Q itself" (p. 33). Kelber considers this final point to be the "death blow" against Robinson's *logoi sophon* view of Q: "Surely, any genre designation of Q must remain unconvincing unless it is demonstrated by intense analysis of the present text" (p. 33). Kelber does not mention that the detailed investigations of Q by John Kloppenborg were designed to demonstrate "by intense analysis of the present text" the nature of Q as an instance of *logoi sophon*. At this point in the essay, then, Kelber addresses the *logoi sophon* thesis in the form in which it was launched by Robinson to inaugurate a program of analysis of Q, rather than discussing the thesis of Q as *logoi sophon* in its strongest form (Kloppenborg).

Instead of addressing the work of Kloppenborg, Kelber turns to the work of Horsley, which works with "sociological forces of power relations" (Horsley) and Q as oral performance. As Kelber indicates, the work of Horsley and Draper conflicts with his own concepts of "sayings Gospel," "biography," and "manual." Kelber resolves this conflict by adapting Schröter's concept of an interface of *Spruchsammlung* and *Biographie* with the proposal that "we should think of Q in its final form as a generic hybrid, participating both in biography and in manual" (p. 39). Q, then, is neither a "list" nor a "gospel"; it is a hybrid of "manual" and "biography."

Kelber's vocabulary is grounded in literary-historical categories that are resistant to oral rhetorical dynamics. This causes Kelber to be "haunted by feelings of anxiety about the sense of instability an oral-derived text brings to hermeneutics. Indeed, Q's meaning in oral performance is not quite the measurable quantity it has sometimes appeared to be in print culture. And yet, from the perspective of oral aesthetics, the designation of Q as a single text with a single meaning may well appear to be a grave misunderstanding" (p. 39). While Kelber uses Horsley's assertion that kingdom materials constitute one single unifying theme for Q to distinguish Q from *Thomas* (p. 41), in the context of discussing Q on its own terms, he asserts that there probably is no single meaning in Q.

Throughout Kelber's essay, then, the reader detects cognitive dissonance produced by natural tensions between a philosophical approach grounded in literary-historical categories and gestures toward oral-rhetorical approaches grounded in sociological-anthropological categories. Many observations are informative and strong. Other assertions, however, reveal the absence of an approach that is readily comfortable and familiar with orality. The natural home of the discourse in Kelber's essay is philosophical inquiry rather than rhetorical orality.

Richard A. Horsley: Polarities in a Political Mode

Richard Horsley's essay is a political exploration of Q driven by discourse that creates polarizing frameworks to investigate the nature of orality in peasant culture. While Kelber's essay creates epistemological alternatives from a philosophical position polarized against Robinson's view of Q and *Thomas* as "sayings of the wise," Horsley creates a list of opposites from a social-political position to create a framework for the oral performance of Q in the context of village life in Galilee. On the one hand, the approach enacts the dynamics of the beginning stages of "new paradigm" investigation as described by Thomas Kuhn. On the other hand, the approach generates a contracultural environment of interpretation where major alternatives are presented as polar opposites. Where Kelber presents alternatives to create hybrids, therefore, Horsley presents alternatives to create opposites.

By my count, Horsley's essays introduce at least ten polarities. The initial four are socio-political in nature:

1. Elite culture versus popular culture;
2. Great tradition versus little tradition;
3. Israelite "established order" tradition versus "resistance and rebellion" tradition;
4. Herodian and other elites of Tiberias versus surrounding villages and ordinary residents.

The next six concern oral and written communication:

5. Print culture versus oral culture;
6. Writing versus oral composition;
7. Copying versus composing;
8. Quotation of scripture versus presentation of images, motifs, and patterns from cultural memory;
9. Individual sayings versus speeches;
10. Public transcript versus hidden transcript.

In Horsley's essays in this volume, the first term in the list is negative: hegemonic, oppressive, and destructive. The second term, in contrast, is positive: rebellious, resistant, and life-giving. The socio-cultural perspective in the essay, then, is from popular culture upwards, rather than elite culture downwards. Many biblical scholars would undoubtedly choose the first term as positive rather than the second term. Who wants to side with rebellious and resistant culture over against a culture that establishes order? Many interpreters read the Bible for the purpose of establishing order. This, for Horsley, is the issue. Should interpreters read the Bible from a perspective of dominant, elite culture, or should they read it from a perspective of subordinated, popular culture? Horsley's argument is that a majority of the population lived in popular culture in antiquity and a minority lived in dominant culture. Rather than presenting the view of a minority of the population who were born or adopted into dominant culture, the Bible, in Horsley's view, presents the perspectives of a majority of the population who were forced to live in environments of subordinated, oppressed culture.

The polarized terms listed above provide a framework for Horsley to analyze and interpret the clusters of sayings in Q 6:20–49 from the perspective of rebellious, life-giving, popular culture. This culture uses oral performance as its mode of communication. Any use of writing, therefore, is an oral usage. The question for Horsley is if biblical interpreters can find a way to analyze written texts as oral-derived compositions. While the irony in Kelber's essay is the approach to Q as a "final text," the irony in Horsley's essay is the approach to a reconstructed, written text as an oral text. Horsley sees no traces of "writing composition" in the portions of Q he analyzes. The written texts before him are "oral-derived." Horsley's models are Jeremiah and his scribe Baruch. Jeremiah initially dictated to Baruch for over a decade the oracles God spoke to him, and Baruch wrote them on a scroll. When the king destroyed the scroll, Jeremiah again recited the oracles and Baruch wrote them on another scroll. Horsley's point is that Jeremiah carried these oracles in his memory, without any recourse to writing. The written text was an oral-derived text. Jeremiah retained the oracles in memory, so he could recite them again, when the written text was destroyed, and his scribe could write them down again, in virtually the same form they existed in the initial instance (p. 19). Horsley might have explored major variations of length and wording in manuscripts of Jeremiah, using data from Qumran in particular, to suggest that "oral" composition grows and varies as much as, or even more than, "scribal" composition. But he prefers an approach to oral performance as "reliable" recitation from memory.

Horsley, and the scholars on whom he depends, have substantive evidence to support the case that members of popular culture energetically promulgate polarized pictures of their relationships to those who have power over them. The misleading thing, of course, is that if "an outsider" asks members of the subordinate popular culture if they see the bosses, landlords, and political leaders over them as their enemies, they will tell about their good relationships with them and access to them, by which they receive many benefits. In other words, the "public story" they present regularly does not emphasize their negative views toward them. This takes us to one of the most profound aspects of Horsley's essay. Using insights from James Scott's *Domination and the Arts of Resistance: Hidden Transcripts* (1990), Horsley argues that Q 6:20–49 represents the "hidden transcript" being performed by Galilean Christians. But it is more than this. "Q portrays 'Jesus' as having boldly declared the hidden transcript in the face of the power-holders, in pronouncing woes against the Pharisees and prophetic condemnation of the Jerusalem rulers" (p. 22). The challenge that Horsley sets for himself, then, is to analyze Q 6:20–49 as a presentation of the "hidden transcript" that Galilean Christians have promulgated "publicly." How could this be done?

Supported by insights from James Scott's work on hidden transcripts and John Miles Foley's works on oral tradition, Horsley adapts Bernard Brandon Scott and Margaret Dean's "sound mapping" approach to written texts to display the rhythm, alliteration, balance, and allusions in Q 6:20–49. The baseline for him is the existence of "measured verse" in the speeches, that sound like poetry and exhibit the presence of "oral performance" (p. 56). The display of the text is, indeed, convincing. The display of the text is guided by the conclusion that "[k]ey markers of oral-derived texts are the repetition of words, sounds, and verbal forms, and parallel lines and sets of lines." (p. 66). Then Horsley interprets the "context, register, and cultural tradition" of Q 6:20–49 from the perspective of renewal of covenant, in particular as it exists in the Community Rule and Damascus Rule found at Qumran. The analysis of Q 6:20–49 is convincing. The content of the sayings, the focus on poverty-wealth, indebtedness-giving, etc. supports his reading of the text as one of the hidden transcripts of Jewish tradition made public among Galilean Christians.

In the midst of Horsley's interpretation of Q 6:20–49, however, a number of questions emerge. Here are some of the questions: (1) How did Q 6:20–49 become a written text? (2) Did any manifestations of "writing" come into Q 6:20–49 in the process of embedding it in a larger written text? If not, why not? (3) How can interpreters begin to analyze the differences between the "oral-derived" text of Q 6:20–49 and the "written" text of the Sermon on the Mount? It will, in fact, be important to include the Sermon on the Mount in the discussion. Horsley has not seemed to notice, for instance, that the recitations of scripture in the Sermon on the Mount do not have the technical form of "scribal quotation" but the oral form of "proverbial speech" (p. 70). How does one account for this oral aspect of the Sermon on the Mount?

Horsley's model for the writing down of Q 6:20–49 seems to be the relationship of Jeremiah to Baruch, but here he faces a problem of the relation of orally performed text in Aramaic to a written text in Greek. Horsley mentions this as a "problem" (pp. 52–53), but it either does not occur to him to use insights from the *Progymnasmata*, which tell us how people learned to compose in Greek from the dictation of a *grammateus*, a teacher of writing, or he is opposed to using such evidence. He, as many other NT interpreters, continue to be unaware, it appears, that Theon's *Progymnasmata* in particular exhibits many aspects of the interface between popular and elite culture in Mediterranean society and culture, as exhibited by its extensive use of Cynic *chreiai*. The absence of insights from the *Progym-*

nasmata in this volume weakens the discussion in substantive ways, since these manuals show how people learned how to write "orally performed speech" in Greek. (See Kennedy 2003.)

As stated above, Horsley offers a solution to the existence of Q 6:20–49 in Greek by suggesting that the writing down occurred "in the villages or 'regions' of Tyre, Caesarea Philippi, and the Decapolis" (p. 53), which is a very interesting suggestion. It is precisely in these locations that one can appropriately think of *progymnastic* teaching of Greek writing to be occurring. Instead of investigating the discussion of the *Progymnasmata* by NT interpreters, Horsley uses significant space in his introduction (pp. 11–15) to launch a "death blow" to Kloppenborg's and Arnal's argument that village clerks (*komogrammateis*) in Galilee were the likely writers of Q in Greek. Horsley's identification of the "surrounding regions" as a locale for the composition in writing of Q is a most interesting proposal. Even though Horsley uses the relationship of Jeremiah and Baruch as the major model for how Q may have been written, he does not tell the reader if he thinks Q first was written down in Aramaic, or whether it was translated from Aramaic into Greek while it existed solely in an "orally composed" form, then the Greek version of it was written down in the villages and regions of Tyre, Caesarea Philippi, and the Decapolis.

Another question Horsley does not address is the relation of the writing activity at Qumran with the "orality" of the Community Rule and Damascus Rule he analyzes for analogs to the covenant renewal performance that was the context for the composition of Q 6:20–49. He includes a number of very good paragraphs about Hebrew text and memory, using insights from excellent essays from Daniel Boyarin, Martin Jaffee, and William Scott Green. Horsley's omission of the *Progymnasmata* from the discussion, however, leaves a gap that makes it impossible to discuss in a substantive manner how Q 6:20–49 might have migrated from an oral performance environment located in Aramaic language to an oral-derived text written in Greek. Here a perspective of "ABK" (Anything but Kloppenborg) haunts his essays. Since Kloppenborg's analysis is the "unacceptable opposite" of the analysis Horsley enacts, there can be no admission of the presence of *chreiai* in Q, even if there are narrative introductions to Jesus' sayings, which are the special characteristic of a *chreia*.

A number of items in Q 6:20–49 that Kloppenborg and others have judged to be "redactional" at a stage of writing could help to support Horsley's thesis. For example, careful attention to the introductory exhortation in Q 6:27 may help with the argument that the "register" of this section is covenant renewal. In the context of an oral performance of a covenant renewal discourse as Horsley describes it, it is likely that "But I say to you who hear" (Luke 6:27a) would be heard as a tag that evokes "Hear O Israel" (Deut 6:4) in the Shema. The focus on the *topos* of "love" in Q 6:27b–38, then, reconfigures "Love the Lord your God with all your heart, with all your soul, and with all your might" in the following verse of the Torah (Deut 6:5). Since this exhortation is not present in reconstructed Q, one could argue that the Greek writer of Luke 6:27–38 has transmitted an "oral tag" related to the "oral-derived" dynamics of this text as covenant renewal by adding this introduction to Q 6:27–38.

There is one part of Horsley's display I consider inaccurate. Horsley has misread Q 6:27–38 in a manner that creates an inaccurate "balancing" of the verses. Q 6:36–38 are, in my judgment, 1, 2, and 3 that form the balanced conclusion to 6:27–38. Q 6:39 presents another tag in the form a narrative introduction, "He also spoke to them an analogy (*parabolē*)." After the section that reconfigures the Shema (Q 6:20–38), Q 6:39–45 introduces a question that opens the next section of the speech. This section elaborates "by analogy" (see Theon *Progymnasmata*) the covenant-renewal *topos*, which Q has reconfigured by that point into "love as God loves." As Draper observes, Q continues after the "sayings" of Jesus with two miracle stories (Luke 7:2–17). We will see below that these function as *paradeigmata* that Jesus himself enacts. This is a natural "next step" in an "elaboration," which exists at the interface of oral composition and *progymnastic* written composition. This, however, is a topic for the discussion of Draper's essay.

Jonathan A. Draper: Contextual Register in a Continuum

Jonathan Draper's essay exhibits an awareness of a continuum between oral and scribal composition that Kelber does not address and Horsley appears not to accept. Draper knows that oral performers tell stories in addition to giving speeches. Therefore, he includes narrative material as well as sayings material in the section of text he analyzes. Kelber and Horsley, in contrast, operate in a mode characteristic of much "rhetorical" analysis of NT texts that presupposes that "oral" performers can only present a "speech." Again, careful attention to the *Progymnasmata* removes this misunderstanding. An oral performance may be a matter of elaborating *topoi* by telling stories, as well as by formulating proverbial, balanced speech.

One of the keys to Draper's essay is the well-grounded insight that there are no "original performances" or "original texts." Rather, "[t]here are only particular performances, varying according to circumstances" (p. 72). This means that Luke 6:12–7:17 is a "particular performance," which an interpreter must analyze in toto. This is a major difference from Horsley who, in spite of some statements to the contrary, enacts his interpretation as though he were working with an "original performance" that could be rewritten through dictation. This appears to come from using Jeremiah and Baruch as his model for how Q became a written text. When the "original" scroll Baruch wrote was destroyed by the king, Jeremiah dictated "once again" the oracles God had given him to proclaim, and Baruch wrote them down "again." The way Horsley tells this story suggests that he at least implicitly thinks of an "original text" dictated to Baruch and written down, then destroyed and written down again through dictation. Draper insists that each performance would have been "a particular performance" containing certain variations from one another. The task of interpretation, then, is to analyze the "particular performance" that stands before the interpreter.

Another key to Draper's essay is his understanding that there is "a continuum between 'primary orality' and 'textual orality,' in which oral forms persist even after a person may become literate" (pp. 72–73). Every oral text from antiquity available to interpreters today is an "oral-derived text," namely it exists only in written form. This is not a substantive problem, however, in Draper's view. An oral-derived text will exhibit its "orality" in its sound balance, alliteration, assonance, binary oppositions, measured verse, and rhythm (p. 81). If it is not an oral-derived text, it will not have these qualities. Foley's use of the work of A. N. Doane, not cited in Draper's essay, helps to confirm Draper's assertion. Doane posits four kinds of interfaces between orality and literature:

1. the scribal transcription of a performed event,
2. the oral "autograph" poet who serves as his or her own scribe;
3. the literate poet who knows the tradition well enough to emulate an oral performance in writing. (Doane: 76, cited in Foley 1995:74);
4. a scribe who may be thought of as composing in the oral traditional manner, an act [Doane] calls "reperformance." Doane describes the last kind of scribe in the following manner:

> Whenever scribes who are part of the oral traditional culture write or copy traditional oral works, they do not merely mechanically hand them down; they rehear them, "mouth" them, "reperform" them in the act of writing in such a way that the text may change but remain authentic, just as a completely oral poet's text changes from performance to performance without losing authenticity. (Doane: 80–81, cited in Foley 1995:74–75)

In the light of these four alternatives, Draper's insight about the continuum between oral and written texts is highly welcome. Still another key to Draper's essay is his understanding that "Galilee was not a truly oral culture, since writing was known and used even if the majority of the members of that culture were illiterate" (p. 75). The important thing in this kind of setting is to be aware that "Oral texts written down do not lose the most characteristic features, although clearly the paralinguistic features will be lost—gesture, intonation, pause, pitch, and so on" (p. 76).

Draper's "rhythmographic" representation of Luke 6:12–7:17, following guidelines from Scott and Dean's "sound mapping," divides the sections of the text accurately, in contrast to Horsley's, which makes a mistake at 6:36–38, as discussed above. Then his analysis on the basis of tenor, field, and implied and real communicative event is highly instructive and suggestive. Draper comes close to observing that a "key" to 6:27–38 is the Shema, when he writes that "They are required of 'all Israel': 'to you who hear'" (p. 95). Instead of suggesting that Luke 6:27–38 is likely initially to evoke the Shema in the hearing of the audience, he moves directly to an analysis based on the "Holiness Code" in Lev 18–20. The verses Draper displays suggest that Luke 6 does in fact reconfigure the Shema on the basis of stipulations in the Holiness Code. I think he misses a part of the "orality" of Luke 6, however, when he does not notice the likely oral resonance with the Shema when the text has Jesus say, "But I say to you who hear" (6:27a).

Having asserted the importance of narrative as well as speech in the covenant discourse, Draper does not comment on "He also told them an analogy" (*parabolēn*) in 6:39. Again, the likely reason is the absence of information from the *Progymnasmata* in the discussion. *Parabolē* (analogy) is a key *topos* for hearers in the Mediterranean world. "Can a blind man lead a blind man?" introduces the analogy of "seeing" to explain the nature of "hearing." The question introducing the analogy sets the context for the six references to "the eye" in 6:41–42. When the speaker moves to the analogy of trees that bear fruit in 6:43–45, then onto a question that focuses on "doing what I tell you" (6:46), the hearer waits to hear if the speaker has moved away from the *topos* of "seeing." The speaker signals the conclusion to the speech by asserting, "I will show you" what the person who comes to me and hears my words and does them is like (6:49). The final analogy presenting the two houses is designed to remove "the blindness" to which the speaker referred at the beginning of the section. With the conclusion (6:46–49), the "eye" of the hearer is able to see the ability of the person who "hears the words and does them" to withstand all kinds of difficulties (6:47), in contrast to the ruin of the person "who hears and does not do them" (6:49). The hearer has "seen" all of these things, of course, "by analogy."

Draper's analysis is correctly informed, in addition, when it includes the two healing stories in Luke 7:2–17. As he observes, the reference to "When all his words were completed in the hearing of the people" is a metonymic reference to Moses at the end of Deuteronomy (again showing the importance of the evocation of the Shema in Luke 6:27). This reference, however, is simply a transition to two healings that evoke the declaration that "A great prophet has arisen among us!" in Luke 7:17. Again, the absence of the *Progymnasmata* from the analysis is noticeable. At this point, the Mediterranean hearer will know that the speaker has moved beyond "analogy" to "example" (*paradeigma*). The story teller now shows the hearer by example how Jesus enacts the blessings of covenant renewal amidst

God's people, in a context where a centurion enacts the teaching of "loving your enemies." The key *topoi* in the first healing story are the "love" of the centurion which led him to "build" the synagogue. The centurion is showing "by example" how to enact the "love" the speaker talked about in Luke 6:27–38 and the "building" the speaker talked about in Luke 6:48–49. Then when Jesus heals the only son of the widow of Nain, as Draper observes, the storyteller shows the "covenant renewal enacted by the 'prophet like Moses'" (p. 97). This is the final presentation "through example" in the oral performance. As Draper says, Jesus becomes the "prophet like Moses" who renews the covenant through his speech and action.

Conclusion

There are significantly different "signals" among the essays in this volume written by Werner Kelber, Richard Horsley, and Jonathan Draper. All of the authors attack the "print culture perspective" that, in their opinion, drives modern biblical interpretation. Yet each approaches the problems in a different way. Their attack is noticeably aggressive, and one of the reasons may be their focus on Q, which is both "strongly asserted" and "highly disputed" in the field of NT studies. The intensity of the "fight" over Q creates a "performance arena" (Foley 1995:79–82) in which polarization is the most natural way to proceed. Inasmuch as the essays are designed to introduce a "new paradigm" for analyzing discourse in the Gospels, one might consider it natural that Kelber's and Draper's essays, in particular, adopt such an aggressive, polarizing position. Only Draper's essay, which is nurtured by extensive information about oral performances in South Africa in particular, limits its oppositional modes of thinking to the conflict between elite culture rulers and popular culture subordinates. Draper knows from firsthand experience that orality and literacy mingle together is multiple ways.

In their analyses, Horsley and Draper are pursuing issues of rhetorical elaboration, which have been investigated in the synoptic Gospels since the 1980s. Much of their analysis is looking at "rhetorical elaboration," the "working out" (*exergasia* [Greek] or "refinement" *expolitio* [Latin] of a "topic" (*topos* [Greek], *locus* [Latin]) or "subject" (*res* [Latin]), which can also take the form of the "working" (*ergasia*) or elaboration of a contextualized saying (*chreia*, Mack and Robbins). Neither author, however, uses insights from these investigations which could help them to exhibit the nature of the oral-derived text they are interpreting. In fact, it is not clear that Draper and Horsley have a clear grasp of the widespread "elaboration techniques" that were taught during the final stage of grammatical training, when students were taught how to "compose" in writing on the basis of oral recitation to them. As I have tried to show, their analyses could be improved and assisted in a number of ways if they were to incorporate insights from these manuals into their work.

Though I have articulated perhaps more disagreements than usual in this response, I want to make it clear that I am deeply appreciative, and deeply indebted, to the conversation taking place in these essays and the courage that is being taken to display aspects of orality in the written texts before us. I consider the issues of orality to be very important for New Testament interpreters to master. It is clear, however, that we are only at the beginning stages of learning how to approach them. I applaud the courage and energy present in these essays and look forward to the time when insights from them will incorporate more robust rhetorical analysis and interpretation of all of the NT writings.

The Riddle of Q
ORAL ANCESTOR, TEXTUAL PRECEDENT, OR IDEOLOGICAL CREATION?

John Miles Foley

In medieval literature it is conventional to begin with the "modesty" *topos*—words to the effect that the writer or speaker, supposedly handicapped by a lack of expertise or knowledge, can offer only a qualified and necessarily limited view of the matter at hand. In most such cases the idiomatic force of this strategy is less to indemnify the writer or reader against criticism than to rhetorically amplify the tale-telling that follows. Asking readers or listeners to excuse an unfortunate but unavoidable liability amounts by agreed-upon convention to securing the authorial high ground.

Let me start by affirming that no such rhetorical *topos* is intended here. As an outsider to the field of biblical scholarship, I truly am at a marked disadvantage in commenting on this thought-provoking symposium on Q: the papers by Werner Kelber, Jonathan Draper, and Richard Horsley, as well as the responses by Joanna Dewey and Vernon Robbins. My home field is oral tradition, principally ancient Greek, early medieval English (Anglo-Saxon), and contemporary South Slavic, which I examine chiefly from the perspective of comparative studies, anthropology, and linguistics. What I can perhaps contribute here thus derives not from a professional immersion in the history of New Testament research and scholarship, then, but precisely from its absence. That is, I will attempt to comment on the manifold different ideas about Q by adducing comparative parallels, by citing and briefly exploring verbal ecologies from other times and places. Like the folklorist who cautions that any oral tradition is best understood stereoscopically—by attending to both the "emic" (internal or ethnic) and "etic" (external or analytical) realities—I will try to supply a comparative perspective on what my colleagues in this symposium are discussing from a specialist point of view. In the spirit of inquiry and an ongoing heuristic, I will phrase most of my comments not as pronouncements or air-tight affirmations, but rather as suggestions and proposals.

General Questions

For the outsider, the first concern has to be the very viability of the concept of Q, however the individual scholar may construe this document, performance, or instance of tradition. In other words, what leads us to believe that there ever was a Q, no matter what we suppose it was?[1] There seems to be no manuscript or fragment, no summary, not even a reference to such a source. While none of these lacunae are really very surprising, given the oral-aural context out of which the gospels emerge, the issue of Q's very existence does in fact arise if we are willing to start from the beginning and ask a disarming question: why do a substantial number of scholars adhere to the Q hypothesis and commence their investigations from the presumption that it (whatever it was) lies behind surviving gospel texts?

The easy answer is the correspondence between the speeches of Jesus in Matthew and Luke. How else are we to explain such close links except as second-order reflexes of an Ur-text? And indeed, centuries of editing and collating, and particularly of sorting manuscripts into family trees stemmata, have honed our research methods, and not only in biblical studies, with the result that we have trouble imagining any other dynamic. The standard editions of Homer's *Iliad* and *Odyssey* were compiled by collating manuscripts, sifting variants, and building a "best text" that most faithfully "re-created" an envisioned (ontologically edenic) Ur-Homer.[2] Wherever possible, editions of medieval poetry based in oral tradition have been constructed along similar lines: one surveys and analyzes the progeny in order to sleuth out the identity of the now-lost ancestor, all the while assuming the inevitable, deterministic rules of textual genetics.

But recent research has shown that this procedure is based more on ingrained ideology than on the actual dynamics of transcribing oral performances and copying manuscripts. Witness after witness steps forward—whether Byzantine Greek romance, Anglo-Saxon poetry, South Slavic oral epic, or others (see, respectively, Jeffreys and Jeffreys 1971; O'Keeffe 1990; and Foley 2004a:144–91)—to put the lie to lock-step stemmata that assume the simplex model of one text giving birth to another, parthenogenetically it would seem. We may have depended on an unchallengeable (because unexamined) textual procedure to order the shards of once-living traditions into what we conceive of as their original form, but

---

1. For an overview of what it tellingly calls the "Q document," see the Wikipedia entry at http://www.answers.com/topic/q-document?method=5&linktext=Q%20document.

2. In this context it is interesting to consider the physician-fieldworker Elias Lönnrot's mid-nineteenth-century project of (re-)constructing an envisioned Finnish epic, the *Kalevala*, by combining collected poems, sequencing them narratively, and himself composing material to fill the interstices. See further Foley 2002:51–52; DuBois 1995; and Honko 1998:169–76.

the phenomena of oral transmission, subjective transcription, and even re-composing during "mechanical" copying reveal that we have been insisting on an outdated, misleading Newtonian approximation when we should be confronting the Einsteinian complexity of the situation.

From a comparative perspective, then, there seems little reason to place one's faith in an Ur-text called Q as the literal and lettered source of the gospel correspondences, no matter how similar the wording may be. In fact, there is every reason *not* to do so: in the period during which the gospels took shape, the nature of literacy and, more fundamentally, of the technology of text-creation, -transmission, and -consultation was vastly different from the default set of textual practices in place today. Consider what didn't exist: the familiar and comfortable concepts of the standard work or mass readership for that work, the single ubiquitous printed form (available from online booksellers at a mere click), legal copyright or some other inertial force that privileges the single version and constrains variability, and so forth (cf. my discussion of the twin myths of object and stasis in Foley 1998a). The 131 texts of Homer apparently on deposit at the Alexandrian Library make this point indelibly, as does the modern insistence—totally without objective evidence of any sort—that there must have been a master-edition assembled by Aristarchus or another of the librarians (cf. Foley 1990:20–31; on recording materials and practices in ancient world, Haslam 2005). They didn't have the technology, they didn't have the concept, and even if they miraculously managed to construct such an anachronism they couldn't have mustered a readership.

Comparative studies thus point toward, at the maximum, a non-textual, oral traditional precursor, which we may choose to call Q. But even that modified hypothesis raises some problems. Oral traditional entities are by their very nature instances rather than items. That is, they figure forth one version of an idea or story by enacting its potential, but they do not—indeed cannot—serve as the sole basis for the next version or generation of the idea or story. Because they are rule-governed but flexible expressions, oral traditional units and patterns will owe their allegiance primarily to the network of pathways that make up the tradition, just as any sentence we utter owes its shape and structure to rule-governed fluency in whatever language we happen to be using.[3] The question of how far an oral traditional Q can predetermine a written gospel text is a difficult one, involving variables such as social context, translation from oral to written semiotics (not mutually exclusive, of course), individual and col-

---

3. For a discussion of how the technologies of oral tradition and the internet operate in strikingly similar ways, see, incipiently, Foley 2002:220–25, and, more substantially, the Pathways Project (www.pathwaysproject.org), which will include a conventional book (*Pathways of the Mind*) suspended in a network of electronic appendages. Examples of eEditions and eCompanions can be found, respectively, at www.oraltradition.org/zbm and http://oraltradition.org/ecompanion/.

lective patterns of expression, and the like. But it is clearly a question that needs to be addressed even if it cannot be easily answered, and several of the contributions to this collection are in one way or another pertinent.

Let me summarize these few thoughts before responding to each of those contributions as best I can. From a comparative perspective, the absence of evidence for the existence of Q is expectable and explicable. We do not expect documentary evidence for something that may never have reached documentary form or, if it did, could not have been centrally distributed in a multilithed format or "consumed" by a mass readership. At the same time, the very terms in which the discussion has proceeded reveal our contemporary culture's abiding ideological need for an author, a point of origin, a well-ordered succession of texts, and a literary dynamics that reinforces our submerged notions about how verbal art arose and was transmitted.[4] If we are able to extricate ourselves from that imposed, culturally rooted (even tautological) mind-set, and to see what was actually possible in the era in which the gospels took shape, then I believe we must come to the conclusion that Q—if indeed there ever was a Q—must have been an oral traditional entity of some kind, and that it could have served as a "source" only secondarily, to the limited extent that one instance informs another. This isn't the kind of orderly, exclusive, literary model we are accustomed to employ in negotiating the often confusing because "partial" remains of ancient works, but it does have the advantage of engaging the problem of interpretation realistically. Toward the end of this response I will offer a proposal for an alternative model.

Werner Kelber: Process and Genre

In "The Verbal Art in Q and Thomas," Werner Kelber undertakes to dislodge the riddle of Q from form and source criticism. From the perspective of this outsider, he seems to succeed quite admirably by querying the notion that a tradition can be represented as a linear historical evolution and employing a narratological explanation of the gospels as "a reconfiguring of the traditional legacy." This model allows for both the correspondences and differences that have been noted among the gospels as well as establishes the basis for an oral traditional Q. Likewise, his objections to Robinson's thesis of a genre identified as *logoi sophon* seem well founded, and I would further (and I hope sympathetically) observe that the Robinson thesis assumes a historical-textual dynamics but depends for its overall efficacy on imposing a blanket "literary history" on rather disparate texts.

---

4. One is reminded of the depth of this ideological need by some of the more inventive strategies editors have summoned in order to explain what the manuscript record alone cannot: the "lost Latin intermediary" has served this function for medieval poetry that lacks an ostensible source in the correct language, for example, usually without any trace whatsoever of the elusive creature itself.

Kelber affirms the approach taken by Richard Horsley and Jonathan Draper, whose work will be treated separately below, agreeing with them that Q must have been an "oral-derived text."⁵ Greatly to the credit of all three scholars, this new hypothesis recognizes the extent to which our modern investigations have been predetermined by textual ideology. As Kelber puts it, "Horsley's [and Draper's] work on Q contributes toward a deconstruction of our print-based hermeneutics and launches a re-imagining of Christian origins in their historically appropriate environment." We wouldn't try to imagine Ernest Hemingway's novels as bardic performances, so why should we falsify the provenience of ancient works in order to fit our cognitive categories? Kelber thus provides a refreshing and fundamental intervention that forces us to understand Q and the gospel network on their own terms, as closely as circumstances permit at any rate.

And what is the benefit of thinking about Q in this way? Kelber is echoing the findings of many scholars in many traditions, ancient through modern, when he observes that "understood orally, the speeches in Q encapsulate a world of words, phrases, ideas, and images that resonate with a map of experiences and associations shared by speakers and hearers. In short, Q as an oral-derived text relies heavily on extratextual factors, shifting meaning from production to performance." That is, oral traditional entities inherently engage larger-than-textual fields of implication, depending on idiomatic fluency at both ends of the communicative interchange.⁶ Since one simply can't contain all of that interchange in a conventional text, it's no wonder that different instances or avatars vary systemically, or that we will always seek in vain for purely textual explanations of how various instances are related. Along with what we have recently learned about the instability of all texts, oral-derived texts demonstrate an additional flexibility that stems from their identity as instances rife with more-than-textual implication rather than controlled, circumscribed items.⁷

Toward the end of his essay Kelber confronts the related question of the *Gospel of Thomas*, and comes to the conclusion that the ancient genre of "list" or catalogue is the most apposite model. I can affirm that the list is a widespread form in worldwide oral tradition, ancient through modern, existing both as a freestanding form and as a subgenre within larger genres such as epic. Its purpose is customarily to preserve in memorable

---

5. For the initial proposal of the term "oral-derived texts," see Foley 1990:5–8, where they are defined as "manuscript or tablet works of finally uncertain provenance that nonetheless show oral traditional characteristics" (5). A more nuanced model, consisting of a four-part media morphology, is presented below.

6. On the dynamic of *traditional referentiality*, cf. Foley 1991:xiv, 6–8, and passim; also Bradbury 1998.

7. For an excellent example of how this kind of implication can be investigated by modern scholars, see Amodio 2005.

form the identity-history of a group or people by memorializing folk history, and its structure is usually non-narrative (except for biographical or genealogical patterns). One is reminded of the "Catalogue of Ships and Men" in the second book of Homer's *Iliad*, or the genealogy of the gods and goddesses in Hesiod's *Theogony*, or the king-list in *Beowulf*, or indeed the catalogues of combatants in any of several modern epic traditions across eastern Europe through central Asia and Africa (see further Lord 1991:221–22; Foley 2004b:184), as well as of the self-contained lists found in oral traditions worldwide. There is, in short, widespread evidence of this genre and its central importance for the cultural and religious identity of the people who maintain it as a staple of their oral traditional ecology. It may well be that Q should be added to this group.

In regard to Kelber's specific comments on the *Gospel of Thomas* as a "sayings gospel" rather than a list, I cannot comment except to observe that once again we have numerous parallels in international oral tradition. A convenient example is the Anglo-Saxon "Maxims" poetry, which reaches us in two separate but related manuscript instances dating from the last third of the tenth century at the latest. Composed in the Germanic language of Old English, these collections of poetic statements proclaim cosmological, meteorological, theological, and other verities and are linked through syntactic and phonological patterning. Such gatherings of proverbial wisdom are neither trite nor "minor," as literary criticism that privileges familiar textual forms has too often claimed, but rather a kind of repository of culturally significant knowledge that seems to have been valued not as an item but a living heritage, an index or lemma of what it meant to belong to that culture.

In what has been called "Maxims I" in the Exeter Book manuscript, we glimpse an expressive strategy somewhat similar to that employed at the start of the *Gospel of Thomas*. Here are the opening lines, which cue the kind of speech-act soon to be underway (Krapp and Dobie: 156–57, lines 1–4a, translation mine):

> Ask me with wise words! Don't let your heart be hidden,
> concealed what you most deeply know! I won't tell my secret to you
> if you hide your mind-craft and your heart's thoughts from me.
> Clever men should exchange songs.

This brief prologue situates the utterance to follow as precious, secret information that should be shared among "clever men," and portrays its oral publication as a societal duty. Phrased in riddling language (and the riddle is a subgeneric element here), these lines authorize the speech-act socioculturally. Although we know next to nothing about the ethnographic context of the maxims in pre-Conquest England, they do provide an engaging parallel to the *Gospel of Thomas*, especially in the built-in generic imperative to share their living, guiding contents—not through the medium of the text but orally and in performance. As Kelber puts it in relation to the *Gospel of Thomas* and more broadly the sayings gospel genre, "the unifying aspect . . . is its demand for interpretation." It demands to be embodied.

Jonathan Draper: A Living Analogue

Theorizing about ancient texts can be productive; indeed, all of the contributions to the present collection certainly illustrate that premise. But consulting a living analogue can also offer insights of a different and complementary sort, and it is this second type of approach that lies at the basis of Jonathan Draper's remarks. He is confronting the same problem as Kelber and Richard Horsley, namely "the twin assumption that Q is a written source, which can be analyzed like other literary sources, and that it is the earliest and therefore the most authoritative source for the quest." But while his observations harmonize with these other papers, they also gain another kind of authority through his evocation of South African oral tradition as an analogue.

Contemporary South Africa offers an especially apt parallel because of its media history and present media situation. As Draper notes, before the arrival of missionaries and the Bible, oral tradition was the exclusive technology of communication among indigenous peoples. But the advent of literacy, powerful as it was, did not signal the immediate and universal shift from oral tradition to reading, writing, and print that some scholars, working mainly from theoretical paradigms rather than real-world observation, have predicted. Instead of the envisioned Great Divide, orality and literacy came to interact in rich and interesting ways, and still today, in Draper's words, "the oral forms and traditions remain operative, even in writing."

As numerous examples brought forward in recent years indicate, this is in fact the typical situation: not only cultural groups, but even single individuals demonstrate complex expressive repertoires (cf. Foley 2002:36–38 and passim). The same residents of a Serbian village who pen letters to relatives who are working as *Gastarbeiter* in Switzerland never consider using the technology of writing to manage epics, lyrics, magical charms, genealogies, funeral laments, and so forth. Within ecologies of oral tradition, various ways of communicating—distinctive and functional discourse styles that anthropologists call "registers"—may involve reading and writing, or they may not, and in many if not most cases the reality is a mixture of voice and page, not simply one or the other (Foley 1995, esp. 49–53; 2002:109–24).

To fit this spectrum of forms I have proposed a four-part model that may have resonance for the early Christian situation: a system of flexible categories that includes *oral performance, voiced texts, voices from the past,* and *written oral poetry* (see further Foley 2002:38–53). The first category, *oral performance*, reflects theorists' first approximation of oral tradition—a live speech-act conveyed by a performer to a present audience wholly without recourse to texts of any kind. Although for many this has been taken as the "pure" (and sometimes exclusive) form of oral tradition, it actually proves much less common than one might suppose. *Voiced texts* take shape as written artifacts, although they are meant primarily or only for performance. *Voices from the past* provides a category for those ancient and works, like Homer's *Iliad* and *Odyssey* and the anonymous *Beowulf*, that reveal both internal and external signs of having been derived from oral tradition, with the recognition that their specific media history has perished since their recording. Finally, *written oral poetry* recognizes those not uncommon works that, although composed in writing for readers, nevertheless employ the oral traditional register—and its built-in idiomatic implications—to communicate "more than textually."

I will have more to say about the nature of Q in terms of this morphology toward the end of my response, but for the moment let me concentrate on Draper's affirmation that the Q material in Matthew and Luke amounts to an "oral-derived text" rather than "oral tradition." This distinction is a crucial one for at least three interrelated reasons. First, by such a reclassification he avoids the unsustainable hypothesis that Q (or any other work) emerged from the multi-media world of early Christianity as pure oral performance, transcribed from an event and converted to an artifact. Complementarily, he acknowledges the complexity of the orality-literacy mix without abandoning the link between Q—and by implication the gospels—and the matrix of oral tradition. Third, he situates Q in a context that has innumerable parallels worldwide and throughout history: an ecosystem, as it were, of communicative species with a host of different characteristics. Draper's commitment to a realistically complex media-mix, as opposed to a binary opposition that doesn't match what humanity actually does in most instances, is admirable on all these scores.

The key to Draper's argument seems to me to be the establishment of a "discourse register," a specialized language that is not merely mnemonically supportive but also idiomatically echoic. Very importantly, he does not settle for the Parry-Lord concept of metrical formulas, which is based on a Greco-Roman concept of the poetic line, but adapts Dell Hymes' work on ethnopoetic structure in Native American oral traditions (cf. Foley 1995, esp. 17–27; more broadly, Hymes 1981, 1994). What Hymes accomplished was to open up the possibility that verse increments, and other units as well, could be defined according to parameters largely outside Western experience, such as breath-groups and pattern-numbers. Once one realizes that our default concept of poetic structure is highly parochial and that "poetry" needs to be conceived much more broadly to answer the world's diversity, then units of utterance typical of oral traditional registers can begin to emerge. Draper's ethnopoetic representation of the Covenantal

Discourse on the Plain reveals some of the endemic structure that is foregrounded when the material is understood on its own terms.

In short, then, I certainly concur with Draper that "the search for an original text of an oral-derived text is an illusion, indeed results in neutering the tradition and systematically *mis*-understanding its performative significance (italics his)." By receiving such texts—poised between orality and literacy—on their own terms, and by recognizing the structure and the expressive register that underlies them, we will be in a far better position to interpret them.

Richard Horsley: How Oral Performances Live

In "Performance and Tradition: The Covenant Speech in Q," Richard Horsley is concerned above all with embedding this hypothetical source-work into its genuine sociocultural context. This means, first and foremost, escaping the "presuppositions of print-culture" so much a part of nearly every aspect of our daily lives today and recognizing the "live communication that was involved in the oral recitation of Gospels, gospel stories, and the speeches of Jesus." Of course, these concerns in many ways dovetail with Kelber's concentration on process and genre and with Draper's focus on a living analogue and oral-derived texts, but for Horsley the investigation centers on issues of what is meant by text, context, register, and tradition, with special reference to the expressive structure and arc of the Q speeches that serve as the primary platform for the Q hypothesis.

For *text* what is most important to Horsley is not to mistake the libretto for the performance. This is essentially the same caveat as the linguist's reminder that any script is not itself language, but rather a prompt for or encoding of language—a fundamental but very often overlooked distinction. Texts were not simply processed silently and alone in the ancient world: they were also (and much more frequently) read aloud, shared vocally, experienced orally and aurally. If we aspire to a modern reception of Q that matches its composition and transmission, Horsley argues, we will need to pay attention not to the unsegmented, silent prose into which our print-culture ideology has synthetically reduced such works, but to what he terms Q's "intelligible units of communication," that is, its "speeches and discourses focused on particular issues." To this caveat he adds an emphasis on relational *context*, which involves a focus on the religious, political, and economic aspects of the environment in which Q purportedly arose. The latter emphasis harmonizes with Horsley's view of text, again stressing that scholars must avoid treating Q as an artifact or museum-piece removed from performance and reality.

In addition to these paired concerns, Horsley underlines the significance of *register*, or, as Dell Hymes has put it, the "way of speaking" (Hymes 1989:440 defines "registers" as "major speech styles associated with recurrent types of situations"). This is, of course, a fundamental concept in any form of communication. Sociolinguistics starts with the premise that the expressive instrument or vehicle matches the expressive goal, so that the particular form of language (a poetic variety, for example, in whatever way poetry is made and received within a particular tradition) provides the best possible tool for accomplishing the task at hand. To cite a few real-life situations, South Slavic magical charms employ a register packed with anachronisms and a specialized color-vocabulary, both of which aspects would be out of place—and effectively unintelligible—in the narrowly defined South Slavic lyric poetry register as well as in more broadly defined everyday speech on the streets of Belgrade.[8] Although the very same woman might well be fluent in all three of these communicative streams, and might conceivably practice all three on the same day, she would never mix modes. Instead, she would choose the designated tool for the particular purpose, "dialing in" to the appropriate way of speaking for the given speech-act. At the same time, and this is crucial for Horsley's reasoning, she would be alerting her audience to the nature of the speech-act, tapping into their fluency to signal the kind of performance they would then have reason to expect.

From this point Horsley moves to the importance of *tradition* for understanding the coded message of Q and the gospels. As has been established in myriad different oral-traditional scenarios, the audience receives the message not as an epitomized document whose primary source of signification is itself and its linear relations to other documents, but as a multivalent utterance bristling with idiomatic implications. "Tradition" is no mere monolith (another concession to the "communication-as-tangible-item" assumption that drives our modern textual ideology), but rather a plastic, rule-governed way of speaking that contains implicit directions on how to understand it—directions that the fluent audience knows how to follow but the far-removed, textual scholar struggles to hear. What Horsley is advocating is a form of ethnopoetics (Hymes 1989:440; DuBois 1998), which operates on the central conviction that we need to receive Q, the gospels, or for that matter any human communication not according to our default rules for reading texts but in harmony with the assumptions and coding that were operative as part of their creation.

Before illustrating how he would ethnopoetically score the performance libretto for Q 6:20–49 to help the reader (in a basic sense the re-performer) glimpse its truer structure and correspondences, Horsley mentions three problems that highlight the "special importance of Israelite tradition for hearing Q as oral performance." The first of these problems—that the tradition was not unitary and existed on different social levels—is a familiar one worldwide, often overlooked or minimized by

---

8. On the Serbian magical charms and their special register, see Foley 1995:99–135; 2002, esp. 190–95. An audio of a charm performance is available online at http://www.oraltradition.org/hrop/eighth_word.

collectors and scholars seeking to rationalize the inherent multiplicity of oral tradition to a single, convenient, textual unity. One thinks of the manifold different genres clustered around the *Siri Epic* mythology of the Tulu people in southern India, for example (see further Honko 1998:245–53). Or, more generally, consider the various dialectal and idiolectal forms of all oral traditions, which do not conform to a single standard any more than all English-speaking citizens of the world (or even within a small town) speak precisely the same language.[9] Diverse living performances simply don't coalesce to fulsome prelapsarian unity; we can't reduce oral traditions to books without denaturing them.[10]

The second problem has to do with the Israelite popular tradition taking shape in Aramaic while Q, one must suppose, existed in koinê Greek. Horsley's explanations seem to provide a logical social framework for the transferral or dual-language existence, but I do not have the specialist background to judge which, if either, is likely the factual scenario. What I can offer, drawing on comparative studies in oral tradition, is the observation that a dual-language vehicle is a fairly common phenomenon worldwide. All this apparent miracle requires, after all, is a single bilingual speaker who can perform in two different linguistic registers. Present-day or recent examples include the sharing of *Manas* oral epic across the Turkic languages of central Asia (cf. Reichl 1992), and the bilingual Bosnian oral epic singers Djemail Zogi and Salih Ugljanin, who could perform the same tale in both South Slavic and Albanian (see http://cc.joensuu.fi/~loristi/1_03/dus103.html; Kolsti 1990). If we understand that such migration amounts simply to construal and expression within two linguistic systems rather than the conversion of one artifact to another, a transition and interplay between Aramaic and Greek may not appear so problematic.

Horsley's third issue is perhaps the most crucial and, at the same time, the most elusive for those of us who have trouble imagining communication outside our default textual presumptions. He maintains, and there are myriad comparative parallels to bolster his assertion, that "culture involves more than particular items such as names, place-names, and motifs, but broader patterns, connections, and 'discourses,' as well" and that "the very concept of *register* implies such cultural realities as discourses devoted to certain memories and other cultural patterns." In other words, he is insisting, together with Kelber and Draper, on interpreting Q and the gospels

---

9. Compare the idiolectal, dialectal, and pan-traditional levels of South Slavic oral epic structure as demonstrated in Foley 1990: chs. 4–9.

10. In addition to these engines of variability, Horsley also mentions several specific measures that we text-based scholars usually choose to disregard, or at least submerge: the unwieldiness of textual technology and low literacy rates in the ancient world. On the virtually universal intervention by which oral epics become books—namely, through the agency of an outsider with an external agenda—see the collection of viewpoints in Honko 2000.

on their own terms, which will not usually coincide with the text-driven habits we bring to interpretation.

To the question of how we can come to understand these broader patterns and their significance, of how we can gain admission to the performance arena (as I have described the challenge elsewhere[11]), I start with a double statement: we can never become the original audience, but we can do better than subscribe to mindless and automatic conversion of oral- and performance-derived utterances to flattened texts. By paying attention to the units and shape of the work, by remaining open to the ethnopoetic possibility that it may well be organized in unexpected ways and therefore may well *mean* in unexpected ways, we can at least make some progress toward understanding its depths. What Horsley's (and Kelber's and Draper's) work encourages is a hermeneutic that matches the phenomenological dynamics of Q and the gospels, that "reads" them on their own terms, via their own cognitive categories, as well and as thoroughly as we can. If we cannot conquer space and time and insert ourselves into the world of Q, at least we use a more finely calibrated hermeneutic lens to bring Q and the gospels into clearer focus.

Joanna Dewey and Vernon Robbins: Responding to the Responses

I append here just a very few words about the helpful responses made by two colleagues in biblical studies to the three essays on Q. As with the essays themselves, my lack of appropriate expertise does not permit a specialist engagement with their thoughts and comments, but I hope to offer a few useful observations from a comparative perspective.

Joanna Dewey's succinct summary of what the three authors share is extremely helpful, and to my mind on the mark: (1) the unit of meaning must be the entire discourse and not the individual saying; (2) the speech derives its meaning from its cultural tradition; and (3) the performance event is "the shaper of the discourse." I would add only that one does not need to prescribe any single level of structure and signification in oral and oral-derived works to the exclusion of others; while the discourse as a whole may represent the overarching pattern informing the speech, there may also be smaller units within it that bear an idiomatic function of their own. Elsewhere in oral traditions one finds copious evidence of different-sized "words" or thought-bytes, all the way from entire story-patterns to

---

11. On *performance arena*, cf. Foley 1995:47–49. This term "designates the place where the event of performance takes place, where words are invested with their special power," and thus names a virtual, ritual, action-circumscribed space rather than simply a geographical or temporal location.

scenes and on to phrases.[12] Oral performers seem to be able to fluently manage a tiered act of expression, which their original audiences successfully process without choosing one channel to the exclusion of others.

On the matter of what constitutes the whole performance, and particularly of the stability of the hypothesized Q (all this in her response to Horsley's ideas), there are many analogues that could be cited. Suffice it to say that, whether it became a manuscript or not, there would remain a degree of variability within limits. First, and here I find Dewey's caveat applicable, it would be unprecedented for an oral discourse to absolutely stabilize (pseudo-textually) as long as it lived in performance (cf. again Honko 2000). Living processes live through continual re-creation, not through fossilization. She refers to the famous incident concerning the *Mwindo Epic* and the bard Mr. Rureke, and I have myself observed similar phenomena during fieldwork in the Former Yugoslavia: no matter what the genre, each telling will differ—sometimes in order, sometimes in "inclusiveness" (though this is at heart a textual measure), sometimes in other ways. One could add the vexed notion of the "cycle" (an ordered anthology) that has compromised our understanding of how stories interrelate in modern-day oral epic traditions from central Asia and Africa, or even in the ancient Greek Epic Cycle that mostly perished before, like the *Iliad* and *Odyssey*, it was recorded.[13] Briefly put, if each "part" is an instance of the tradition rather than a jigsaw piece tailored to fit snugly with its neighbors to make a well-ordered (textual) whole, then the concept of cycle is semiotically inapposite.

As for scribal influence, we have in the past been very naive about this dimension of recording and transmission, unthinkingly imposing a print-culture frame of reference where it cannot be anything but culturally foreign and anachronistic. Reacting against the false notion of verbatim recording and transmission, Dewey is certainly right to implicate scribes in not simply the copying but also the actual refashioning of texts. On one point, however, I would offer a word of caution. Research in early medieval English scribal practices has revealed that scribes read and re-created out of a knowledge of the oral traditional register (cf. O'Keeffe 1990), and an analysis of even a modern-day transcriber of an oral performance has shown that the transcriber clearly re-made the work he was hearing—adhering to the rules of the register (as one would respect the rules of the broader language when attempting any sort of communication) but varying within them, thus making the traditional work also his own (cf.

---

12. On "words" as minimally phrases and maximally whole performances, see Foley 2002:11–21. For an application of the concept to Homeric epic, cf. Foley 1999a: chs. 5–7.

13. On the misleadingly textual nature of the term "cycle" as applied to oral traditions, see Foley 1999b.

Foley 2004a:144–91). This is another reason why "either/or" models, which Dewey sensibly argues against, do not serve us well.

Vernon Robbins advocates the same "spectrum" model instead of the either/or binary of the Great Divide, citing Draper's contribution as a healthy comparative perspective on the early Christian situation of mixed orality and literacy. With this kind of thoughtful, realistic observation I cannot help but agree. His discussion of Horsley's essay finds ten dichotomies that he feels characterize Horsley's "conflict model," and asks whether interpreters should read the Bible "from a perspective of dominant, elite culture or should they read it from a perspective of subordinated, popular culture," commenting that many biblical scholars would favor the former approach. At the risk of overstepping my expertise, I would suggest that this is precisely the problem with most scholarship that seeks to deal with oral and oral-derived works, biblical or otherwise: precisely because the academy's culture is fundamentally the culture of the book, we tend to predetermine the scope of our research and opinions by the very cognitive categories with which we deliberate. If Horsley is advocating attention to popular culture, the "little tradition," oral culture, oral composition, cultural memory, and so forth, he happens to be entirely in tune, for example, with UNESCO's worldwide program of Intangible Cultural Heritage, the most ambitious investigation and preservation project for oral tradition and related forms in the history of our species.[14] And there is after all the matter of balance. We have suffered under long centuries of privileging elite culture, the "great tradition," print culture, writing, and so forth, and it seems high time to open up the inquiry to confront the non-official, sociohistorical realities surrounding such works of verbal art.

Because of my lack of broad acquaintance with New Testament scholarship, I am not able to comment specifically on Robbins's repeated complaint, particularly in regard to the Horsley and Draper essays, that the *Progymnasmata* and attendant activities were not sufficiently taken into account in this collection of Q scholarship. Perhaps such manuals parallel the rhetorical handbooks of the later Middle Ages, which likewise contained a selection of *topoi* and instructions on how to use them. To the extent that this kind of rhetorical guide provided a hypostasis of oral-performative expressive strategies, it may have promoted the writing of oral-derived works. In the case of the medieval handbooks, however, the mechanical deployment of rhetorical figures—always necessarily from an external point of view—differed dynamically from the "inside" deployment of oral-traditional patterns as part of a learned and understood register. It's one thing to erect a building based on someone else's blueprint; it's another matter to execute the construction fluently from inside a coherent, shared style.

---

14. Visit http://portal.unesco.org/culture/en/ev.php-URL_ID=2225&URL_DO=DO_TOPIC&URL_SECTION=201.html.

Conclusion: Reception, Embodiment, and Voiced Texts

Let me use Robbins's citation of A. N. Doane's four kinds of interfaces between orality and literature as a bridge to my concluding proposal. Although quite helpful descriptively as a way to open up multiple possibilities for how a work gets committed to written form, Doane's catalogue includes no reference to what I take as a crucial aspect of orality-literacy mixes: the *reception* end of the communication. Just as important to the understanding of how oral and oral-derived works were composed and committed to texts is a corresponding focus on how they were apprehended by those who used them.

To give equal emphasis to the linked phenomena of composition and reception, I have proposed using the four flexible categories of oral tradition sketched above, with the entire circuit of communication indicated for each as follows:

	Composition	*Performance*	*Reception*
Oral performance	Oral	Oral	Aural
Voiced texts	Written	Oral	Aural
Voices from the past	O/W	O/W	A/W
Written oral poems	Written	Written	Written

Oral performance is very straightforward, with all interlocutors present and directly participating in the performance arena; within this category composition and performance may or may not be simultaneous. With *voiced texts* we enter the realm of the written, as works are composed in a literate fashion but intended (at least initially) only for active oral performance, in which form they are characteristically received. The *voices from the past* category covers those ancient and medieval (and later) works that stem from oral tradition but survive only as texts; by both recognizing their origins and admitting our lack of knowledge about the particulars of their provenience, we can avoid an oversimplified perspective from either side. *Written oral poems* are composed in an oral-traditional register, and, ideally at least, received via that same channel, but with the difference that they are composed in writing and experienced through silent reading. By employing this media morphology it is possible to plot the location of diverse forms of oral and oral-derived works, to foster tenable comparisons and contrasts, and at the same time to give needed emphasis to the experience at the "other end" of the circuit—whether the performer's designated partner is a living audience (itself of different possible sorts) or a latter-day reader trying to make sense of the work according to the contract of meaning under which it came into being.

Strictly speaking, then, I would characterize the oral-derived gospel texts as *voices from the past*, that is, works based in oral tradition but interacting in some way(s) with the technology of the written word. This category allows us to investigate their ethnopoetic structure, as do Draper and Horsley in their contributions to this volume, without committing to the gospels as transcribed oral performances (as we cannot responsibly do). It also harmonizes with the most current and defensible view of oral traditions—namely, that they can interact with writing and reading in various ways, from composition through reception, and including scribal intervention. This view also licenses influences from other texts, such as the *Progymnasmata* cited by Robbins, as long as the integrity of the oral traditional register remains central to the overall scenario.

Now, if indeed Q actually existed (as opposed to being merely a reflex of textual ideology), and if that "source" was indeed behind the creation of Matthew and Luke (in some as yet unspecified way), and if it was furthermore an oral-derived text (as our three main contributors agree), then how would it fit into the four-part morphology? Before elaborating my proposal, let me repeat that the morphology is meant as a flexible taxonomy and helpful heuristic rather than an all-or-nothing, deterministic grid. It reflects a great deal of real-world research on actual interactions of orality and literacy, representing observed phenomena rather than theoretical abstractions, but it remains a way to think about media interactions rather than a set of mutually exclusive, unbridgeable categories. Nonetheless, because the morphology addresses both reception and composition, and is founded on actual rather than imagined scenarios, it offers a singularly incisive interpretive tool.

We can start by classifying Q as likewise a *voice from the past*, a designation that effectively reinforces the status quo. Under this rubric Q is understood as a text with roots in oral tradition; we would be both insisting on an oral-written media-mix and concurrently declaring an honest agnosticism about the particular details of its history and provenience. This seems a reasonable first step—allowing for oral or written composition and performance alongside aural or written reception, and avoiding the reduction of realistic complexity to an unsustainable either/or hypothesis.

But we can take a further step by proposing that Q was, more specifically, a *voiced text*. That is, I suggest that even if it was composed in writing, Q was composed for performance. Another way to say the same thing is to argue that it was an oral-derived text meant for oral performance, for enactment, for embodying. In place of the text-ideological model that would place Q at the head of a stemma leading to Matthew and Luke, with the silent but woefully anachronistic assumption that the influence was of the canonical text-to-text sort that has become the only option of print culture, I suggest that Q was a work intended and destined for *embodiment through oral performance*, and that its "descendants" were individualized re-embodiments by Matthew and Luke.

Around the world and throughout history *voiced texts* share the marked characteristic of creating and sustaining a "textual community," as Brian Stock has shown for early medieval texts (see further Stock 1983, 1990). Expertise in performing the libretto is often the province of a single specialist, who reads aloud (I would say "enacts") what amounts to a prompt-book for an experience. By its very nature that performance is never exclusively textual, of course, nor is it a one-time event. The singularity of the libretto engenders a plurality of experience(s) for both performers and audiences because the very act of performance—of resurrecting the living reality from the textual cenotaph—is what matters.

If Q existed, then, it may well have been a *voiced text*, an oral-derived script for performance that would in turn give way to the *voiced texts* of Matthew and Luke. In addition to shedding light on the media-mix certifiably a dimension of the gospels and presumably of Q of well, this explanation would account for the phenomenological impulse to re-embody the drama of the gospels, to give the Christian story life via the somatic as well as semiotic ritual of iteration and reiteration. When you voice a text, wherever and whenever you do, you cause it to live and to mean by being present; when you perform within a community, you bind the community together in a shared experience that far supersedes the authority of any artifact. That is the inimitable power of voice—to give presence, literally to "em-body," and to do so not via *ipsissima verba* ("the very words themselves," a concept much indebted to textual thinking), but via *ipsissima agenda* ("the very enactings themselves").

It is also a power that Walter Ong understood, and one that he helped us understand in deep and revolutionary ways throughout his unparalleled career. For that reason let me close by remembering a remarkable exchange between Ong and a well-meaning undergraduate student that took place at the 1984 Oral Literature Symposium at the University of Missouri-Columbia; although revised versions of the papers read at that conference quickly reached print in a collective volume entitled *Oral Tradition in Literature* (cf. Foley 1986), this particular oral exchange—as the untextualized will o' th' wisp it was—has never been published.

After a challenging paper entitled "Text and Interpretation: Mark and After," in which he considered the oral traditional roots of New Testament works, Ong was confronted with the following question from the student: "If Jesus' message was so crucial for so many people, why didn't he oversee a standard, authorized, written version of it?" Media anachronisms aside, we can appreciate where this question is coming from—straight out of a cultural habit of mind that assumes that textuality is the one true apotheosis of the word and that the communication resides wholly in the artifact, self-contained and resistant to tampering. The only way to be sure of continuing accurate transmission, so goes the ideological tale, is to insulate the message from human fallibility, to delete the living person from the transmission. But Ong, as gifted a scholar as we have had in the field of studies in oral tradition, was somehow unhampered by the cultural baggage that so often obscures our experience of such matters, and he answered his questioner with disarming simplicity. "He chose not to leave a written record of his message," Ong replied, "because it was far too important."

Part Two

MORAL ECONOMY AND HIDDEN TRANSCRIPT: APPLYING THE WORK OF JAMES C. SCOTT TO Q

ESSAYS

Moral Economy and Renewal Movement in Q

Richard A. Horsley

James C. Scott's broad purpose in *The Moral Economy of the Peasant* was to explain the occurrence of peasant revolts—in twentieth century Southeast Asia and more generally, as he read widely in studies of particular instances and comparative studies of peasant revolts. He found unsatisfactory previous approaches to peasants as individual actors with particular goals and previous explanations of the motivation of popular rebellion, as rooted in the quantitative degree of exploitation or in "relative deprivation" or in the "J" curve of "rising expectations." Scott laid out an alternative theory, which appears applicable also to popular movements such as that evident in the sequence of Jesus-speeches known as Q.

In bringing the work of Scott to bear on Q, we are broadening the consideration of the movement that produced and found expression in this sequence of Jesus-speeches from their previous focus on "social context" and "social formation." Perhaps because of the modern western habit of thinking of Jesus and his followers mainly in religious terms it has been difficult to conceive of movements of Jesus' followers as engaged in *politics*. This reluctance to think of Jesus and his movements in political terms has been reinforced perhaps by the kind of social scientific studies previously brought to bear on Jesus and Gospel traditions as rooted in the Galilean peasantry. In *The Politics of Aristocratic Empires*, for example, John Kautsky argues that the genuinely political actions and decisions that determine peasants' lives are taken in aristocratic circles well above the level at which peasants operate in their village communities. In contrast to the social banditry in Galilee and Judea, which Hobsbawm would label as "pre-political," however, the popular prophetic and messianic movements that appear to provide the closest parallels to the movement(s) spearheaded by Jesus of Nazareth were taking political initiatives, actions to which the official political-military measures were reactions (Horsley 1984; 1985). It could easily be said that in first century Palestine, peasant movements and

143

protests were the principal political forces driving historical events (Horsley 1986). The theory that Scott develops in *Moral Economy of the Peasant* can help us understand where the Jesus movement that comes to expression in Q fits in the historical dynamics of Roman-dominated Judea and Galilee of the first century C.E. Further illumination of that Jesus movement and its expressions in Q can be gained from Scott's subsequent research and reflection on more hidden and everyday forms of peasant resistance in *Weapons of the Weak* (1985).

Scott's theory of the complex combination of factors that leads to peasant revolts can be summarized in six steps—with apologies to Scott for oversimplification—and then applied to the Jesus-movement evident in Q in the same six steps (all references not otherwise indicated are to *Moral Economy*, Scott 1976). In the application of Scott to Q below, I am presupposing my previous analyses of the political-economic-religious structure and situation in Galilee (on the basis of extra-Gospel sources; Horsley 1995; 1996) and the application of that analysis to the origin of Jesus movement(s) (Horsley 1999).

Moral Economy and Popular Revolt among Various Peasantries

1. In close examination of southeast Asian peasant societies and more general historical and ethnographic studies, Scott discerned what he called the "moral economy" of the peasantry. Obliged by custom and often by force to meet the demands for their products by lords, landlords, the state, and/or creditors, peasant families are faced annually with the problem of feeding themselves (vii, 2–3). Besides its physiological dimension of enough calories to "reproduce" the producers, moreover, subsistence has social and cultural implications. "In order to be a fully functioning member of village society, a household needs a certain level of resources to discharge its necessary ceremonial and social obligations.... To fall below this level is not only to risk starvation. It is to suffer a profound loss of standing within the community and perhaps to fall into a permanent situation of dependence" (9; cf. 1985:236–40). Peasantries develop a common sense of their right to minimum subsistence, which is a matter of social-economic justice. Scott's emphasis on economic rights and a sense of social participation or failure recognizes that peasants, like elites, have a sense of the moral structure of their society and a political consciousness. Peasants judge others as morally responsible for their predicament and act to claim their rights when they are violated (1976:189).

2. Precapitalist village communities, says Scott, were organized around maintaining subsistence for their constituent households, by minimizing the risk to which they were exposed by their obligations for taxes, rents, weather, and so on. Peasantries developed principles of reciprocity, mechanisms of redistribution, and other social arrangements to assure subsistence

to the members of village communities (5–6, 9, 176). Central to the moral standards of the village community was a basic notion of equality. The possession of a minimum of land necessary for support of the family and the performance of essential social tasks was basic to the village sense of justice. The basic principles of this peasant moral economy usually had some sort of religious sanction, usually in their deep roots in popular tradition (Scott: 10). Peasant religion tends to differ from that of the dominant classes precisely in its stress on these principles of justice (Moore: 497–98). Village egalitarianism does not hold that all families should be equal, but insists that all should have a living. Among pre-capitalist peasantries where villagers remained in control of local community affairs, they maintained certain mechanisms whereby contributions of the better-off kept the weakest from going under. The pressures of community opinion enforced adherence to such mechanisms by the better-positioned families. In Andalusia, for example, "The idea that he who has must give to him who has not is not only a precept of religion, but a moral imperative of the pueblo" (Pitt-Rivers: 62). Villagers studied by Scott, like those in many cross-cultural studies, offer "a living normative model of equity and justice . . . a peasant view of decent social relations" (40–43). The fundamental right to subsistence that tended to be observed in precapitalist village communities thus provided the moral principle to which the poor might appeal, whether to their neighbors or in dealings with their lords and rulers (176–77).

3. Recognition of this moral economy among peasantries leads to a different approach to the occurrence of revolts and resistance movements. Instead of looking for the percentage or amount of the peasant product taken by lords and/or the state, we must begin with peasants' traditionally grounded belief in their fundamental right to subsistence and then examine peasants' relationships to other villagers, to elites and to the state with regard precisely to this economic right (5). "This moral principle forms the standard against which claims to the surplus by landlords and the state are evaluated. . . . The test for the peasant is more likely to be 'what is left' than 'how much is taken'" (7, 19, 31). "The moral economy of the subsistence ethic can be clearly seen in the themes of peasant protest. . . ." Two themes prevailed: first, claim on peasant incomes by landlords, moneylenders, or the state were never legitimate when they infringed on what was judged to be the minimal culturally defined subsistence level, and second, the *product* of the land should be distributed in such a way that all were guaranteed a subsistence living (10). Scott has thus arrived at a much more precise sense of the basis of peasant politics and, given the rarity of peasant protest and especially peasant revolt midst the ubiquity of intense exploitation, of understanding why and when protests and revolts occur.

4. Political-economic transformations under modern colonial practices, including the transformation of land and labor into commodities, tended

to violate the moral economy and threaten the subsistence rights of peasants, some in ways that led to the conditions susceptible to peasant revolts (3–4, 9, 196). In Southeast Asia "colonial regimes were likely to press even harder in a slump so as to maintain their own revenue.... In the midst of a booming export economy, new fortunes for indigenous landowners, officeholders, and moneylenders, there was also growing rural indebtedness and poverty and an increasing tempo of peasant unrest.... The explanation ... [is] new insecurities of subsistence income to which the poorer sector was exposed" (10). The experience of the Southeast Asian peasantry with the fiscal practices of the colonial state is analogous in many respects to the experience of the European peasantry, where taxation was the most prominent single issue in the large-scale rebellions during the European state-making of the sixteenth to the nineteenth centuries (96).

5. Given the moral economy of the peasantry increasingly violated by escalating exploitation resulting from transformative effects of the state and a new economic system, Scott finds that certain factors tend to lead to revolt or non-revolt. One of the most important is the state's power of repression (195). "Tangible and painful memories of repression must have a chilling effect on peasants who contemplate even minor acts of resistance" (226). Another key factor is derived from the central role of economic security for the peasantry. Peasants may resist most seriously at the thresholds where they are threatened with loss of their self-sufficiency as smallholders, i.e., where they "might lose the land that gives them their fairly autonomous subsistence ... and they face having to become dependent clients. A second threshold occurs when the subsistence guarantees within dependency collapse" (39). These thresholds also have a cultural dimension insofar as they involve minimal cultural decencies, such as caring for elderly parents and crucial rituals, as well as subsistence economic resources (177–78). The ability of village communities to adjust to deteriorating conditions and to protect their component members, however, can delay the crossing of that first threshold (194). Scott found the social strength of this moral economy and its traditional mechanisms that protected the village poor, varied from village to village, region to region. "It was strongest in areas where traditional village forms were well developed and not shattered by colonialism.... It is precisely in areas where the village is most autonomous and cohesive that subsistence guarantees are the strongest" (40–41). On the other hand, similarly cohesive social composition, with strong communal traditions and few sharp internal divisions can make some peasantries inherently more insurrection-prone. A less differentiated peasantry will experience economic shocks in a relatively more uniform fashion insofar as its members share more or less the same economic circumstances. Communitarian structures, moreover, have a greater capacity for collective action. It is easier for the peasants to organize if an existing structure of local cooperation has remained intact. And

their "little tradition" is a ready-made source of motivation for collective action. "The more communal a village structure, the easier it is for it to collectively defend its interests" (201–2).

6. Finally, as Scott points out, even "false starts" of revolt and social-religious movements (e.g., Hoa Hao and Cao Dai in southern Vietnam, Iglesia Ni Cristo in the Philippines) can often reinforce the bonds between peasants and serve (paradoxically) both as an alternative and as a prelude and stimulus to revolt (207, 219–20). Evidence of nascent symbolic withdrawal can be found in movements among those who are exploited yet with little prospect of revolt. The views or grievances evident in a social-religious movements provide a telling indication of the degree to which they identify with or oppose the values of the elite (231). Even a religious movement whose orientation might seem otherworldly often articulates sharp criticism of the existing order and an alternative symbolic universe that contains seeds of potentially social-political disruption. And such movements can also cultivate inter-village communications and alliances along with the newly articulated dissatisfaction with current conditions that anticipate more explosive future events (237). "Since peasants' freedom to define and elaborate their own culture is almost always greater than their capacity to remake society, it is to their culture that we must look to discover how much their moral universe diverges from that of the elite. . . . This symbolic refuge is not simply a source of solace, an escape. It represents an alternative moral universe in embryo—a dissident subculture, which helps unite its members as a human community" (238, 240).

Moral Economy and the Israelite Renewal Movement Evident in Q

1–2. Reading Scott's *Moral Economy of the Peasant* might be more compelling at first glance to those of us who (also) deal with the Hebrew Bible than to those who deal only with Synoptic Gospel materials. The Mosaic covenant in Exod 20, the covenant law code in Exod 21–23, and many provisions in the Deuteronomic code and the Holiness code (esp. Lev 25) are immediately intelligible as articulations of the "moral economy" of ancient Israelite peasants. The special provisions included in various Mosaic covenantal codes—exhortation to lend liberally to a needy neighbor, gleaning, prohibition of interest, sabbatical rest of the land, sabbatical release of debts and debt-slaves, redemption of land by the next of kin—constituted the social mechanisms by which Israelite villagers attempted to keep each member household economically viable. It is also evident that the prophet Micah was referring to one of those mechanisms in 2:5—the periodic redistribution of (communal) land. Underlying all of these provisions, of course, was the principle that the land belonged ultimately to Yahweh and had been parceled out as a gift to each family or lineage as its own inheritance (e.g., Lev 25:23). A story such as that about Naboth's vineyard (1 Kgs 21) indicates that Israelite kings were put on notice that the peasantry as well as their prophetic spokespersons such as Elijah had a clear sense of their social-economic rights.

Most of the social mechanisms mentioned in Israelite law codes were designed to keep the land, the basis of subsistence, in those lineages. Subsistence rights and the broader "moral economy" of the peasantry were thus deeply rooted in Israelite tradition. Judging from elite sources such as Josephus, moreover, at least some of these social-legal mechanisms to protect the subsistence rights of peasants were still practiced in late second-temple times. The sabbatical rest for the land was still observed, apparently sanctioned by the temple-state, in early Roman times and the sabbatical cancellation of debts was still practiced, as evidenced in the *prosbul* devised by Hillel to circumvent it. If some of these social-legal mechanisms were still officially observed and discussed, then almost certainly they were still alive among the Judean and Galilean villages, in the "little tradition."

This should lead us to take much more seriously the references and allusions to traditional Israelite covenantal laws and teachings in Q discourses. But before proceeding to examination of key speeches in Q we should take note of the awkward situation we are in as would-be historians of the ancient Israelite "little tradition" with regard to our sources and how we use them. It is evident from a combination of archaeological and textual evidence that the fundamental social form in ancient Israelite society was the peasant village. It is equally evident from the content of the laws in the Covenant law code and the later Deuteronomic and Levitical codes that the provisions and mechanisms such as liberal lending, prohibition of interest, and sabbatical release of debts applied mainly to relations among villagers, that is, to "the moral economy of the peasant." Yet our sources all belong to the Jerusalemite "great tradition" of literature written or edited by scribes supported by the temple-state. In using these sources, therefore, we must take into account the interests of the scribal elite as representatives of the temple-state aristocracy. Hence we cannot read the "little tradition" or the "moral economy of the [Israelite] peasant" directly out of the written texts that derived from the elite. We can only extrapolate and project on the basis of those written texts, with critical awareness of its particular interests.

When we come to the Jesus-speeches in Q we are apparently dealing with texts derived from the "little" or popular tradition (Scott 1977; Horsley and Draper: ch. 5). That these speeches do not quote, but rather seem to allude, for example, to laws in as the Covenant Code (Exod 21–23) is probably one key indication of their popular derivation. They have not been conformed to the written texts of the "great tradition" by subsequent generations of scribal copyists. Given the limited sources, there are only two ways in which we as historians can discern that the Q speeches may be alluding to and/or derived from and/or expressions of the Israelite popular tradition and covenantal principles of Israelite moral economy. One is by comparison with what we project onto earlier generations of Israelite villagers from the law-codes that are extant only in the written texts of the Jerusalemite great tradition, that is, what later became the biblical texts. The other is by comparison with the texts discovered at Qumran, produced by a scribal community more or less contemporary with the Q speeches.

Several of the speeches in Q articulate the concerns of the moral economy of the peasantry rooted in the Mosaic covenant, its principles and mechanisms. Most elaborate is the covenant renewal speech in 6:20–49. Q-scholars tend to focus on individual Q sayings as artifacts isolated from their speech-context and to interpret them according to modern scholarly categories, such as "sapiential." As noted in my article in part I above, however, it is clear that the "love your enemies" section of the speech in 6:27–36 not only alludes in numerous ways to traditional Mosaic covenantal teaching, but is a continuation of that tradition. Most obvious perhaps are the comparisons between Q 6:27 and Lev 19:17–18, between Q 6:29 and Exod 22:25–26; Deut 24:10–13; cf. Amos 2:8, and between Q 6:36 and Lev 19:2 (Horsley 1986; 1987:255–73). That the broader framework of the speech is a renewal of Mosaic covenant can be seen from comparison with covenantal texts in Exod 20; Josh 24; and the contemporary covenant renewal texts from Qumran, in 1QS 1–4 and CD (Horsley and Draper: ch. 9). The "love your enemies" section of the Q covenant speech thus focuses on local economic relations that are disintegrating into mutual hostility. Jesus' renewed covenantal teaching calls basically for return to the mutuality that will maintain the component family units of villages to remain viable members of those village communities. "Love your enemies, do good, and lend," not harassing each other for previous debts, and coming to each others' aid in times of difficult circumstances: those are the basic principles of the moral economy in any number of different peasant cultures, according to Scott's cross-cultural studies.

Two other Q speeches also focus on concern for basic subsistence in peasant households: the "Lord's Prayer" in Q 11:2–4, 9–13, and the exhortation in Q 12:22–31 about single-minded pursuit of the "kingdom of God" program that constitutes the theme that links the Q speeches as a whole series. In the Lord's Prayer people of the Q communities petition God for maintenance of their subsistence bread and cancellation of their debilitating debts that make them vulnerable to creditors, even to loss of their ancestral land. The petition for cancellation of debts, with its clear allusion to and basis in Israelite covenantal tradition, includes the principle of mutual-cancellation of debts by villagers: "cancel our debts as we herewith cancel those of our debtors." That is a renewal of one of the key Israelite social mechanisms by which households were to be kept viable in the village community, the cancellation of debts (known from all of the covenant law-codes and subsistence-maintenance mechanisms, Exod 21–23, Deuteronomy, and Lev 25). The point of the exhortation in Q 12:22–31 is apparently that if community members will only focus on the general goal of renewal of Israel (kingdom of God) then subsistence will not be a problem, presumably because of the renewed spirit of mutuality among members of the village community. It is surely significant that Matthew understood that this exhortation belonged together with the explicitly covenantal teachings on Q 6:27–36, such that he included it in his version of the covenantal renewal speech in Matt 5–7 that has the same overall structure as Q 6:20–49.

The same covenantal concern for subsistence is articulated in two other Q speeches that mock the opulence and exploitative practices of the rulers and their representatives. The rhetoric in Q 7:18–35 mocks Herod Antipas, the Roman client ruler in Galilee, for his luxurious life-style of soft raiment and fancy palace—all based on the products of peasant labor. And the (covenantal-prophetic!) "woes" against the Pharisees in Q 11:39–52 indict them for pressing the peasants to tithe rigorously from their scarce resources and for not using their scribal authority to alleviate the burdens of those who are heavy laden with taxes/tithes (Horsley and Draper: 285–91).

This reading of these Q speeches as statements of concern about the moral economy of ancient Palestinian and Syrian villagers is further supported by several parallels elsewhere in the teaching of Jesus. Matthew includes Jesus' parable about cancellation of debts in Matt 18:23–33 that parallels the petition on debts in Q 11:2–4, and Mark has Jesus address the same problem in conversation with the wealthy young man in 10:17–22 in an explicitly covenantal context that insists on the principle of non-exploitation among community members. We also happen to have evidence from a generation before and a generation after Jesus' activity in Galilee and the early development of Q discourses that concern about unjust seizure of their produce in taxes and their indebtedness to wealthy creditors, i.e., basic threats to their subsistence, could drive the peasantry to protest and revolt. According to Josephus accounts, the popular messianic movements just after Herod's death attacked royal fortresses/storehouses in order to "take back" the goods that had been seized (and taken) there (*Ant.* 17.271–76). And one of the first actions of the insurrection in Jerusalem in 66 was to burn the archives in order to destroy the records and to prevent recovery of debts (*B.J.* 2.427).

3. Were we to follow Scott's distinctive approach to peasant protest and revolt as rooted in the people's right to subsistence, we would no longer seek to establish the percentage or absolute amount of taxation, but rather look for the factors that combined to threaten their subsistence. Moreover, once we have learned from Scott's *Weapons of the Weak* about

peasants' hidden forms of resistance such as sequestering produce from the tax collectors, which render the official rate of taxation functionally irrelevant, we are forced to devise a more subtle and nuanced approach anyhow. Also, more directly pertinent to interpretation of Q, if its speeches reflect and/or were addressed to and supposedly resonated with Galilean and other common people, then we must take into account not just their poverty and indebtedness, but both the social-cultural meaning of the threat to their subsistence and their indignation at the injustice of their circumstances. Both the blessings-and-woes that begin the covenant-renewal discourse in Q 6:20–49 and the speech addressed to anxiety about subsistence in Q 12:22–31 appear directly to address the discouragement and self-doubt that poor indebted villagers might feel about their "failure" as members of the community. And the prophetic declarations of woes against the Pharisees in Q 11:39–52 and of condemnation of the Jerusalem ruling house in Q 13:34–35 (and the not-so-veiled commentary on Antipas in Q 7:24–25), as well as the blessings and woes in Q 6:20–26, appear to articulate their indignation.

4. As Scott points out, despite high levels of exploitation, peasants have seldom mounted outright revolt. But both in 4 B.C.E. after the death of Herod and again in 66 C.E., widespread revolt erupted among the Galilean and Judean peasantry. In between emerged the Jesus movements, one of which produced/resulted in Q. With Scott's more nuanced approach, we can look for how the new order imposed by Rome through client kings was impacting the Galilean (and Judean) peasantry. Different from but corresponding to the dramatic changes that accompanied the introduction of the capitalist system under colonial rule of nineteenth and twentieth century peasantries, Roman imperial rule brought dramatic and relatively sudden changes that seriously impacted peasants in Palestine. Prior to the Roman conquest, there was one layer of rulers, the Jerusalem templestate. When the Romans imposed Herod as king, and he in turn retained the high priestly and Temple apparatus, the peasant producers suddenly came under multiple layers of rulers and demands on their produce.

The rigorous collection of taxes under Antipas may have been an even more decisive factor in the origin and spread of a Jesus movement in Galilee. Under earlier empires and even under Rome prior to Antipas Galilee had been ruled and taxed by distant rulers. One can imagine that under regimes ruling from a distance Galilean peasants may well have deployed some of those hidden forms of resistance that Scott discusses, sequestering crops, etc. and paying only part of taxation. Given the less than rigorous apparatus in modern Malasia, "the official collection of the Islamic tithe in paddy is only a small fraction of what is legally due, thanks to a network of complicity and misrepresentation" (Scott 1985:31). When the Romans assigned Antipas to rule Galilee, however, he immediately rebuilt Sepphoris in the center of western Galilee as his capital and within twenty years built a new capital city, Tiberias, on the Lake. From these capital cities conveniently located with commanding surveillance over and immediate access to every village in Galilee, tax-collection was suddenly more rigorous and hidden forms of popular resistance less effective. The presence of their rulers directly on the scene in Galilee must have become a major factor in the increasing pressure on Galilean peasant subsistence (on Antipas's regime and newly built cities as a key factor in the emergence of the Jesus movement(s) see further Horsley 1999).

Like the "booming economy" under modern colonial regimes, the "booming economy" of the new Roman imperial order in Palestine—Herod's lavishly rebuilt Temple and newly founded cities in honor of the emperor, the high priestly families' newly built mansions in the New City in Jerusalem, the burgeoning estates of Herodian families in northwest Judea, and Herod Antipas's spanking new cities in Galilee (Horsley 1995: ch. 7)—coincided with increasing poverty among peasant producers. And similar to the increase in rulers' demands that aggravated peasant conditions in early modern times in Europe, the suddenly unchallengeable political-economic power of the Roman client regimes of the Herodians and Jerusalem temple-state ratcheted up the pressure on ancient Palestinian peasants.

5. Scott's generalizations based on a fairly wide selection of comparative materials are particularly suggestive for historians of early Roman Palestine and students of the Jesus movements, including the one connected with Q. It has to be striking, given the infrequency of widespread peasant revolt generally, that Galileans and Judeans put up a fierce resistance to Herod's conquest of his "kingdom" in 40–37 B.C.E., then revolted when the tyrant died in 4 B.C.E., and mounted an even more widespread revolt again in 66–70 C.E. Similarly striking is the seeming quiescence of the people during the reign of Herod the Great and again under Antipas and the early Roman governors. Striking, finally, is the emergence of the Jesus movements more or less midway between the increasingly tightened new Roman-imperial order in Galilee under Herod and Antipas, and the steadily expanding unrest in the 60s and the outbreak of the great revolt in 66, that is, as the Galilean peasantry began to feel the economic pressures of demands by multiple layers of rulers.

The principal factor in all of these revolts or movements is the new and continuing economic pressure on the peasantry under Roman rule, following the weakness of late Hasmonean rule, particularly when juxtaposed with the strength of the tradition of independent rule integral to Israelite popular tradition. Survey of the location and circumstances of large (royal) estates in Palestine (Applebaum, Fiensy, and Horsley 1995: ch. 9) suggest that they were still concentrated, as in previous times, mainly in the Great

Plain, the rich agricultural lowland between Samaria and Galilee, and in "the king's mountain country" northwest of Jerusalem. They were apparently spreading, however, indicating that some peasants were losing control of their land and becoming dependent share-croppers or worse (via the usual debt-mechanism). That Herodian officers of Agrippa II in Tiberias still had their estates "beyond the Jordan" suggests that despite the intense economic exploitation of Herod Antipas earlier in the century and their difficult economic circumstances addressed in Q speeches (6:20–21; 11:2–4; 12:22–31), Galilean peasants had not yet been reduced to dependency. Indeed, that Galilean and Judean peasants still had the ability to organize and take common action (in Jesus movements and in semi-organized revolt in 66–67) suggests that conditions of Galilean and Judean peasants were more like those in Morelos in 1910, where the Zapatistas were based, than like those in Sedaka in 1980 (cf. Scott 1985:242–44). Yet the concern of Jesus movements with debt as well as poverty and hunger and the outbreak of widespread revolt in 66 all suggest that the new pressures were pushing the Galilean and Judean peasants toward the first threshold delineated by Scott. That is, in the Jesus movement addressed in the Q speeches, we can see peasants threatened with loss of their traditional lands and semi-independence, motivated by indignation at the violation of their subsistence rights, responding to the call to renew their traditional mutuality and solidarity in resistance to the pressures and incursions of their rulers. There would be little point in the admonitions to "lend" and otherwise engage in mutual economic support in Q 6:27–36 if the addressees, having already become mostly dependents, were at the second threshold of absentee landlords withdrawing their guarantees of minimal security for share-croppers.

6. Scott's comments that traditional communal structures of peasant villages that have not decisively disintegrated from the pressures of outside forces can function both as a factor contributing to revolt or a factor deterring revolt is highly suggestive for Jesus movements such as the one linked with Q. On the one hand, the people living in an intact communal village structure can more easily mount cooperative action rooted in their "little tradition" and communal structure. On the other hand, the more communal structures enable the villagers to redistribute the pressures so as to avoid or postpone subsistence crises. Suggestive in the same direction are his observations about how a "false start" or a religious movement may serve as prelude to revolt. Both of Scott's observations point to the possible effects of the Jesus movement, its effective relationships and interaction with (other) Galilean people.

Again, if we assume that Q consisted of discourses addressed to ordinary people (and was not simply a device for preservation of Jesus-sayings), then discourses such as 6:20–49; 11:2–4, 9–13; 12:22–31 were concerned with people threatened with poverty, hunger, and debt, encouraging them to respond to God's bringing the kingdom with mutual caring and renewed cooperation in their communities. While the underlying values of the peasant moral economy are similar, the disintegration of the communal structures in "Sedaka" had progressed beyond what Q discourses represent in ancient Galilean villages (cf. Scott 1985:178, 180–81, 191, 235). Indeed, since we may project that these discourses must have resonated with audiences of people or they would not have been perpetuated, these discourses would have built and reinforced horizontal bonds among community members. If other Q discourses resonated similarly with Galileans, we can imagine that Q 7:18–35; 12:2–12; 11:39–52 and 13:28–29, 34–35 helped solidify their dissent from the values represented by Antipas, the Jerusalem rulers and their scribal and Pharisaic representatives. "While folk culture is not coordinated in the formal sense, it often achieves a 'climate of opinion' which, in other more institutionalized societies, would require a public relations campaign. The striking thing about peasant society is the extent to which a whole range of complex activities ... are coordinated by networks of understanding and practice.... No formal organizations are created because none are required [given the communal village structures]" (Scott 1985: 300–301). That is, "Jesus" or the Q performers did not have to organize new communities.

Virtually all of the discourses in Q articulated an alternative symbolic universe of Galilean Israelites, focused in the symbol of the kingdom of God, which weaves through the sequence of discourses like a thematic red thread. That is, in terms of Scott's concept of "moral economy," Q speeches crystallize and renew a "moral universe that diverges from that of the elite." Scott's exploration of how peasant politics are rooted in this "moral economy" thus provides a new vision for the hungry historical imagination of biblical interpreters. Scott provides an alternative to the old debate about whether Jesus and his movements, like certain contemporary popular movements in Palestine, constituted what was in effect a revolt, or were absolutely anti-revolutionary. Approaching Q discourses with the help of Scott's "moral economy" might lead to the conclusion that, in their time, Q discourses must have supplied cultural dissent, an alternative symbolic universe, and social links among the oppressed. Q represented "an alternative moral universe in embryo—a dissident subculture, which help[ed] unite its members as a human community and as a community of values" (238).

Oral Performance of the Not-So-Hidden "Hidden Transcript" of Q

Still other, related work of Scott enables us to discern how oral performance of Q speeches may have provided both an ideology and a motivation for the communities of the movement that heard them performed. As mentioned in the introduction to this volume, Scott's richly documented comparative article, "Protest and Profanation" (1977), is highly suggestive in opening our understanding of Q speeches as rooted in the Israelite "little tradition." We noted in that essay how the Q speeches resonated with the hearers by making numerous metonymic references to the Israelite popular tradition that evoked the rich resources for resistance and renewal deeply ingrained in it. The "kingdom of God," the symbol placed at key positions in most Q speeches, hence clearly the dominant theme of the whole sequence of speeches, is thus also the symbol under which the speeches evoke the renewal resources of Israelite tradition. So a couple of Scott's many observations seem pertinent for understanding how the Q speeches do the "work" of "the kingdom of God" in performance before the communities of renewal movement.

Scott comments that in some popular movements religion and politics become joined in a utopian vision of a revolutionary new order. A religious charter becomes the basis for more far reaching revolutionary goals (1977:225). Such an observation provides an overarching perspective from which to comprehend how the Q discourses in 6:20–49; 7:18–35; 11:2–4; 12:22–31; and 22:28–30 might have resonated with their audiences. To focus on the covenant speech analyzed in my article above, the communities of a movement that regularly celebrated a renewal of the Mosaic covenant as a charter for community sharing and solidarity may well have understood this as a revolutionary new order in which the tables were turned, the poor enjoying the benefits of the kingdom while the rich were dethroned from their power and privilege. This seems all the more likely when we notice that other speeches in Q also condemn the wealthy in the ruling house in Jerusalem and their Pharisaic retainers.

Scott further observed that "ideology . . . may often be experienced by peasants . . . as a kind of magic charm, an esoteric religious knowledge that is capable, by itself, of transforming the world" (1977:220). This observation takes us well beyond the attempt, some decades ago, by Norman Perrin and others, to use the concept of "tensive symbol" to understand the phrase "the kingdom of God." We must be careful not to over-interpret. But perhaps we should take seriously the possibility that, if audiences of Q speeches heard "blessed are you poor, for yours is the kingdom of God" as a declaration of God's new action of deliverance and "seek first the kingdom of God and all these things [food, clothing, shelter] will be added" as an exhortation, then they, in response, would have been motivated almost magically, as it were, to "love your enemies, do good and lend" and not to worry about their threatened subsistence, since the world was obviously being transformed! Ironically, for New Testament scholars, Scott reminds us to take religion and magic seriously as symbols at work in popular culture subject to high degrees of stress and distress.

Besides resonating with the hearers by metonymically referencing Israelite popular tradition, the Q speeches resonated with hearers as a no-longer-so-hidden transcript. In the Introduction above it was explained how Scott's insights into usually unrecognized modes of popular politics, including the "hidden transcript" and the jolting public declaration of that hidden transcript (Scott 1990) enable us to discern the character of Q as communication. On the one hand, the Q discourses are clearly performed among communities of a Jesus movement, i.e., among the subordinated, and not in public where the dominant would have been listening. That is why "Jesus" could condemn the Jerusalem ruling house and its Pharisaic retainers in no uncertain terms (Q 11:39–52; 13:28–29, 34–35) and not be apprehended and executed immediately. On the other hand, precisely those Q speeches represent "Jesus" as "speaking truth to power." In such Q discourses "Jesus" is again brought to voice declaring the hidden transcript directly in the hearing and "in the face" of the dominant.

Cultivating the hidden transcript in safe sites, says Scott, creates a discourse of dignity, negation, and justice (1990:114). This seems to be a principle function of some of "Jesus'" speeches in Q, such as 12:22–31. And this is surely one of the functions of most Q discourses. Just as Brer Rabbit stories lent a sense of pride and satisfaction to slave audiences (1990:164), so Jesus' covenantal admonitions in Q 6:27–42 would have lent a similar sense to ancient Galilean audiences called to respond to God's gift of the kingdom. The beatitudes and woes, the covenantal blessings and curses, like the "symbolic reversals of folk religion," constitute the equivalent of a radical counter-ideology. Both "are aimed at negating the public symbolism of ideological domination" (1990:199). As Scott comments about the "counter ideology" contained in the hidden transcript, so the proclamation of the kingdom of God and renewed covenant in Q 6:20–49, along with the Lord's Prayer and the discourse in 7:18–35, presented a counter-ideology that enabled people to resist their rulers and their pressures that were threatening to disintegrate their family and village community lives.

But Q speeches performed in village communities went beyond the usual hidden transcript. They represent Jesus as proclaiming that God's decisive action in establishing the kingdom was already underway and proceeding with utter certainty. Insofar as they present Jesus as having already declared the coming of the kingdom and the attendant condemnation of the rulers directly in the face of power, moreover, the Q speeches instill in their hearers a confidence in the immanent realization of a revolutionary new social order of justice and sufficiency, in the apparent absence of their rulers whom God has condemned.

Just as "the hidden transcript is continually pressing against the limit of what is permitted on stage" (1990:196), in potential resistance of the subordinated to the dominant, even more does Q's presentation of Jesus as declaring the agenda and resentment of the people "on stage," as it were, push against and expand the limit of what is permitted. This is partly because "it is only when this hidden transcript is openly declared [as in the Q discourses] that subordinates can fully recognize the full extent to which their claims, their dreams, their anger is shared by other subordinates with whom they have not been in direct touch" (223). That we have the Q discourses at all must mean that they resonated with people in such a way that the movement expanded and these very discourses "lived to tell about it."

The Jesus Movement in the Villages of Roman Galilee

ARCHAEOLOGY, Q, AND MODERN ANTHROPOLOGICAL THEORY

Milton Moreland

Introduction

Early Roman (ER) Galilee has been classified as an agrarian society in the midst of a struggle to conform to the pressures of a colonial administration. A small administrative base dominated this society and wielded control over the majority peasant producers whose labor was the underpinning of the economy. While we can be confident of this basic societal reconstruction, we are less certain about the details of the types of struggles the peasants faced, the pressures exerted by the administrative elites, and the resistance measures the peasantry and other non-elite classes in the society employed. Although we have enough archaeological and literary data to reconstruct basic societal patterns, to a large extent the details about the lives of agrarian villagers in ER Galilee are unrecorded. In order to debate the details, part of our task involves using models that have been established by the labor of those scholars who have observed the minutiae of the many contemporary and past societies whose information about peasant ideology, class struggle, and administrative ideologies are still intact or are recoverable. The detailed research into peasant ideologies and struggles in the midst of colonial pressures provided by James C. Scott is one analysis that is beneficial to our cause.[1] Whether identified or not, all

---

1. In anthropological and political theory Scott is often referred to as a "moral economist," in distinction from a "political economist." As illustrated below, moral economists are interested in agrarian populations and focus on kinship, patron-client relations, and other economic institutions in village contexts, while political economists emphasize the personal investment logic of peasants in market economies. For the purposes of studying ancient, pre-capitalist societies—because of their examinations of the logic and inter-workings of village social structures—moral economists provide relevant analogical data and assess-

159

reconstructions of the past are based on analogy or the use of models. In this study I intend for analogical reasoning to take center stage, rather than simply being the unacknowledged theoretical underpinning. While the socio-economic setting of ER Galilee is not directly equivalent to any one particular society studied by Scott, the analytical typology established in his work is valuable to our reconstruction attempts.[2] What Scott offers is an expansive, cross-cultural model that describes how agrarian populations were forced to think and work when faced with the typically abusive power structures of a colonial administration. Because of the paucity of data that derive from Galilean Roman period village settings, historians must use studies like Scott's in order to gain insight into the complexities of "social rights" and "village morals" that prevailed in pre-industrial, pre-capitalist rural settings during times of escalating colonial control. By using Scott's model of peasant societies we are better able to ask questions about the types of social and economic conditions that prevailed in the villages of ancient Galilee.

The task of developing a plausible historical reconstruction of life in ER Galilee is complicated by the nature of the extant literary material that mentions this area of the Roman Empire. Many scholars have noted the problems of using Josephus, the New Testament Gospels, and the Mishnah as our primary sources of information. Recognizing the often biased and deficient nature of the literary sources, the goal of this paper is to develop a reconstruction of ER Galilee that depends primarily on recent archaeology, aided by relevant anthropological theory. After establishing a plausible reconstruction of the Galilean setting, I draw on a critical study of the literary sources—particularly the Sayings Source Q—in order to reconstruct the various ideas and actions of the Jesus Movement in this setting. For several decades scholars have been attempting to read the sayings attributed to Jesus in Q as a response to the pressures of the colonial administrative programs established in ER Galilee by the Roman client rulers. I not only agree that this is the appropriate lens through which to view the sayings, as a Galilean social movement I think the Jesus Movement must be understood as a response to the Roman administrative control.[3]

---

ments of village life. For a critique of "moral economists," see Popkin. Similarly, see the critique of the "homogeneity theorist" by Cancian.

2. A full defense of employing modern anthropological theories in comparative and analogically based research on ancient societies can be found in Wylie: 136–53.

3. Regarding the notion of the Saying Source Q as a written document, see the summary description by Jonathan Reed 2000: 178–81. Reed's four major conclusions are: (1) Q "was a literary document written in Greek," (2) there was a group responsible for the text—a "Q community"—that defined itself in the document by establishing "ethical and theological boundaries to distinguish its group from the larger society," (3) the Q community "collected and preserved

To imagine an ER Galilean group that ignored the extreme societal pressures that were put in place by the Roman/Herodian administration is impractical.

During the past two decades the scholarly labor that has been exerted on this type of assignment has succeeded in identifying many of the major alternatives we have when we ask who the first followers of Jesus were in the Galilean context. For example, we can choose between radical itinerants, social prophets, a network of village scribes, and/or peasant artisans. The ultimate goal of this essay is to illustrate several ways that Scott's ideas regarding agrarian social order and forms of resistance, peasant political consciousness and moral structure, and the nature and transmission of "hidden transcripts" can help us specify who might have been attracted to the movement that was associated with Jesus. More precisely, by comparing the ideology of peasant groups with the ideology found in the sayings of Q, I will propose that quite regularly the social patterns, modes of resistance, and social ideology that are evident in the sayings are actually *at odds with* the general assessment of peasant ideology and action that is described by Scott and other anthropologists interested in agrarian peasant societies. While I think Scott's analysis of peasant ideology is appropriate to our study of Q, it is not because he provides a rationale for reading Q as a *peasant* text. The value can more accurately be found in helping us explain why it is likely that few peasants actually joined the Jesus Movement in ER Galilee, and why the movement was ineffectual as a stimulant for any observable social, economic, or political change in the region. Scholars have advanced various reasons that help explain why the Jesus Movement died out, moved away from Galilee, or was subsumed by other groups without much notice. Jonathan Reed, for example, observes that "the Q community . . . marginalized itself and was never a major concern to Judaism as a whole in Galilee" (Reed 1999:108; also see 2000:61). Scott prepares us to better understand why the Jesus Movement did not generate a substantial following in this region.

Before moving to my analysis of Scott and the relevance of his theories for the study of Galilee and the Jesus Movement, I pause to make one clarification regarding my use of the term "peasant."[4] In the process of reading recent anthropological studies on agrarian cultures, one becomes keenly

---

traditional material and adapted it to their situation, whether by juxtaposing sayings, modifying them, or adding new ones," and (4) regarding the genre of Q, it is a sayings collection that "lacks a literary design with a concomitant narrative world."

4. A review of the origins of the category "peasant" in modern anthropology, and a critique of the use of the term as descriptive of modern groups is found in Kearney. Similar to the category "primitive," Kearney demonstrates the ambiguous use of the term "peasant" in modern anthropology and its roots in post–World War II scholarly conceptions of "the other," making it all the more important to

aware of the need to maintain distinctions between the wide variety of peoples who lived in the ancient world, beyond the obvious designations of elites, retainers, peasants and slaves. The thesis of this paper is based on the postulation that the so-called "peasant" class was distinct from other non-elite groups in ancient agrarian societies such as full-time village artisans and craftspeople, fishers, village priests, and others involved with trading and manufacturing. When using Scott's idea of the "moral economy of the peasant" as a theoretical basis for speaking of the Galilean peasants, it is necessary to maintain Scott's general use of the term, which is in agreement with the definition used by the majority of scholars who study agrarian peasants.[5] Thus the term 'peasant' in this study refers to "small agricultural producers, who, with the help of simple equipment and the labour of their families, produce mostly for their own consumption, direct or indirect, and for the fulfillment of obligations to holders of political and economic power" (Shanin: 3).

Although peasants were usually involved in the part-time production of other goods, their primary existence was based on subsistence crop production. It should be noted that my use of the term differs from the modern notion of "farmers": producers who intend to draw an income from their crops (Heilbroner and Milberg: 22; Kautsky: 272; cf. Scott 1985:234). Peasants also differ from ancient "cultivators" who were not obligated to produce a "fund of rent" (Wolf: 10). Peasants were always exploited by the elites; they subsisted on the bare essentials of life. While I do not downplay the variety of similarities between most non-elite members of an agrarian society—and I am aware of the differences that exist among those who use the term 'peasant' to describe other groups in the ancient world—I am nonetheless interested in maintaining the distinctions between the peasant class and all other non-elite segments of the population (Scott 1978:178–79). In much of Scott's work, the idea of a "moral economy of the peasant" is specifically based on the social structures and ideas that derive from subsistence farmers in agrarian societies.[6] While the notion of a moral economy may be applicable to village artisans or economically oppressed village traders, it is not necessarily the case that the model fits the social and ideological structure of any group besides the agrarian peasants.[7] As

---

carefully identify the exact meaning of the term in our historical reconstructions of ancient societies.

5. On defining the term "peasant," and the widespread use of this definition, see the summary statement in Shanin: 3–9.

6. For Scott's distinction between "poor peasants" (those who fit into his model), and "rich peasants" (having "high incomes, abundant land, small families, reliable crop yields, and outside employment opportunities"), see 1978:25.

7. For example, I would contend that Crossan's use of the term "peasant artisan" to describe Jesus and his first followers is too broadly conceived (1998: 346–50).

will become clear in the course of this essay, it is precisely this group of subsistence farmers who would have been less likely than other non-elite people to join the Jesus Movement in Galilee. By maintaining this distinction, we are able to ask more detailed questions about who might have been part of the group responsible for the Saying Source Q.

The remainder of this paper is divided into three sections. First, I examine the key elements of Scott's thesis regarding the moral economy of the peasant that are amenable to the study of ER Galilee. Second, I examine the socio-economic conditions of ER Galilee, paying attention to the similarities and differences between this setting and those societies referenced in Scott's model. In the final section of the paper, I observe particular internal markers in the Sayings Source Q that can be used to better understand the social world of the Jesus Movement in ER Galilee. In particular I am interested in the ways in which the Q sayings appear to be at times responsive to the characteristic peasant struggles and ideologies that Scott illustrates; yet at times they appear to be contradictory to the ideology of the peasant's subsistence ethic. In conclusion, I argue that this comparison shows that the Jesus Movement in ER Galilee, rather than representing a clear peasant ideology, more likely represents the ideology of a group of disenfranchised retainers or what might be called a "dissident intelligentsia" (Scott 1976:198), who were drawn from a mixture of mostly non-elite, non-peasant individuals. I am arguing that while the ideology of the Jesus Movement made some significant inroads into the villages of early Roman Galilee, it did not play a noteworthy part in reforming the "little tradition" of the indigenous peasant population. While the groups associated with Jesus contained "the seeds of political and spiritual dissidence" they did not activate a significant movement of political or social dissent; followers of Jesus did not mobilize the rural population of Galilee.

Applying Anthropological Theories to Early Roman Galilee

All the elements of peasant life mentioned below revolve around the foundational need to maintain a stable economic and social environment within the village context. "This precapitalist normative order was based on the guarantee of *minimal social rights* in the absence of political or civil rights" (Scott 1976:184). In varying degrees, peasants viewed the elites as obligated to insure basic rights of subsistence. In this system—based on reciprocity and more generally mandated by a deeply entrenched system of honor—Scott notes that village patrons were responsible to ensure "a wide range of economic and social protection to dependents in return for their labor and support" (1976:176). This traditional village ethic was threatened in agrarian societies that encountered periods of significant growth in their administrative structures. As the majority of *The Moral Economy of the Peasant* illustrates—and as is often referenced in other anthropological studies—in pre-capitalist societies peasant hardships increased in direct proportion to the expansion of the colonial administration (56–113; Moreland 2004). This hardship did not necessarily lead to additional poverty, but it usually involved heightened economic and social instability. Traditional security and risk-sharing measures of agrarian farmers were eroded as a result of the social and economic shifts that typically occur with colonization. This is not to say that pre-colonial agrarian village contexts were exemplary settings of communal life. Indeed, one must take for granted that pre-Herodian villages in ER Galilee were socially stratified settings in which the local village elites and the dominant political authorities in the region (for example, Syrians, Phoenicians or Hasmoneans) regularly exploited their positions to the detriment of the majority peasant population (Freyne 2000:113–35). It is likely that villages differed one from the other with regard to the extent of stratification, tax burdens, kinship connections, and property ownership (Scott 1977:9). Regardless of the extent of stratification in individual villages, Scott illustrates the point that colonial efforts to regulate tax collection, for example, are detrimental to an already precarious situation. As village leaders align with the colonial authorities, the stability of village subsistence ethics and reciprocity becomes increasingly undependable for the subsistence farmers.

For scholars interested in the economic conditions of Galilee in the early first century, it is increasingly common to focus on the socio-economic shifts that accompanied the Herodian building projects in the region. Regarding economic consequences of colonizing efforts in rural settings (particularly Vietnam, Burma, Cambodia, Laos, Malaysia, and Thailand), Scott examined the following tangible results.[8] Due to the close proximity of new urban and administrative centers, tax payments were more easily demanded. Urban sites that were established within traditional rural settings functioned as centers of operations for administrators whose livelihood stemmed from tax payments. Additionally, new jobs and markets were created in the urban centers, resulting in the disruption of village crafts and a shift in village based trade patterns (1976:62). Landlords and local elites often moved to cities where they were more protected and benefited from other economic arrangements. "Both their personal and timely assistance to needy tenants, and the collective services they had once maintained, diminished or disappeared with their physical withdrawal" (1976:76, 175). Militias and courts were enlarged with the spread of the colonial administration, thus better able "to enforce contracts that violated the moral economy of the peasantry" (65). In times of desperation, rather than being able to depend on the honor-based relationship with the local elites, subsistence farmers were constrained by new forms of administrative controls that stripped them of their village-based safety net. The growth of the state also negatively affected the peasants' abilities

---

8. Scott has recently responded to and reflected upon his work in Southeast Asia, see Scott 2005.

to subsist by non-agrarian means: less property for villagers to cultivate, new limits on fishing in traditionally unrestricted lakes and streams, and limits on the collection of wood and hunting in local forests (63–64).

These economic shifts negatively impacted the traditional redistributive norms that were foundational to the peasant village. When the subsistence ethic was well supported, peasants could often count on the village elites to supply a wide variety of economic relief measures in times of extreme threats to survival. The growth of administrative centers was hazardous to village based risk-sharing measures. Conversely, the economic benefits that accrue with the establishment of colonial administrative centers favored the landholding elites. With Scott's help we are better able to imagine the challenge of colonial expansion from the peasant's viewpoint:

> First, it exposed an ever-widening sector of the peasantry to new market-based insecurities which increased the variability of their income above and beyond the traditional risk in yield fluctuations. Second, it operated to erode the protective, risk-sharing value of the village and kin-group for much of the peasantry. Third, it reduced or eliminated a variety of traditional subsistence "safety-valves," or subsidiary occupations which had previously helped peasant families scrape through a year of poor food crops. Fourth, it allowed landholders, who had once assumed responsibility for some of the hazards of agriculture, not only to extract more from the peasantry in rents but also to collect a fixed charge on tenant income, thereby exposing the peasantry more fully to crop and market risks. Finally, the state itself was increasingly able to stabilize its tax revenue at the expense of the cultivating class. (1976:57)

In pre-colonial settings, agrarian villages functioned to provide subsistence farmers with the necessary safety nets that ensured against the inevitable difficulties of natural and economic hardships and disasters. Agrarian farmers were tied to the land, to the village elites, to the kin-group, and, as much as possible, to diminished risk. The precautions that were taken to live according to the principals of "safety-first," in coordination with the positive relationship between local elites and peasants in the village network were ultimately responsible for the survival of the subsistence farmers. Anything that threatened the day-to-day stability of the peasants' lifestyle or hindered the relationship with the village elites was detrimental to their traditional means of insurance. Colonial administrative restructuring of the social fabric of rural life was damaging to the safety concerns of the peasants. When local elites aligned themselves with new colonial administrators, nothing of benefit resulted for the poor rural villager. Socially and economically, the peasants lost the ability to ensure themselves against environmental setbacks and loss (droughts, crop-failures, market insecurities, etc.). Local elites became further removed from the daily affairs of the subsistence farmers at the same time that increased economic pressures arose from the newly centralized colonial administration.

Faced with new economic pressures and threats to their moral economy from these socio-economic shifts, agrarian villagers exhibited diverse reactions. After encountering severe exploitation and the upheaval of their traditional subsistence ethic, rather than political revolts, opposition to administrative pressures was most often demonstrated in clever resistance measures and extreme self-reliance. Scott has observed that peasants do not rebel in order to gain social status or to remove themselves from a subsistence level of existence: "[T]he vast majority of peasant risings with which I am familiar were without doubt largely *defensive* efforts to protect sources of subsistence that are threatened or to restore them once they have been lost. Far from hoping to improve their relative position in the social stratification, peasant rebellions are typically desperate efforts to maintain subsistence arrangements that are under assault" (1976:187; 1985:xvii, 295–96).

Scott elaborates another common peasant reaction to exploitation: increased labor and personal hardship: "The choices may include putting all of the family to work, eliminating valued ceremonial obligations, emigrating, sharing, poverty, seeking charity, or serving in a landlord's gang against one's own fellow-villagers; and, as this list suggests, they usually entail great human costs" (1976:203–4). Rather than public resistance, one of the most common reactions of the peasant to the pressures of the elites is seen in the extremely laborious lifestyle changes that the agrarian peasant shoulders. In an attempt to maintain their insecure existence—brought on by the new colonial pressures—peasants were more likely to attempt to increase labor and production and "curtail consumption," rather than strike back at the forces that inflicted their suffering. As Eric Wolf has stated regarding the pattern of reduced caloric intake as a common peasant survival tactic: "Such efforts to balance accounts by underconsumption go a long way towards explaining why peasants tend to cleave to their traditional way of life, why they fear the new as they would fear temptation: Any novelty may undermine their precarious balance" (16).

The idea that the peasant is "more often a helpless victim of violence than its initiator" is a key factor to remember in our reconstructions of ER Galilee (Scott 1976:203). A related element is the fact that when peasants rise together in public revolt other non-peasant members of agrarian societies usually aid them (Scott 1977). Peasants are clearly not the only group that is exploited by the elites, and the elite population itself is not always in agreement about economic matters. Scott provides several useful insights into the role that non-peasants play in attempting to shape peasant response to oppression. For example, he notes that peasants are keenly aware of their class relations and are cognizant of times when they experience additional exploitation. Thus, "they do not need outsiders to help them recognize a pattern of growing exploitation which they experience daily." But he continues, "This does not mean outsiders are inconsequential. On the contrary, they are often critical to peasant movements, not because they convince peasants that they are exploited but because, in the context of exploitation, they may provide the power, assistance, and supralocal organization that helps peasants *act*" (1976:173–74; cf., Kautsky: 304–6).

Associated with this notion of the role of non-peasant outsiders are the references Scott makes to carriers of the hidden transcript in *Domination and the Arts of Resistance*. While not arguing that these carriers necessarily inspire revolt, these socially marginal, non-peasants, by virtue of having more time for imaginative thought and more ability to travel, are the human agents who assist in creating, elaborating, and disseminating the hidden transcript. Scott says, "The carriers are likely to be as socially marginal as the places where they gather. Since what counts as socially marginal depends so heavily on cultural definitions, the carriers will vary greatly by culture and over time." These might include "itinerant entertainers of all kinds," "renegade lower clergy, would-be prophets, pilgrims, marginal sects and monastic orders, mendicants, and so forth." Others who primarily assist in conveying the transcript, "while perhaps less active in elaborating a dissident subculture," include "journeymen, craftsmen on tour . . . petty traders, vagrants, [and] healers." Thus non-peasants play key roles in the creation, elaboration, and transmission of the hidden transcript, and "they may provide the power, assistance, and supralocal organization that helps peasants *act*" (1990:123–24, also see Scott 1977).

The Early Roman Setting of Galilee

Despite the increase in archaeological activity related to ER Galilee, we face several challenges in our attempts to describe the socio-economic world of the majority peasant population of this region. For example, notwithstanding several recent attempts to clarify the cultural and ethnic affinities of the population of Galilee in the first century CE, it is difficult to determine the cultural roots of the inhabitants. The task of describing the social setting of the ER Galilean villagers would be less complicated if we could be more certain of the long-term history of this population. If these villagers had been residents of Galilee for many centuries—descendents of an ancient Israelite village population—we could more readily link the cultural and "ethnic affinities" of these agrarians to a long-standing tradition that might better enable us to describe how they would react to the socio-economic pressures of the Herodians, and the ideology and socio-political concerns of the Jesus Movement (see Horsley 1995; 1996). Unfortunately, the extent to which Galilee was populated prior to the Hellenistic period is still debated. The archaeological survey of Zvi Gal and the results of other archaeological fieldwork in the region have convinced most archaeologists that the area was very sparsely populated during the Persian period. After the eighth century the population level was minimal—likely due to mass deportations by the Assyrians. Because of the dearth of evidence that supports the idea of a continuous "Israelite" population in the region, it is difficult to assume that Roman period Galileans were descendants of Israelite ancestors. The archaeological data suggest that the Assyrians had a major impact on the occupation of the region for several centuries. The area of Galilee was a hinterland of the Assyrian and Phoenician administrations and was sparsely populated by agrarian villages. This low population lasted until the Late Hellenistic (Hasmonean) period, at which time there was a gradual influx of people into Galilee. This population increase continued throughout the ER period. Thus we are left to ask, where did the inhabitants of the ER Galilean villages come from? A few conjectures about the growth of Galilee during the Hasmonean period can be suggested.

Some scholars have suggested that the area was almost entirely populated by Judeans (see Aviam), yet there is no evidence that people moved to Galilee from Judea in mass during the Hasmonean or Herodian periods. The only solid evidence for a new Judean population in the region is the use of stone vessels and Mikvahot in some ER Galilean settlements. These practices do indeed have clear associations with the "purity concerns" of some of the residents of Jerusalem, but we cannot be certain that Judeans brought those practices with them as they moved north into Galilee. While one should not deny the clear connections of some inhabitants of Galilee with traditions and rituals that were popular in Judea, the ancestral connection with Judea cannot be assumed.[9] Even if these are "ethnic markers" that suggest some Judeans moved to Galilee after the Hasmonean capture of the region, we cannot be confident that the majority of Galilean villagers were Judeans. The archaeological evidence suggests that Judeans did not move to Galilee in mass until after the First Revolt; the Judean influx into Galilee did not begin in earnest until the mid–second century C.E.

The expansion of village settlements in Galilee in the Late Hellenistic and ER periods was in many respects due to the establishment of protective measures by the Jerusalem-based Hasmoneans (for example, their establishment of a fortress at Sepphoris). With the advantage of a regular armed presence in the area, people from the surrounding regions were allowed to more easily take advantage of the fertile Galilean valleys and the western shore of the lake. The new inhabitants began building settlements on fairly remote, well-protected hillsides, like the small village of Nazareth—similar to the previously established Phoenician-based outposts in Galilee that are in evidence throughout the Persian and Hellenistic periods. They also began building small agrarian settlements in the valley floors and on the Kenneret lakeshore. This type of settlement practice

---

9. For detailed analyses of the "Jewishness," or better, the "Judean identity" of ER Galilee, see Chancey; and Reed 2000.

became even more widespread after additional protective arrangements were instituted by the Herodian dynasty (i.e., urbanization).

In the Late Hellenistic period, the region of Galilee appears to have been comprised of a network of recently formed agrarian villages that were successively administered by the Assyrians/Phoenicians, Hasmoneans, and Herodians. Most likely as a consequence of Hasmonean administrative directives, by the Late Hellenistic period these villagers were beholden to the Jerusalem based administration, though one should not overestimate the economic interests that the Hasmoneans had in this northern region. The archaeological and literary records have little that recommends anything more than limited oversight of the region by the southern administrators. Galilee was part of the Hasmonean hinterland, as it had been Syro-Phoenician hinterland for several centuries prior.

It is only during the time of Herod the Great that we see a significant interest in deliberately re-colonizing the Galilee. As was typical of Roman administrators around the Mediterranean, Herod held dominion in his region by demonstrating his military might and by establishing administrative and economic centers in the form of walled cities. Of course, Herod's most elaborate building projects were not immediately in the region of Galilee but there should be no doubt that new economic pressures were exerted upon all the subsistence farmers of this region. Nevertheless, direct incursions into Galilee were already well underway at Sepphoris by the first century B.C.E., and with the ensuing administration of Herod Antipas, the interest in exploiting and developing Galilee through urbanization projects greatly increased.

Regarding the development of Sepphoris, while there was a settlement on the hill that the city occupies from at least the Iron Age, the site was essentially a small village or a military outpost until the end of the Hasmonean Period, not an urban center. Only with the building projects of Herod and especially his son Herod Antipas—beginning in 4 B.C.E. and continuing throughout the first century C.E.—do we see the dramatic expansion of Sepphoris as a city in the heart of the Galilee. Sepphoris was located in a prime administrative position: overlooking one of the most fertile agricultural regions in all of Palestine, with easy access to the east-west corridors crossing the valley from the lake to the Mediterranean, which linked Galilee to the rest of the world.

In the case of Tiberias, there is a similar history. The building of the city was begun by Herod Antipas around 17–23 C.E. and continued into the middle of the first century. The city was positioned in an area that would have allowed for administrative control over the trade passing through the region along the lakeshore road, and dominance over the lively fishing industry that was primary to almost all the villages scattered around the lake (Hanson). There should be no doubt that with the rise of these cities came many of the same pressures on peasant life that have been illustrated by Scott. As Crossan and Reed have stated regarding the cities of Sepphoris and Tiberias, "New architectural styles, larger structures, and expensive materials were introduced into Galilee by Herod Antipas, yielding two miniature Caesareas, just as that city itself was Rome in miniature" (69).

From the extant archaeological evidence it appears that the Herodian administrative structure in lower Galilee did not employ a complex military organization to keep the peace in the rural settings. It should also be mentioned that there were no major natural disasters or extreme environmental conditions that would have driven the peasants into deeper poverty during the years projected for the existence of the Jesus Movement in Galilee (ca. 30–60). A basic overview of the material remains of the inhabitants of Sepphoris should illustrate the contrast between the wealth and prestige of this city in comparison to other major Greco-Roman cities in the region like Tyre, Caesarea, or Scythopolis (Reed 2000:94–96, 117–31). Relative to these other Roman cities, the inhabitants of Sepphoris were not extremely wealthy. They appear to have been unable to afford most luxury items. There is evidence for some trade with outside regions in the form of imported fine wares, and there are some domestic decorations that imply attempts by some of the residents to try to reproduce signs of wealth with cheaper replicas. But there are no large quantities of imported marble, and fewer public building projects (i.e., hippodrome, temple, or gymnasium) that date to the early first century. Sepphoris was a larger city than the surrounding villages (around nine thousand to twelve thousand in contrast to many villages between one hundred and one thousand inhabitants), but we have yet to excavate any major signs of extreme wealth. There is no doubt that the urban context—by its very presence in an agrarian society—was abusive to the peasant class, but the severity has to be examined in each regional and village setting.[10]

We are hampered by the fact that there is very little archaeological or literary data that derives from the rural or village culture. It is difficult to know the extent to which the inhabitants of the villages may have been affected by the development of the urban centers. Most rural sites that have been identified as having been occupied in the early Roman period remain unexcavated. Of course, studies like those of Scott help us imagine the social conditions of the rural population, but we must remain cautious about claiming the most extreme conditions for the peasants of ER Galilee. The recent studies of Freyne, Horsley, Kloppenborg, Reed, and Arnal have described many of the key shifts in the socio-economic conditions of Galilee that resulted from the new Herodian administrative pressures, and

---

10. On the exploitative nature of the urban-rural relationships, there is almost unanimous agreement among theorist that it favors the urban elites, for example: the theoretical model of the ancient city elaborated by M. I. Finley; the description of agrarian society by Lenski; and the description of the exploitation of peasants in aristocratic economies by Kautsky are all explicit about this fact.

that likely are the stimulant for the social movement that is associated with Jesus. There is little doubt that the Roman administration of the Herodian dynasty had many of the same impacts on the agrarian villages of Galilee that are documented in the anthropological studies of Scott (among others). The urbanization projects of the colonial government increased the need for taxes, as well as made tax collection more accessible. Most likely, this resulted in increased debt, the forfeiture of land rights, and a greater need for monetization and mono-cropping. These socio-economic shifts have been surmised from the literary evidence, and increasingly from the archaeological evidence as well (most recently, see Horsley 2005, and Herzog). Furthermore, as Scott illustrated, these economic changes typically lead to fundamental shifts in the subsistence ethic of the peasants. Landlords and local elites become further alienated from the rural farmers, urban centers are increasingly draining any surplus from the agrarian peasants, and fewer economic safety nets are available in the villages.

Regarding these principal conclusions, a comment on the debate about the nature of urban-rural relations in ER Galilee is warranted. The 1993 study of pottery distribution in first-century Galilee by D. Adan-Bayewitz is probably the most significant obstacle against the notion that the establishment of Sepphoris had an extremely detrimental effect on the rural population. Rather than a lack of trade between the city and the village, Adan-Bayewitz argued the wide spread distribution of pottery from the village of Kefar Hananya suggests a more reciprocal relationship between the urban and rural settings. Since the pottery produced in Kefar Hananya was widely used in ER Sepphoris, he concludes that the urban settings functioned as a central market for the village producers who carried their products to the markets and were personally familiar with the inhabitants of the cities (228–34; and Adan-Bayewitz and Isadore Perlman). Several scholars seeking to illustrate the very negative consequences of the new urban centers have interpreted his data differently. For instance, Horsley has suggested that because pottery making was "dependent on the availability of the right kind of clay, pottery-making would have been specialized in certain locations." He concludes, "The distribution of pottery, therefore, does not appear to be a good indicator of intraregional mobility and cultural interaction, let alone of interregional economic and cultural contact" (1996:72). Nevertheless, the possibility remains that some of the small village industries had something to gain by the fact that Sepphoris and Tiberias provided them with larger populations that needed their goods and provided them with a wider consumer network through the urban markets. Besides Adan-Bayewitz, several articles by J. Strange and D. Edwards (1988; 1992) also suggest, based on the archaeological and literary evidence, that there existed much better relationships between the rural and urban environs than is typical in agrarian settings.

Arnal's well argued assessment of the village-to-village and village-to-city relationship provides a needed bridge between those who have argued for a more beneficial role of the city in Galilean economics and those who have seen no reciprocity between the urban and rural settings. Arnal concludes,

> Thus, at the very least . . . there appears to have been a fairly elaborate network in place to channel, in spite of technological and geographical difficulties, produce and other goods to the main cities, as well as throughout the region. By extension, other sorts of ordinary intercourse evidently could have taken place on a routine basis between close-by settlements, and so for the inhabitants of one village to have dealings on a frequent and even casual basis with those of another is unlikely to have [been] unusual or worth remarking. (127)

Arnal's statement appears to fit quite well the conclusion of G. Lenski regarding the nature of urban and rural settings: "these relationships which developed between the villages and the urban centers were essentially symbiotic in character, but with definite overtones of parasitism" (206).[11] In light of recent anthropological studies of peasant societies (like Scott's) it is at least plausible that the new urban centers had limited benefits for some members of the agrarian villages; though one has to suspect that those most likely to be able to take advantage of any new economic rewards were the village elites, not the majority subsistence farmer.

Besides any potential benefits for agrarian villagers that arguably accrued due to the influx of people moving to the new cities in Galilee, the natural environment of this region supplied several opportunities to provide for a subsistence lifestyle through non-agrarian means. Depending on the region in Galilee where one resided, a subsistence farmer might have supplemented his or her means of living by working in olive oil, pottery, or wine production, or by fishing, hunting, and collecting wood. Additionally, some areas of Galilee would have supported small family plots, in addition to the normal farm production. Nevertheless, it is reasonable to expect that with the increase in Herodian administrative controls, traditional means of supplementing one's livelihood were progressively limited. As a case in point, regarding the management of the fishing industry around the lake, K. C. Hanson has persuasively argued that the Herodian administration had tight control of the lake's produce and related commerce. Overall, it is probable that the colonial government negatively affected the majority of peasants in much the same way that colonial pressures have affected other agrarian based societies.

---

11. Prior to this conclusion, he notes, "[T]here was a steady flow of goods from the peasant villages to the urban centers. In return, the villages received certain services of a political, cultural, religious, educational, and commercial nature, together with a small number of necessary or desired commodities such as salt, tools, or other manufactured objects not produced in the villages themselves" (206).

Finally, it is also worth mentioning that in spite of the more oppressive conditions for peasants that must have followed the building projects of the Herodian administration, there were several instances recorded by Josephus of economic benefaction to the Palestinian population during severe conditions. For example, even during Herod the Great's reign, relief was sought for the inhabitants of his region by appealing to the Egyptians for food supplies in the famine of 28/27 B.C.E.; and in 20 B.C.E. Herod provided relief from taxes for the population (*Antiquities* 15.299–316, and 365; see, Richardson: 222–23, 236–37). Of course, this implies both that taxes were overbearing and that the administration could make concessions in times of extreme economic affliction. While we should not make too much out of these examples, they do suggest that at least a basic norm of reciprocity—as part of the deeply ingrained Roman system of honor—was intact during the ER period between the urban elites and the non-elite classes. At the very least, even a ruler like Herod needed to appear to be interested in supplying the peasants with a subsistence level existence, if for no other reason than to acquire public acclaim and honor from his fellow Roman aristocratic elites (Lendon: 116). These seemingly kind acts of the colonial administration toward the subsistence farmers demonstrate the power of the Herodians, and the disenfranchisement of the majority peasants. Herod's beneficence would have increased his claim to being the patron over the client populace. In return the peasants became increasingly indebted to a secluded Roman client king that had very little in common with the village elites and their system of subsistence ethics.

The Early Jesus Movement in Galilee

In the midst of the socio-economic and moral shifts that resulted from the urbanization projects of the Herodians, the Jesus Movement had its origins. For many scholars who are familiar with the Galilean context in the early first century, the most plausible reason for the rise of this movement was the socio-economic shift that accompanied the colonizing efforts in the area. In light of this scholarly trend, it has become increasing prevalent in recent scholarship to examine the sayings of Jesus that are attributed to the sayings source "Q" in order to better understand the social agenda of the group responsible for the document. The sayings found in this collection are thought to be a direct response to the changing conditions of the Galilean villagers. While I agree with the basic results of much of this scholarship, one should not forget that it is unlikely that the Jesus Movement was effective in any of its attempts to change the socio-economic conditions of ER Galilee. While we should read the sayings of Jesus as responses to the social world of Galilee, we should not assume that the majority of the Galileans found the ideology of the Jesus Movement to be desirable. In the final section of this essay I will draw attention to several observations that will suffice to set the stage for my final contention: that the ideology of the sayings of Jesus in Q, especially in its final literary form, does not correspond to the peasant subsistence ethic. While many reasons can be suggested for why the Jesus Movement evidenced by Q did not engender a significant and resilient community of followers in Galilee prior to the Byzantine period—spreading instead to the major urban centers in the Roman world—the basic ideological conflict between the Jesus Movement and the agrarian village is a factor that must be seriously considered.

There is no doubt that the sayings of Jesus in Q are interested in the basic economic structures that are central to peasant concerns. We can observe several intersections between these sayings of Jesus and the socio-economic world of the Galilean peasants. The positive interest in the redistributive norms and risk-sharing measures that are at the core of peasants' subsistence ethic can be seen in a variety of sayings attributed to Q. For example: the desire for daily bread and debt release (11:3–4); not being anxious about food and clothes (12:22–31); getting what you ask for (11:9–10, 11–13); the ability of the shepherd or woman to find the lost sheep or coin (15:4–7, 8–10); not being anxious before the synagogue (12:11–12); the command to offer forgiveness to a brother (17:3–4); the promise of being taken in (10:16); and the idea of the house built on rock as a metaphor for those who hear and act on Jesus' words (6:47–49), all illustrate the positive aspects of joining this movement.

For peasants, these elaborate promises of divine security appear to fit well with the basic desire for safety and for maintaining a subsistence lifestyle. These sayings also implicitly suggest the idea that the peasants were in fact struggling with the negative impact of agrarian administrative structures. If the audience was well fed, clothed, housed, and actually had the doors opened to them when they knocked, the rhetorical force of these sayings would be greatly diminished. Additionally, the explicit condemnation of earthly treasures (12:33–34), and the negative attitudes toward wealth (16:13) suggest that the group was intentionally trying to appeal to the peasant class. Typically, it is this set of sayings that have caused many scholars to assume that the message of Jesus was well received by the Galilean peasants.

But the ideology of this Jesus Movement appears to transcend or breach the bounds of acceptable ideology for the security-seeking agrarian villagers. For instance, there are many sayings that ask the audience to take risks or give up possessions that are rightfully theirs, and abandon their traditional kinship based obligations and lifestyles. These demands were unacceptable to peasants who valued the security measures available in the traditional village setting. If the Q group was formed during the time of the Herodian administration, with all the aforementioned economic pressures and threats to traditional village life, it is hard to imagine that the suffering peasant class would be receptive to a group that required more non-traditional ideals. Rather than suggest a reinforcement of or a return to the desired life of the agriculturally based village peasant, in several key sayings, the group demanded an abandonment of stability. If the Jesus Movement in Galilee had rural peasants in mind as part of their audience, what they were asking the peasants to do was in direct conflict with peasant notions of safety first and/or redistributive norms and risk-sharing measures.

For example, while it might be argued that the ideology of Q 6:27–30 (love your enemies) would be appealing to peasant ideology (based on its appeal for altruism), the premise of these sayings ignores the typical safety-first condition of peasant existence. While the mention of corvée in Q/Matt 5:41 (go a second mile) reveals that the Q group's audience was familiar with this type of forced labor, the solution the group offers is once again contrary to peasant notions of avoiding risk and protecting one's self.

In Q 9:57–60; 14:26–27; and 17:33 we find a set of sayings against traditional family values. These sayings appear to fly in the face of peasant ideology. The Jesus Movement positioned itself in support of the "reign of God" over the security of the peasants' this-worldly, security-driven ideology (Kloppenborg 2000:386). The suggestion of homelessness and the implicit rejection of family structures directly contradict the notions of safety-first, and the ideals of a kin-based village structure. In spite of the admittedly hyperbolic nature of these sayings, the fact remains that the movement demanded rather drastic, even radical, measures from its members, if not in physical displacement, at least in the call to abandon central tenets of peasant ideology.[12]

Q 10:2–11 (the discourse on mission) is at the heart of many attempts to reconstruct the original constituents of the Jesus Movement. These sayings are problematic to the peasant subsistence ethic on several levels. Like Q 6:27–30, these instructions refer to the positive aspects of receiving from those who will give and vise versa (seemingly in support of peasant redistributive norms). This is what Crossan has referred to as commensality, defined as "a strategy for building or rebuilding peasant community on radically different principles from those of honor and shame, patronage and clientage. It was based on an egalitarian sharing of spiritual and material power at the most grass-roots level" (1991:344).[13] While I think

---

12. As Burton Mack observed, "These sayings are fundamentally and intentionally hyperbolic. If the analogy with the foxes and birds were pressed, even a Cynic would have no trouble finding a 'home' for the night. So the import must be that commitment to the Jesus movement takes priority over even such basic ties to conventional social arrangements as those constitutive for the family" (1988:634).

13. Similarly, Kloppenborg suggests, "The admonitions to love one's enemies and abusers and to suffer insult and seizure without retaliation are grounded in the assertion that only actions which surpass the ordinary expectations of reciprocity are truly meritorious. And it is stepping outside the bounds of general reciprocity that one comes to be a child of God (6:35c)" (1989:214).

Crossan's understanding of what Jesus and his Galilean followers intended is essentially correct, it should not go unnoticed that it is exactly this radical departure from the peasant norms of reciprocity—the norms that have their roots in the administrative patronage system that Q seemingly abandons—that must have led to the essential rejection of the Jesus Movement among the peasants of Galilee. While the commands for itinerancy should not be understood as a direct revelation of the members' actual lifestyle practices (like the hyperbole of Q 9:58), the core substance of these sayings is fundamentally opposed to the peasant ideology described by Scott. The requirements simply do not fit within the parameters of the safety-first precautions of the agricultural worker. As was elaborated previously, the peasant is tied to the land, to the kin-group, and, as much as possible, to a risk-free lifestyle. For the Q group, these elemental parts of peasant ideology are abandoned. These sayings of Jesus propose that by giving up security you will meet your genuine "kin-group" of the reign of God. But convincing a subsistence farmer that this departure from the norm was desirable is arguably a lost cause when one factors in all the aspects of the subsistence ethic.

Finally, with regard to the resistance measures that Scott observed in typical peasant communities, we can observe the Q response to exploitation in several of the sayings. The Q saying with the most similarity to peasant ideology might be the lack of resistance that is called for in Q 6:27–30. Yet, as was just observed, these commands for doing more than is called for appear to exceed the parameters of the subsistence lifestyle. Additionally, the decree to proclaim what was whispered (Q 12:2–7) does not fit with typical peasant ideology. This pericope contradicts the need for security by demanding risk-taking and public acts.

These brief considerations of several sayings in Q suggest both that this Jesus Movement was in fact interested in reaching out to peasants, and that the group would have met stiff resistance because of their explicit departures from the peasants' basic desire for safety and for maintaining a subsistence lifestyle within the village network. On the one hand, these sayings promised divine security and basic economic stability (i.e., food, debt release, and millennial hopes). On the other hand, they exploded peasant ideology with their radical idea that advised that living in the reign of God meant abandoning the subsistence ethic. From this initial comparison between Q and the 'moral economy of the peasant' a clear reason for the peasant rejection of this group begins to emerge.

The negative aspects of the Q sayings in comparison to peasant ideology are made even more explicit in several other sayings that are found as part of the apocalyptic interests found in these sayings. For example, in Q 12:51–53 ("striking the earth with fire," "bringing no peace," and "father against son and son against father"), the Q group heightened its notion of rejecting normal village-based security measures and ethics in order to join a group that promised a new family in the reign of God. While the group continued to maintain a negative portrayal of wealth and abuses of power (Q7:22, 25; 10:21–24; 11:43, 47; and 14:16–24), to a large extent the focus of these apocalyptic sayings helps to explain their rejection and provides a condemnation of their opponents (Kloppenborg 2000:204–5). In conclusion, I will observe the explicitly mentioned locales of that rejection, and summarize the reasons why it seems likely that the Q group failed to attract a following from the Galilean peasant majority.

Within Q there are abundant indications of the failures experienced by Jesus and his followers. As Kloppenborg's literary analysis revealed, in their written form many of these sayings contain "abrupt shift[s] of rhetorical stance, from instruction to prophetic woe" (2000:147).[14] The primary examples are: Q 6:22–23 (the beatitude for the persecuted); 7:31–35 (the rejection of John and Jesus by "this generation"); 10:13–15 (woes against Galilean towns); 11:32 (the Ninevites condemn this generation); 11:49–51 (this generation will pay for persecuting and killing prophets); 13:25–27 (the master rejects the lawless ones); and 13:34–35 (Jerusalem kills the prophets). In an effort to understand this rejection within the peasant context of ER Galilee, I will focus on the woes against the Galilean towns (10:13, 15).

Of the three settings, Chorazin, Bethsaida, and Capernaum, the latter may be the most interesting. Reed's study of the setting of Capernaum reveals a mid-sized, Jewish, agricultural and fishing village on the edge of Antipas's kingdom. With the absence of large public buildings, mosaics, frescoes, and marble, the village was apparently not occupied by any elites whose wealth made these affordable. Instead, regarding the level of Herodian administrators, Reed suggests that Capernaum was most likely the home of "some low-level bureaucrats or officials with a modicum of wealth" (2000:165). Furthermore, as a setting located both on the lake and on the regional north-south trade route, Capernaum offered its inhabitants ready access to other parts of the region.

While a more complicated picture of Bethsaida is found in the literary sources, and the archaeological evidence of the ER period is less secure, for our current overview we can reasonably assume for this site many of the same features that were found in Capernaum: no evidence of great wealth, primarily a fishing and agricultural village, on the north-south trade route, primarily occupied by peasants and fishing laborers with some low level administrators.[15] Additionally, in the literary sources Bethsaida is clearly tied to Herod Philip who is said to have founded the "city" in 30 C.E. in

---

14. Where he is speaking directly of Q 10:12–15 within the instructional context of 10:10–11 and 16.
15. On the (still disputed) location of Bethsaida at et Tell, just to the North of the lake on the east side of the Jordan, and the literary and archaeological evidence about the setting, see Arav and Freund; and Strickert.

honor of Julia. In spite of this auspicious founding, the archaeological remains reveal a rather small village with little evidence of royal wealth.

These pictures of Capernaum and Bethsaida suggest settings in which a group interested in developing a program of resistance against the exploitative norms of the Herodians may have found "ears to hear." The truly wealthy members of the ER Galilean society were not located in these villages; neither does there appear to have been significant exposure to military control.[16] There is no reason to doubt that the peasants in these villages would have faced the normal struggles of the subsistence lifestyle. With the establishment of Tiberias just to the south, which led to greater administrative control and the expansion of the fishing industry, it is probable that residents of these towns felt the negative impact from the new administrative structures: more tax collection by the elites, monetization of the economy, less village economic safety-nets, etc. The fact that these villages were located on a significant trade route within an active lake environment (with non-Jewish cities in close proximity) arguably adds to the relative complexity of the social classes that might have lived in these places. Thus, as the literary evidence in the Gospels suggests, if most of Jesus' first followers came from this region, it appears that the membership could have derived from a variety of social groups: people associated with fishing, with trading, with agriculture, with low-level administration. Yet, as I have argued, the least likely group to accept the message was the majority, agriculturally based peasant population. We might surmise then that one of the factors in the eventual rejection of the Jesus Movement in these lakeside villages was the growing tension between the peasants, who were tenaciously clinging to the basic security of the village kin-group setting (even as it was under duress from the new urban elites), and the radical ideals of the Jesus Movement, which was pressing the population to resist the powerful by means of a major ideological shift.

Since peasants were so clearly interested in the reality of economic conditions (survival tactics), rather than in ideological campaigns, the Jesus Movement's promises of food and debt release might have originally had some reception. Clearly, the group was interested in many aspects of economic critique that fall within the typical confines of the "hidden transcript." But as the group became more concerned with elaborating on "the presence of divine activity" and less interested in clearly supporting the basic principles of the peasant's moral economy, the members may have found themselves further marginalized and alienated. For the peasants,

---

16. With regard to the Centurion mentioned in Q 7, Reed states quite clearly, "In fact, it is historically implausible to suggest that a Roman Centurion and upwards of one hundred Roman Legionnaires were stationed at Capernaum. Roman troops only periodically passed through Galilee, such as to quell the revolt at Sepphoris upon Herod's death, but no troops were stationed in Herod's kingdom or his son Antipas's tetrarchy" (2000:162).

the risk management elements that are implicit in the patron-client relationship (even in rather severe conditions), and the redistributive norms of the village setting, must have been more appealing than the radical option offered by the Jesus Movement.

Finally, conjectures about the small ER village of Chorazin bring us even closer to a setting where acceptance of the ideology of these sayings attributed to Jesus is doubtful. Located two and one half miles from, and 270 meters *above* the lake, this small village differed from the other two sites in both size and resources (Yeivin: 301–4). Although the archaeological evidence in the ER period is scarce, we can infer that Chorazin was a very small hamlet focused almost exclusively on agricultural production. Thus it would constitute a typical example of a fairly remote peasant village. By virtue of its setting on a steep rise above Lake Kinneret, the inhabitants would have been less likely to participate in the various trade or industrial jobs available on the lake, and they would have had less contact with the Herodian administrators from the urban area of Tiberias.

If Jesus and his followers actually went to this small agricultural village promoting the ideology that is encapsulated in a saying like Q 9:60: "leave the dead to bury their own dead," or Q 14:26: "If you do not hate your father and mother you cannot be my disciple," then it seems reasonable to conclude that they would have been turned away. Based on what we know of the peasant moral economy from Scott, it is likely that all the notions of divine security and action that the Q group could promise would not have compensated for the drastic ideological shift in peasant norms that they called for.

While there are many other avenues that need to be explored, I conclude by suggesting that Scott's analysis of peasant ideology has helped to construct a description of both the positive and negative aspects of the ideology of the Q sayings from the perspective of the agrarian peasant. Based on this description, it is easier to understand why the Jesus Movement was ineffective in bringing about real economic or societal change for the Galilean peasantry, and why this group was opposed by the Galilean agrarian villagers. As the Woes against the Pharisees suggest, the followers of Jesus found themselves increasingly marginalized and essentially powerless against those who were more able to maneuver in the Herodian economic structure. In ER Galilee, the ideology and practices of the "Pharisees," as representatives of the normal exploitative, yet subsistence guaranteeing, elite based patronage system, were actually more acceptable to the peasant class than the idealized reign of God and the demands for a new type of reciprocity that were proclaimed by the members of the Jesus Movement. In the midst of all the socio-economic pressures brought on by the Herodian administration, and the threats to the "moral economy of the peasants," the Jesus Movement responded to the Herodian elites and the local leaders who had aligned themselves with this colonial power with a philosophy that threatened core elements of the agrarian village organization and ideology. It is little wonder that Christianity eventually became a movement that had its greatest following in the large urban centers outside of Galilee.

Going Public with the Hidden Transcript in Q 11
BEELZEBUL ACCUSATION AND THE WOES

Alan Kirk

I

Patterns of subordination in ancient agrarian societies conform in important respects to the forms of personalized domination analyzed by James C. Scott. Such societies are steeply stratified in terms of wealth and power. With varying degrees of success ruling groups attempt to exert political, economic, and cultural hegemony over the agrarian producers, and the relations between elites and subordinated groups serve the purpose of material appropriation (Scott 1990:111–12). Through rents, debt, tithes, tributes, and corvées, elites appropriate the labor and agricultural surplus of the peasantry. Coupled with the ecological precariousness of small-scale cultivation, these claims upon surplus mean that peasant families live close to subsistence thresholds.

In Judea, Samaria, and Galilee, Rome ruled either directly or through Herodian client kings and local elites who resided in cities such as Sepphoris, Tiberius, and Jerusalem situated in agricultural hinterlands populated by small-scale cultivators. Such a political-economic structure allows relations of domination to flourish. It is also the matrix of Jesus' activities and the mobilization of the Jesus movement. We will see that Q, in particular the sequence of traditions found in Q 11, is bound up in this matrix. More precisely, we will argue that these materials give trenchant expression to a strategy of resistance that subordinated groups may under certain conditions bring to bear against elite hegemony, a strategy, following Scott, that we will call the *public declaration of the hidden transcript*. After clarifying the key terms used by Scott—the "public transcript" and the "hidden transcript"—we will analyze the Beelzebul Accusation (Q/Luke 11:14–23) and the Woes (Q/Luke 11:39–52), making use in addition of Wolfgang Lipp and Nachman Ben Yehuda's discussions of stigmatization. We will conclude by linking our results to some current questions in Q research.

181

II

Public transcript designates the full range of routinized and scripted public interactions that take place between rulers and subordinated groups. The public transcript is a performance, an elaborate playing of the roles that are determined by unequal power relationships. These public encounters are "power-laden" situations, which means that these rituals of behavior and verbal exchange dramatize and reinforce relations of subordination and domination (Scott 1990:2, 13, 31). For the weak this entails cultivating, on the one hand, a decorum of deference and servility toward the powerful, and on the other, a demeanor of resignation to exploitations, degradations and humiliations, patronizing condescensions, insults, and other outrages to dignity. Scott describes these concrete displays of domination as the symbolic "performance of mastery" that constitutes the contribution of elites to the public transcript (Scott 1990:23–31, 105–13; 1985:198). "Dominant elites extract material taxes in the form of labor, grain, cash and service in addition to extracting symbolic taxes in the form of deference, demeanor, posture, verbal formulas, and acts of humility. In actual practice, of course, the two are joined inasmuch as every public act of appropriation is, figuratively, a ritual of subordination" (Scott 1990:188).

The public demeanor of the weak thus conforms closely to the interests and expectations of the dominant. In other words, *the powerful control the public stage, the place for symbolic display of their hegemony* (Scott 1990:4, 24; 1985:198, 287). Hence the public transcript, with its "continuous stream of performances of deference, respect, reverence, admiration, esteem, and even adoration," seems to indicate that the weak endorse both their subordination and the social and moral order that supports it (Scott 1990:93). What it testifies to, however, is the power wielded by ruling groups that enables their unchallenged control of the public stage. The public transcript of the weak, Scott argues, is in many respects a prudential strategy, a tissue of tactical dissimulation presented to the face of power. The poor choke back their anger and deliver their performance because their overriding preoccupation is with survival—they fear the retaliatory sanctions the powerful can bring to bear on those who openly confront them. But prudent adaptation of the weak to conditions of exploitation "does not imply [their] normative consent to those realities" (Scott 1985:147, also 273–86; 1990:35–37, 152–53).

That the deferential posture displayed by the poor in public encounters may be less than sincere is hardly lost on the powerful, but neither is this necessarily a matter of concern to them. What is crucial for ruling groups is that subordinate groups feel themselves constrained to continually perform public protocols that accord with their powerlessness and inferior status. In other words, it suffices that the weak perceive the existing moral and social order to be inevitable, and manifest this perception in continual "reproduction of hegemonic appearances" in public encounters. What the powerful really fear are ruptures of "the smooth surface of apparent consent." Breaches of deference, defiant challenges from below, openly call in question the dominant order and expose its precariousness. Therefore, elites are preoccupied with maintaining control of the public stage (Scott 1990:45–46, 66–67, 204–5).

III

In contrast to their public displays, oppressed groups cultivate dissident discourses in the sequestered sites of their semi-autonomous social life. *Hidden transcript* is the term Scott gives to this alternative discourse of the weak. The slave quarters, the village, the working class tavern, the coffee house, the moors are the "locations in which the unspoken riposte, stifled anger, and bitten tongues created by relations of domination find a vehement, full-throated expression" (Scott 1990:120; 1985:328). Because of the perilousness of its public utterance, it stays sequestered, unenacted in public. However, under certain conditions, the long-gestating hidden transcript may break through the "smooth surface of apparent consent" to openly challenge power. In such extraordinary occurrences lies the potential for social and moral transformation (Scott 1990:20, 78–81).

As might be expected, the substance of the hidden transcript is critique and negation of the dominant social and moral order, the norms that legitimize relations of domination. Far more than just an activity of negation, however, the hidden transcript generates alternative norms, a "set of contrary values." Oppressed groups construct no less than a "counterfactual social order" that entails "both the reversal and negation of their domination." Stated differently, the hidden transcript envisions a future state of affairs characterized by reversal of present status arrangements, in which the last will be first and the first, last (Scott 1977:12–19, 224; 1985:297; 1990:41–44, 81, 111).[1]

While imperial conquest and colonization introduce complicating factors, generally speaking political-cultural elites and subordinate groups within a particular society hold in common a number of historical, cultural, and moral traditions. The exercise of power by ruling groups frequently is hedged within these traditions, and to that degree it lays claim to a certain aura of moral authority. The moral critique that takes shape in the hidden transcript likewise draws upon traditions and cultural resources held in common with ruling groups. However, it *contests* elite constructions of that tradition; in other words, it engages in a battle, albeit discreetly, for control of the common moral tradition of a society. "The struggle between

---

1. "The hierarchy engendered by the great tradition thus seems everywhere to encourage its own antithesis within the little tradition.... it would appear that every social hierarchy creates the possibility of a world turned upside down" (1977:17–18).

rich and poor in [the Malay village] is not merely a struggle over work, property rights, grain, and cash. It is also a struggle over the appropriation of symbols, a struggle over how the past and present shall be understood and labeled" (Scott 1985:xvii, 310).

In traditional societies the dominant social order is oriented to a sacred cosmic order, with cult, sacred texts, and sacred institutions typically controlled by the cultural-political elites. Accordingly within the hidden transcript of subordinated people there frequently emerges a critique, in effect a *profanation*, of official religion and its institutions. Moreover the oppressed cultivate forms of religion, with more or less tenuous connections to the official cult, that cohere with their discontent with the conditions of their existence. They orient their lives within alternative, authorizing cosmologies, frequently with pronounced eschatological features, and practice concrete forms of religious life that give sacred status to their "desire for relief from the burdens of subordination" (Scott 1977:7; 1985:320; 1990:115, 147, 226). In other words, longed-for rectifications in the social, political, and moral spheres are indissolubly linked with envisioned cosmic transformations.

IV

Subordinated agrarians practice what Scott calls "everyday forms of resistance." These stratagems reflect the preoccupation of subsistence producers with survival; therefore they aim, within the framework of existing hierarchical relations, at minimizing expropriation and securing subsistence (Scott 1985:xvi–xvii, 310; 1987:419, 450; 1990:86–87). Accordingly these tactics are marked by retreat from the threshold of open defiance; in other words, they tend not to be disruptive of the public transcript of conformity and consent. Those engaging in them "disavow, publicly, any intention of challenging the basic principles of stratification and authority" (Scott 1990:96). Such practices as squatting, poaching, pilfering, tax and tithe evasion, shoddy, slow, or shirked labor for landowners, and dissimulation are preferred over direct but perilous forms of resistance such as open breaches of deference protocols, land invasions, attacks on grain stores, tax revolts, and strikes (Scott 1985:xvi, 32–34, 255–65; 1987; 1990:14).

Certain conditions may lead, however, to that extraordinary event: *the public declaration of the hidden transcript* "in the teeth of power." A subsistence crisis may present a threat to peasant survival of such magnitude that low-level strategies that work within the dominant system of social relations cannot cope with it. People who are desperate have nothing to gain by continuing to accommodate themselves to conditions of domination (Scott 1985:xvi; 1990:203–8).[2] A second scenario that might "trigger this passage

---

2. Samuel L. Popkin notes that effective leadership is frequently a pre-requisite for mobilizing collective action even during subsistence crises (*The Rational*

from quiescence to arousal" is closely related: social, economic, and political change (for instance, brought on by imperial domination) on a scale that threatens destruction of the social and economic viability of the weak and undermines the moral structure of the old order (Scott 1977:230–34; 1985:242, 318–33; 1990:219). Finally, societies riven by tensions, factions, and uncertainty regarding questions of legitimacy and moral authority, societies, in other words, in which the solidarity and hegemony of elite groups are perceptibly unstable, are ripe for increased episodes of public defiance by subordinate groups (Scott 1985:273; 1990:55–56, 67, 88, 102, 117, 200–201).

Public declaration of the hidden transcript has potentially "incendiary" effects (Scott 1990:202). Open breach of protocols of subordination, that is, a "public refusal to reproduce hegemonic appearances," constitutes a direct attack on the relations of domination they symbolize. As such it mounts a provocative challenge to the legitimacy of the dominant social order and its representatives, controverting the claims of the latter to moral authority. Most worrisome from the perspective of ruling groups is that public declaration of the hidden transcript has potential *to mobilize a social movement* as others recognize their own convictions, previously kept prudently off-stage, articulated in the unequivocating speech of those who have dared to openly challenge the powerful (Scott 1990:196–223). The sacred dimension of the hidden transcript intensifies the mobilizing effect of its public declaration, for it serves to depict this crisis event as being of transcendent, revelatory import, as the crux of a transformation of cosmic proportions heretofore only dreamed of. Correspondingly, the daring individuals who go public with the hidden transcript may come to be associated with epic, mythic figures of redemption who have long existed as powerfully evocative archetypes in the cultural tradition of the little people (Scott 1977:238–39; 1990:16).

It is easy to see why public declaration of the hidden transcript is "one of those rare and dangerous moments in power relations" (Scott 1990:6, 207). It calls in question the capacity of elites to dictate the behavior of subordinate groups on the public stage, hence the perceived inevitability of their power. This, added to the mobilizing effect of provocative acts of this nature, means that *the powerful must take decisive countermeasures* to eradicate the challenge and repair the torn fabric of apparent consent. They must reassert control of the public stage, make it again the place where the inexorability of their power is on display. By the same token, these countervailing actions must themselves be public. In Scott's words, "Open insubordination represents a dramatic contradiction of the smooth surface of euphemized power. . . . it requires a public reply if the symbolic status quo is to be restored"(Scott 1990:56; also 1987:423). In suppressing dissent

---

Peasant: The Political Economy of Rural Society in Vietnam [Berkeley: University of California Press, 1979], 245–48).

elites must appear to be acting out of moral authority, that is, in the name of the common moral tradition. Typically, therefore, they attempt to *stigmatize* dissidents publicly as *deviant* with regard to traditional values and thus as dangerous threats to the community's well-being. Moreover, it is crucial to this moralizing enterprise that a negative public interpretation be affixed to acts of resistance (Scott 1985:301; 1990:55, 125, 189, 205–6). Ruling groups by definition have enormous power at their disposal, but public deviantizing is the moralizing step preparatory to their resort to coercive measures.

Associating persons with archetypal evil powers is the paradigm instance of deviancy labeling. A person so accused represents the ultimate deviant, for he or she personifies the antithesis, the evil inversion of the values and norms of the community. Accordingly the point of the accusation is to convince the public that the person accused is a virulent social threat (Neyrey 1996:98; Nash 1967:131–32; Douglas 1970:xxvi–xxvii; Marwick 1970:293; Hohmeier 1975:12; Elmer 1996:151–63). Accusations of this sort are attempts to stigmatize competitors for social and moral leadership, thereby radically degrading their public standing and, accordingly, preparing the ground to eradicate them (Marwick 1967:113–114; 1970:293; Douglas 1991:727; Crawford 1970:307–8, 314; Golomb 1988:437–38; Rivière 1970:251–52). Those leveling such charges present themselves as the authentic guardians of the community's moral order.

V

Nachman Ben Yehuda stresses that "processes of deviantization, stigmatization, and degradation can in fact be effectively resisted, neutralized, and even reversed" (1990:222; also Lipp: 1985:16, 99, 117–19, 204; Schur 1980:24, 144). Those labeled as deviants attempt to repudiate the attribution and redirect it back upon their attackers, in other words, to *counter-stigmatize* their accusers as the real deviants with respect to the moral order. Public confrontations become "stigma contests," dramas of "response and counter-response" (Schur 1971:11; also Ben Yehuda 1990:48). Accusers claim and indeed often fill official roles of guardianship of the community's social and moral order. In such cases counter-stigmatization impugns their legitimacy, their qualifications to exercise this kind of authority. In effect, counter-stigmatization attempts to enact publicly the status reversals long envisioned but kept latent in the hidden transcript.[3] To the accusation of

---

3. Lipp states, "[B]ewirkt der Prozeß am Ende, daß nicht nur die Stigmatisierten *auf-*, sondern die Kontrollinstanzen, die auf sozialmoralisch zunächst 'normalen', alltäglichem Bewertungsboden stehen, *abgewertet* werden und in die Etikettierungszone des Defekten, Bösen, Schuldhaften selbst geraten" (1985:204, my emphases). The convergence of critique and status reversal in public stigma confrontations, as a sequel to public declaration of the hidden transcript, is not explored in detail by Scott, but see 1990:6–8, 115, 169, 172, 196–97, 215.

constituting a threat to the community's moral order can be counterposed robust claims to the contrary, namely, that one's activities are highly beneficial, even salvific expressions of that moral order. The openly dissenting group, seeking to mobilize a movement, vigorously counter-interprets itself and its actions as enactments of the community's deepest, most cherished, constitutive values and norms (Lipp 1977:66–68; 1993:22; Ben Yehuda 1990:221; Goffman 1963:10). In Scott's words: "[T]he refusal to reproduce hegemonic appearances is not entirely straightforward. The political struggle to impose a definition on an action and to make it stick is frequently at least as important as the action per se" (1990:206). The battle for interpretation of a particular act or behavior becomes a flash point for the more comprehensive conflict over who has the authority to define the moral and social order of a community.

VI

Beelzebul Accusation (Q/Luke 11:14–23)

All these strategies and counter-measures come into play in Q 11, beginning with the Beelzebul Accusation, which attempts to affix to Jesus the deadliest of all deviance ascriptions. The preceding sections of Q leading up to this confrontation are largely comprised of exhortations that have spelled out the alternative social and moral vision of the Jesus movement, the "counterfactual" set of norms that Scott argues constitutes an integral element of the hidden transcript (see above). The Beelzebul Accusation, therefore, is a counter-attack, the inevitable reaction to Jesus' challenge to the dominant social and moral order. Following upon Jesus' charismatic display of power in a healing and exorcism, "some" (τινές) level the accusation: "By Beelzebul ... he casts out demons." Though they are not identified, it is clear the accusers constitute a specific group with distinct interests, for their hostility contrasts markedly with the positive reaction of "the crowds" (11:14).[4] Leveling deviancy charges is an activity typical of elites who view themselves as guardians of the moral and social order (Malina and Neyrey 1988:42; Becker 1963:163). Hence the vested interest of elites in publicly labeling Jesus, here exercising his charismatic power in conjunction with his broader moral program, a deviant.

The controversy begins with the Accusation and escalates into the Woes (11:39–48, 52). There any residual ambiguity with regard to the identity of Jesus' challengers disappears. They are concerned with working out and scrupulously observing purity and dining rules (11:39–42). Their claim to positions of honor in public assemblies (perhaps an indication of juristic prerogatives), and deferential public greetings (11:43) shows them

---

4. Form critically, 11:14 is an apocopated miracle story, editorially integrated with the controversy which follows (11:15–23), the whole forming an elaborated *chreia* (Robbins 1989).

positioned atop a hierarchical system based on prestige, privilege, and ostentatious display of status differences. More to our point, these are highly predictable, recurrent elements of an elite-dominated public transcript. Scott notes that "a vital sector of the elite-choreographed public transcript will consist of visual and audible displays of rank, precedence, and honor" (1990:105, 133). The erection of public monuments, such as "the graves of the prophets" (11:47–48), was an honor-augmenting activity of urban ruling groups in the ancient world. The continuation of the denunciation into 11:49–51 makes pointed reference to the Temple. Hence those who accuse Jesus belong among the elites of a temple city.

Elites react vigorously and if need be violently to those who mount threats to their hegemony. The public accusation of 11:14 is their opening gambit, a vigorous effort to counteract the effects of Jesus' public activities. The accusation exploits the evocative cultural symbol "Beelzebul" to stigmatize Jesus as belonging in the demonic realm rather than in the realm of God's power (Malina and Neyrey 1988:57, 62). The charge frontally contests Jesus' own public claim in the preceding Mission Discourse that his proclamation and healing activities are enactments of the Kingdom of God (10:9). Far from it: Jesus is aligned with God's archetypal enemy! Thus the accusation asserts that Jesus poses a threat of crisis proportions to the community. Moreover, the charge that Jesus is demonized stigmatizes him as a ritual pollutant of a particularly virulent kind. It classifies him not merely as "unclean," a remediable ritual condition, but as "an abomination, and hence completely outside the community" (Malina 1993:156). The goal in leveling the accusation is to degrade Jesus, to publicly discredit his claims to moral authority and, conversely, to preserve and enhance that of his accusers. If the charge sticks, all that remains is to process and expel the deviant; hence the *deadly* seriousness of the confrontation.

Jesus responds by counter-interpreting himself and his activities in an extremely elevated manner, using culturally-resonant terms, and, correspondingly, counter-stigmatizing his accusers as the real deviants and pollutants (Robbins identifies this as a rhetorical strategy of "counter-definition" [1989:186]). The effect is to reverse status-positions between himself and his elite accusers. Both strategies converge in verse 20, the crux of the speech. First, *counter-interpretation*: "But if by the finger of God I cast out demons, then the Kingdom of God has come upon you." Against the accusation that he stands with Beelzebul radically opposed to the rule of God, Jesus counter-asserts that his healings and exorcisms in fact form the cutting edge of God's reign. "By the finger of God" (εν δακτυλο θεου) is precisely calibrated to counteract the imputation, "by Beelzebul" (εν Βεελζεβουλ). Besides standing *pars pro toto* for the power and authority of God, "finger of God" is itself a highly evocative cultural symbol, making transparent allusion to Exod 8:15, Moses' confrontation with Egyptian sorcerers in the struggle to liberate Israel from Egyptian oppression. According to van der Horst, "there can be little doubt that it is Ex 8:15 (19) that largely determines the function of the expression in Luke 11:20, for there as well as here it is God's sovereignty over the powers of evil and his intervention on behalf of his people through a human agent that is at the foreground" (1997:91). And further:

> It is the Jewish interpretation of God's finger in Ex 8:19 as an invincible power in the struggle against (demonic) evil ... that is in Luke's mind here. This is further confirmed by the consideration that the Egyptian magicians who opposed Moses in Ex 7-8, called Jannes and Jambres in Jewish tradition, were often regarded in haggadic sources as persons who had made a pact with the devil and his demons. (102-3)[5]

Invoking the "finger of God," therefore, has the double effect, first, of identifying Jesus' power with God's, and second, of establishing a direct analogy between Jesus and Moses—cultural hero, divinely commissioned deliverer, and founder of Israel's moral order. Jesus thereby counter-defines himself in extremely elevated terms, diametrically the opposite of the identity imputed by the accusation.

Second, *counter-stigmatization:* If Jesus inaugurates God's rule, if he thereby embodies the divinely ordained social and moral order, what does this say about those who have ranged themselves here against him, the professed custodians of that order? Verse 20 makes this explicit. As we noted, reference to the "finger of God," invoking Exod 7-8, is a hermeneutical maneuver that recasts this dramatic confrontation of Jesus with his opponents in terms of Moses' confrontation with the Egyptian sorcerers. According to Jewish haggadic tradition the Egyptian sorcerers derived their powers from Belial (see Dunn 1988:39-40, referring to CD 5:18-19). The implication? It is the opponents of Jesus that draw power from Beelzebul and stand opposed to God's servant, even as the Egyptian sorcerers opposed Moses. But the stigma goes deeper: the Egyptian magicians confessed the greater power of Moses and its divine source: "And the magicians said to Pharoah, 'This is the finger of God!'" (Exod 8:19). The opponents of Q 11, by contrast, are refusing to acknowledge Jesus, and in a swift turning of tables are thereby assigned status below even that of the Egyptian sorcerers.

VII

Woes (11:39-52)

This program is carried forward into the Return of the Unclean Spirit (11:24-26), the Demand for a Sign (11:29-35), and then to the Woes (11:39-

---

5. Van der Horst is discussing the Lukan version of this controversy. The *Critical Edition of Q* makes the judgment that Luke's "finger of God" reproduces the Q tradition (ed. James M. Robinson et al. [Minneapolis: Fortress; Louvain: Peeters, 2000]).

48, 52). We will focus here on the Woes and briefly, the Announcement of Judgment (11:49–51), where the confrontation culminates in a profaning reference to the Temple.

The denunciations in the Woes play upon recurrent, constitutive elements of an elite-choreographed public transcript: expectations of deference; ostentatious displays of prestige, rank, and cultural superiority. Like the Beelzebul controversy, in a calculated manner the Woes disrupt the public transcript, the "smooth surface of apparent consent," precisely at these its symbolically most sensitive points. Jesus provocatively violates the etiquette of public deference that symbolizes relations of domination. Simultaneously, the critique from below, the long-gestating hidden transcript, breaks into the open, for Jesus' accusations are calibrated to contest the moral prestige and hence the legitimacy of the elites, and so doing to enact a reversal of status positions. The charge of injustice and avarice, offenses exacerbated by myopic attention to purity observance (11:42), is intended to deprive them of their crucial moral authority. Verse 52, "you shut the kingdom of God from people; you did not go in, nor let in those trying to get in," charges the elites with betrayal of the primary religious obligations incumbent on them as custodians of Temple and Torah, namely, to enable the community's vital access to God. This kind of complaint against religious elites, custodians of the "great tradition," is a stock element of hidden transcripts of subordinated groups (Scott 1990:101–2, 147).

Jesus turns his opponents' ritual purity concerns and expertise back upon themselves. With the label "unmarked tombs" (11:44) Jesus stigmatizes his accusers as bearers of virulent corpse impurity, "the most powerful source of contamination" (Eilberg-Schwartz 1990:184), and with the same stroke reverses the pollution stigma attaching to the accusation of Beelzebul-possession. Imputation of ritual impurity, invoked here metaphorically to symbolize moral corruption, amounts to an assertion that the religious elites are disqualified from custodianship of Torah and Temple. This censuring of elites by reference to the moral tradition they ostensibly espouse, embody, and appeal to to justify their power, in other words, the charge that "rulers have violated the norms by which they justify their own authority," is likewise a characteristic element of the hidden transcript of subordinate groups (Scott 1990:94, 103–6; also 1977:14; 1985:317). In this extraordinary case it shoulders its way out to disrupt the "dramaturgy of power," that is, the self-representations of elites on the public stage. Accordingly, it shatters the "*self*-portrait of dominant elites as they would have themselves seen" (Scott 1990:18).

Given the severity of Jesus' disruption of the public transcript throughout this sequence of material, provocations that no ruling group could afford to stand down from, it is hardly accidental, not to say sobering, that the culminating Announcement of Judgment (11:49–51) makes pointed reference to the blood of prophets violently shed. To maintain though our concentration on public declaration of the hidden transcript: verse 51 recounts an archetypal episode of the shedding of righteous blood, the ultimate pollution, between the altar and the sanctuary in the Court of the Priests, one of the holiest spots in sacred topography. Invoking a defiling act that occurred within Temple courts was a stock method of asserting the desecration of the Temple itself.[6] More to our point, the charge that the Temple, the institutional redoubt of the socio-religious elites, has irrupted with ritual pollution at its very heart amounts to a profanation of elite cosmology (Scott 1977). The severe disarrangement of the social and moral order, Q's generative obsession, finds its counterpart in a sacred cosmos disordered right at its nexus.

VIII

A tendency in the past has been to correlate the acerbic units of Q concentrated in this section with a secondary stage of community formation, that is, to take them as evidence of the putative disengagement of the so-called Q community from a refractory Israel after an earlier phase of mission, a phase that supposedly would be represented by the less caustic passages in other sections of Q. Our analysis of Q 11 materials shows that in fact it is precisely in these tense, confrontational passages that Q is *most engaged* with its social context—the patterns of domination characteristic of first-century Palestine. Far from signaling disengagement, these passages form the leading edge of Q's protreptic program of social and moral transformation in Israel. They register with pristine clarity that charged moment when the hidden transcript of oppressed groups breaks through the "smooth surface of apparent consent" to challenge the powerful on the public stage.

---

6. See 2 *Macc* 5:16; 6:3–6; *Ps. Sol.* 1:8; 2:3, 13; 8:13; *Ass. Mos.* 5:3; *Ant.* 20:166–67.

Communities Resisting Fragmentation
Q AND THE WORK OF JAMES C. SCOTT

Melanie Johnson-DeBaufre

In *Domination and the Arts of Resistance*, political scientist James C. Scott sets out "to suggest how we might more successfully read, interpret, and understand the often fugitive political conduct of subordinate groups" (Scott: 17). Scott challenges the notion that the powerless regularly "speak truth to power"; in contrast, he suggests throughout his book that the public performance of the weak and dominated is most often one of dissembling and posturing (1). The subjugated do resist dominating power. But such resistance thrives in the "hidden transcript"—a range of offstage physical and verbal practices that register dissent from the performance of power typically embodied in the "public transcript." This hidden transcript can only be seen directly when it erupts into public discourse in moments of intoxication, charismatic action, or open rebellion. Otherwise, we must look for it in what Scott calls "infrapolitics," that is, the places where the hidden transcript appears—usually disguised and anonymous—in "low profile forms of resistance" (14–19). If historians and cultural critics do not attend to these often-neglected forms of resistance, argues Scott, they risk missing the resistance altogether, and thus fail to explain the communal force behind large-scale eruptions of resistance to domination.

This *Semeia* volume emerges from an attempt to open a conversation about how Scott's work on the "arts of resistance" among subordinate groups might be useful for thinking about early Christian texts and their formation in the context of Roman imperial power. In particular, we explore whether and how Scott's conclusions can make sense of the rhetoric of the sayings source Q. Scott's conclusions about the political lives of subordinates and their strategies of resistance depend upon the assumption that "similar structures of domination, other things being equal, tend to provoke responses and forms of resistance that also bear a family resemblance to one another" (21–22). He admits that in order to make broader assertions about the politics of subordinates he has "run roughshod" over the differences between the various situations of domination (such as North American slavery and French serfdom). He suggests that "culturally specific and historically deep" analyses of each situation would further demonstrate and elaborate his observations (22). In this sense, historians of early Christianity should investigate the details of the systems of domination particular to the Roman Empire.

In this essay, however, I utilize Scott's observations about the conflict and mutuality of subordinates under divisive systems of domination to examine the rhetoric of Q. I suggest that Q deploys two communal images—the children of *Sophia* and the *basileia* of God—to counter the fragmentation and atomization of the powerless that is characteristic of situations of domination.

Before turning to a discussion of these images in Q 7:31–35 and Q 11:14–20, it is important to take note of the common ground between Scott's work and the work of feminist biblical interpretation. Like many feminist exegetes, Scott approaches his material with the assumption that things are not as they seem—that unequal power relations have created a historical record that does not reflect the views and values of subordinated people. These must be reconstructed, he argues, from the gestures, euphemisms, slogans, and folk traditions scattered throughout the public transcript. This approach resembles the way feminists use a hermeneutics of suspicion and read against the grain of texts in order to reconstruct marginalized voices (Schüssler Fiorenza 2001:175–77, 183–86).

Scott approaches his task of reading against the grain in two ways. At the level of theory, he evaluates and criticizes prevailing notions of hegemony, false consciousness, and ideology (70–96). He concludes that these theories are inadequate for understanding the political lives of subordinates and suggests revising these theories based on a new reading of the evidence. For Scott, these theories misread the evidence when they take the public transcript—which shows subordinates as compliant and quiescent—at face value. Recognizing that the expression of resistance in the public transcript is often undesirable for elites and unsafe for subordinates, Scott suggests that, "unless one can penetrate the official transcript of both subordinates and elites, a reading of the social evidence will almost always represent a confirmation of the status quo in hegemonic terms" (90).

At the level of data-analysis, Scott proposes new interpretive frameworks that recognize the euphemisms, grumbling, and symbolic and ritualized inversions of subordinates as significant strategies of resistance (136–82). This alternative approach to the data effectively reads against the grain of the public transcript and its presentation of subordinates as cooperative and obeisant by re-reading these very acts of deference as signs of a lively hidden transcript of resistance. For Scott, this counter-reading is necessary because "the recovery of nonhegemonic voices and practices of subject peoples requires ... a fundamentally different form of analysis than the analysis of the elites, owing to the constraints under which they are produced" (19).

In my own work, I have taken a similar approach to the interpretation of Q (Johnson-DeBaufre 2005). Like Scott, I begin with an interest in hearing the nonhegemonic voices of the early Jesus movement. By analyzing the frameworks of traditional interpretations of Q, one can see that they tend to re-iterate the perspective of the text and, therefore, continue to hide the values and voices of the powerless. I suggest, therefore, that we consider alternative interpretations that can read against the grain of both the text and their prevailing meanings in order to imagine and reconstruct subordinated voices. In this essay, I offer alternative readings of Q 7:31–35 and 11:14–20 that do not re-inscribe the rhetoric of conflict depicted in the texts. Drawing on Scott's observations about atomization and the logic of domination, I suggest that these texts reflect traces of a hidden transcript of resistance to fragmentation by arguing for solidarity in the face of divisiveness.

Reinscribing Fragmentation

As I discuss below, Q 7:31–35 and 11:14–20 present stories of conflict. In the first text, sayings of Jesus are deployed to critique "this generation's" habit of acting like children in the marketplace and slandering Jesus and John. In the second, Jesus counters a charge that he colludes with Beelzebul by claiming that his exorcisms point to the *basileia* of God. It is a common assumption that the bone of contention in such gospel controversy stories is the singular significance or authority of Jesus. Because of this many locate the *Sitz im Leben* of these controversy texts in the process of early Christian identity formation vis à vis other Jews (see Mack: 177–78).

Several Q scholars approach Q 7:31–35 as a text that is part of what has been termed Q's "announcement of judgment on 'this generation'" (Lührmann: 93; see also Kloppenborg 1987; and Jacobson). Within this framework, "this generation" represents all of Israel (Lührmann: 93) or that part of Israel that has rejected Jesus and his teachings as promoted by the Q community (Kloppenborg 1987:167; Jacobson: 183). Some interpreters resist this dichotomy between the Q community and their fellow Jews, but they retain a dichotomy between insiders (the Q community) and outsiders who reject the community or the message (Tuckett: 201; Horsley and Draper: 299).

Within this framework of judgment, Q 7:31–35 criticizes "this generation" because they have rejected the messages of John and Jesus—the messengers of *Sophia* (see Q 11:49). This view associates Jesus and John with the children in the marketplace who pipe and dirge and focuses on the response to John and Jesus as the central problem being addressed by the unit. Thus the children of *Sophia* are those who have responded positively to the message (the Q community), and the people of "this generation" are their Jewish contemporaries who have rejected the Q community and their message (cf. Johnson-DeBaufre 2003). From this perspective, Q 7:31–35 makes sense within the historical-rhetorical context of identity formation among competing groups of first-century Palestinian Jews. Interpreting this text as group-boundary polemic, therefore, ironically produces a text that functions rhetorically to create the very divisions it seeks to criticize.

A similar interpretive trend appears in the exegesis of Q 11:14–20. This text is routinely viewed as attempting to create boundaries between first-century Jewish groups by emphasizing the unique role of Jesus in bringing the *basileia* of God. Despite the argument in 11:19 that Jesus and the sons of his accusers both exorcize on the side of God, most interpreters conclude that the text functions rhetorically to assert the difference between the Jesus movement and other Jewish groups.

The theological expectation that Jesus must be unique vis-à-vis other Jewish exorcists has played a significant role in the exegesis of 11:14–20. Indeed there is a long tradition of exegetical wrangling over the fit between 11:19 and 11:20. Scholars have tried to resolve the apparent equation of Jesus and other Jewish exorcists by putting distance between the two verses with arguments about redactional layers or by proposing alternative and more theologically acceptable meanings for 11:19 (see Kloppenborg 1987:123–24). Michael Humphries, who argues well that 11:19–20 puts Jesus and other Jewish exorcists on common ground, still interprets the passage within the overall framework of community identity formation:

> It is also quite clear, however, that Jesus' response turns the tables on his accusers. Insofar as they refuse to recognize the power of the kingdom in his exorcisms, they find themselves in danger of standing outside the kingdom. No one belonging to the kingdom of God could identify Jesus' exorcisms, or any exorcism for that matter, as satanic. If the accusers do not accept the "quality in common" expressed in verses 19 and 20, if they do not grant to Jesus what they grant to their own sons, then it is precisely this failure of recognition that renders the accusers themselves as deviant. *And so a sharp distinction is indeed established.* The exchange between Jesus and his accusers constitutes a battle over who represents the legitimate expression of Israel. (33; my emphasis)

The view that the community's identity as a "legitimate expression of Israel" is at stake in the text necessitates that the accusation of collusion is answered not only by a defense of Jesus' collusion with God, but also by a process of counter-stigmatization in which the tables are turned and the accusers are rendered outsiders (Humphries: 33; see also Kirk 1998:328–30). Once again, interpreters see a social divide when, as I argue below, the text argues against such divides both in its logic and its imagery.

Fragmentation as a Strategy of the Powerful

If we take some of Scott's insights seriously, we might ask whether these conflict stories reflect the fragmentation of subordinated groups under a system of domination[1]—in this case, the fragmentation of Jewish groups under Roman imperialism. According to Scott, the "logic of domination is to bring about the complete atomization and surveillance of subordinates" (128). Systems of involuntary subordination achieve ideological hegemony when "subordinates are more or less completely atomized and kept under close observation" (Scott: 82–83). Citing Foucault's dictum that "Solitude is the primary condition of total submission," Scott notes that this "totalitarian fantasy" of complete atomization and surveillance is possible only in some modern penal institutions, thought-reform camps, and psychiatric wards (Foucault: 237; Scott: 83). This level of individual atomization and surveillance is impossible in large-scale systems of domination or in peasant societies where subordinates have more opportunity for communal interaction.

For subordinate communities or groups, there are places—such as separate quarters, family groups, or religious gatherings—where subordinates have discursive freedom. These social sites are not only physical spaces, they are also "linguistic codes, dialects, and gestures" (Scott: 121) that are beyond the ken of dominant powers. It is in these social sites where the hidden transcript takes shape as a "nonhegemonic, contrapuntal, dissident, subversive discourse" (Scott: 25). Because the hidden transcript takes shape in these social spaces where subordinates are free from the eyes and ears of the powerful, however, it is no surprise that systems of domination prefer to dissolve and disperse these "sequestered social sites at which such resistance can be nurtured and given meaning" (Scott: 20).

Scott's discussion of the extreme forms of modern domination and their penchant for physical atomization and surveillance of individuals, suggests that the separation, diffusion, and fragmentation of subordinate groups also work in the interest of dominating powers. For example, Scott notes that when subordinate groups are separated from each other by geography and cultural background, domination systems persist despite their "inability to incorporate ideologically the least advantaged" (25). Indeed economic systems that produce the need for smaller groups or individuals to struggle for daily subsistence works to diffuse the collective will of subordinates (Scott: 86). In addition, systems built on the individual

---

1. Scott's analysis draws on studies of institutionalized forms of domination such as slavery, colonialism, serfdom, untouchability, and racism (Scott, *Domination and the Arts of Resistance*, 20). These forms of domination share certain features: (1) ideologies that rationalize power imbalances; (2) rituals and customs that routinize and naturalize these ideologies; (3) status systems based on birth with little room for mobility; (4) a strong sense of the personal power of the ruler (master, Brahmin, etc.) over the ruled (slave, untouchable, etc.); and (5) an extensive "offstage social existence" where subordinates might "develop a shared critique of power" (21).

relationships between patron and client or lord and vassal create a public transcript that assumes that "there are no horizontal links among subordinates" (Scott: 62). Thus it is common for gatherings of subordinates to be carefully orchestrated as "official rituals"—parades, authorized local festivals, gatherings for instruction or punishment—so that it is clear that the assembly of subordinates must be at the consent of "the lord, patron, or master, *who represents the only link joining them*" (Scott: 62; emphasis original). It is no surprise, therefore, that Scott can adduce various examples of efforts on the part of dominating powers to forbid or control the unauthorized gathering of subordinates (62–65, see also 124–28). Scott concludes that, "large, autonomous gatherings of subordinates are threatening to domination because of the license they promote among normally disaggregated inferiors" (65).

If physical separation and diffusion is advantageous to ruling powers, it follows that cultural and ideological fragmentation of subordinates also works in favor of domination. For example, "slave owners in both the West Indies and North America ... preferred to bring together a labor force of the greatest linguistic and ethnic diversity" in order to minimize solidarity among slaves (Scott: 127–28). Studies of the western working class suggest that the groups that have the strongest solidarity and militancy against their employers are groups that have a high degree of homogeneity and "a relative lack of differentiation within (and mobility out of) their trade," such as miners and seamen (Scott: 134–35). Predictably then, it is a common practice across economies for "management to cultivate collaborators and favorites among the workforce" (Scott: 131) in order to encourage competition above camaraderie among workers. Indeed Scott identifies the cultivation of competition between subordinates as the primary companion strategy to atomization and surveillance for achieving ideological hegemony. He suggests that, "the expectation that one will eventually be able to exercise the domination one endures today is a strong incentive serving to legitimate patterns of domination" (Scott: 82).

It should be no surprise then that stories about Jesus' encounters with hostile Jewish authorities and about conflicts between groups of Jews (such as the Pharisees and the disciples) appear in the public transcript of the gospel narratives. In my view, the Gospel narratives—as written and transmitted texts—qualify as part of the public transcript because they are part of the historical record which, as Scott notes, is produced and perpetuated in the interests of elites (87). Like any other public transcript, the Gospels may contain infrapolitical traces of the hidden transcript, but identifying them as such is a matter of interpretation. As many feminist critics have noted, the biblical text may contain traces of resistance or emancipatory visions or may be interpreted as liberatory (sometimes despite itself), however, the text has been produced in and reflects a thoroughly kyriarchal context. This suggests that while we read the gospel conflict narratives in order to get a glimpse of the hidden transcript, we should keep in mind that the inclusion of these texts does not give us direct access to such a transcript. Indeed, for dominating powers, stories of fragmentation among subordinates are acceptable and indeed crucial to cultivating loyalty and discouraging solidarity.

The logic of fragmentation, however, does not go unanswered by subordinates. Scott suggests rather that, "subordinates everywhere implicitly understand that if the logic of domination prevails, they will be reduced to a Hobbesian war of all against all" (128). The threat to ruling powers of social cohesion and solidarity among subordinates, therefore, is also confirmed by the elaborate ways in which subordinate groups create and even attempt to enforce solidarity and conformity among their members (Scott: 129). Sometimes this can turn violent as strikebreakers or police informants are killed or assaulted.

> For the most part, though, subordinates rarely have much in the way of coercive force to deploy among themselves. . . . Conformity, instead, rests heavily upon social pressure. Granting the *relatively* democratic aspect of social pressure among peers, these mechanisms of social control are painful and often ugly. Slander, character assassination, gossip, rumor, public gestures of contempt, shunning, curses, backbiting, outcasting are only a few of the sanctions that subordinates can bring to bear on each other. (Scott: 131)

Slander and outcasting are precisely the kinds of social control that we see in gospel conflict stories such as Q 7:31–35 and Q 11:14–20. If Scott's observations about the efforts of dominated groups to resist atomization are correct, then these stories of social conflict among subordinated Jewish groups may themselves be a trace of a hidden transcript that highly values and promotes group solidarity in the face of dominating power. If this is the case, then it may be useful to look again at conflict or controversy stories in the gospels for signs of a struggle over fragmentation and solidarity within first-century communities.

Fragmentation and Solidarity in Q

Applying Scott's observation that conflict among subordinates may point to a hidden transcript of solidarity, I interpret the rhetoric of Q 7:31–35 and Q 11:14–20 as addressing a problem of fragmentation by advocating group solidarity through communal imagery. In these passages, the sayings of Jesus are deployed to criticize the audience's habit of slandering each other. Both texts advocate that the contentious audience recognize their common identity as children of *Sophia* (Q 7:31–35) and members of the *basileia* of God (Q 11:14–20).[2]

---

2. I have left the Greek term *sophia* ("wisdom") untranslated so that the gender of the word is apparent. The feminine *Sophia* more clearly brings to mind the personification of God in the Hebrew Scriptures and apocrypha (Prov 8:1–36

Wisdom Is Justified by All Her Children

In Q 7:31–35, Jesus criticizes "this generation" for their in-fighting and reminds them of their common identity and responsibility as children of *Sophia*. The passage consists of a brief simile (vv. 31–32), an application of the simile to the world of the audience (vv. 33–34), and a concluding aphorism (v. 35):

> 31 To what am I to compare this generation and what is it like? 32 It is like children seated in the marketplaces, who, addressing the others, say: We fluted for you, but you would not dance; we sang a dirge, but you would not cry. 33 For John came, neither eating nor drinking, and you say: He has a demon! 34 The son of humanity came eating and drinking, and you say: Look! A person [who is] a glutton and drunkard, a friend of tax collectors and sinners. 35 But *Sophia* [Wisdom] is vindicated by [all] her children. (my translation; for the Greek, see Robinson: 140–49)

The passage is part of a larger section of Q that focuses on the values of the movement, of which both John and Jesus are a part (Johnson-DeBaufre 2005:62–77). These units pose questions about the importance of Jesus and John but ultimately redirect the audience's attention to the *basileia* and the least in the movement. At the conclusion of this section, Q 7:31–35 presses the followers of Jesus and John to recognize their common ground.

"To what am I to compare this generation and what is it like?" The text begins with a question that invites comparison. Put colloquially, Jesus says to the audience, "What are the people of our time like? What's wrong with

---

and 9:1–6 and *Wisdom of Solomon* 7:22–8:1) than the neutral and abstract notion of God's wisdom. I have capitalized *Sophia* because God's Wisdom is personified in Q as a parent who has children (Q 7:35) and as one who sends out prophets and sages (Q 11:49). I have not translated the Greek term *basileia* for two reasons. First, the English term "kingdom" implies a territorial sense rather than God's kingly rule or reign, which most exegetes agree is the proper translation of the expression *basileia tou theou* (see Denis Duling, "Kingdom of God, Kingdom of Heaven," *Anchor Bible Dictionary* 4 [1992], 50). Second, I agree with Elisabeth Schüssler Fiorenza's point that: "most reviews of scholarship on the meaning of the expression "*Basileia* of God" do not even discuss its political significance in a context where people must have thought of the Roman Empire when they heard the word" ("To Follow the Vision: The Jesus Movement as *Basileia* Movement," in *Liberating Eschatology* [ed. Margaret A. Farley and Serene Jones; Louisville: Westminster John Knox, 1999], 134). She recommends such terms as "empire" or "domain" in order to "underscore linguistically the oppositional character of the empire/commonweal of G*d to that of the Roman Empire" (ibid.). She notes that "such translation is generally not understood in an oppositional sense, however, but rather as ascribing to G*d imperial, monarchical power." Because of this she chooses to leave the word untranslated in order to "use it as a tensive symbol that evokes a whole range of theological meanings and at the same time seeks to foster a critical awareness of their ambiguity" (ibid.). I agree with Schüssler Fiorenza's assessment of the situation and have also left the term untranslated.

us?" The answer that he gives stings: we are like children sitting in the marketplaces judging each other. One group judges another because they would not join their dance. The other group sneers back that the pipers would not cry at their dirge. Wendy Cotter has shown that the force of the simile lies in the image of the children and its distinctive vocabulary. Although the content of the taunts implies childlike games, the children are "seated" (*kathemenois*) and formally "addressing" (*prosfonounta*) "the others" in the marketplace. This language is consistently used of adults who sit as judges in the agora's civic courts (Cotter: 295–302). She concludes that "no matter how these 'children' adopt dignified behavior, it is plain from the content of their objections, that they are, after all, only shallow children" (302).

The text leads the reader to view the subsequent slanders made against John and Jesus in light of the opening simile. If the speakers are like children play-acting at being grown-up in the agora, their accusations about Jesus and John are likewise childish. The accusations fly between the two groups. We might imagine the two parts of the children's taunts (and the criticisms of John and Jesus) being spoken antiphonally by opposing groups (represented in the chart by *italics* and **bold**):

A		"*We fluted*	*and you* did not dance"
	B	"**We sang a dirge**	*and you* did not mourn"
A'		For John came not eating and drinking	*and you* say he has a demon"
	B'	The son of humanity came eating and drinking	**and you say he is a glutton and a drunk**"

One side (the *italics* group) calls to the other (the **bold** group) and accuses them of not dancing when the *italics* group fluted. Then the **bold** group retorts that they sang a dirge and you (*italics* group) did not mourn. The application then applies this image of the judgmental and uncooperative children to those who judge John and those who judge Jesus on the basis of their eating practices. "Indeed," Jesus says to the *italics* group, "John came not dancing and you ostracize him." "Indeed," Jesus says to the **bold** group, "I (the son of humanity) came not mourning and you criticize him (me)." The *italics* group both flutes and does not mourn and the **bold** group both refuses to dance and sings a dirge; the **bold** group (represented by John) does not eat/drink and says that he who does is a glutton and the *italics* group (represented by Jesus) eats/drinks and says that he who does not has a demon (see further Johnson-DeBaufre 2003).

The aphorism in Q 7:35 reverses the characterizations of the judgmental children by asserting that *Sophia* is justified by all her children. Although "this generation" is characteristically factional and divisive along lines of difference, children of *Sophia* are *all* children who prove her right or "acknowledge her to be right" (Piper: 168). The text affirms *both* John and Jesus and, therefore, all the "children" who flute or dirge, as children who vindicate *Sophia*. Their differences—represented here by eating practices—are insignificant given their common ground as children of *Sophia*. Thus "this generation" can be like children in a marketplace or like children of *Sophia*. With this familial image, the text invites the audience (who are contiguous with "this generation") to understand itself not as children who bicker and judge each other according to their differences, but rather as children of the same parent—the *Sophia* of God—who recognize their common kinship.

The Basileia *of God Has Come Upon You*

The struggle between fragmentation and solidarity appears again in Q 11:14–20, where Jesus is charged with colluding with satanic powers. He delivers a memorable set of sayings that point out that neither empires nor houses divided against themselves can stand. This critique of divisiveness is the first step in his response to those who would place him on the side of satanic powers. Rather than revile his accusers, Q's Jesus uses the common ground between his exorcisms and those of the sons of his accusers to claim that all their exorcisms are on the side of the *basileia* of God (Johnson-DeBaufre 2005:131–64).

The passage consists of a short exorcism scene (v. 14) that provides the occasion for the challenge (v. 15). Verses 17–20 provide Jesus' riposte:

> 14 And he cast out a mute demon. And once the demon was cast out, the mute person spoke and the crowds were amazed. 15 But some said, "He casts out demons by Beelzebul, the ruler of demons!" 16 And others were seeking a sign from him. 17 But knowing their thoughts, he said to them, "Every *basileia* divided against itself is laid waste, and every house divided against itself will not stand." 18a "And if Satan is divided against himself, how will his *basileia* stand? 19 And if I by Beelzebul cast out demons, by whom do your sons cast [them] out? Therefore, they shall be your judges. 20 But if it is by the finger of God that I cast out demons, then the *basileia* of God has come upon you. (my translation; for the Greek text, see Robinson: 222–33)

The accusation from "some" in the crowd grants that Jesus casts out demons, but claims that he performs them with the power of Beelzebul, the ruler of the demons. The name Beelzebul is probably connected to "Baal," the ancient Canaanite enemy of Yahweh.[3] Thus the charge attributes Jesus'

---

3. *Beel* is the Greek transliteration of the Hebrew *Baal*, which means "owner," "lord," or "prince." Michael Humphries provides an important review of scholarship on identifying Beelzebul in *Christian Origins*, 13–22. He concludes that Beelzebul here "is a provincial manifestation of Yahweh's traditional chief rival, namely, 'prince Baal, lord of the earth' (*zbl Bl ars*), whose name here has been shortened to the simple form of 'Prince Baal' (*Bl zbl*)" (30).

power to exorcize to a foreign or non-Israelite deity. It is "an effort to label Jesus as an outsider," as in league with the enemies of Yahweh (Humphries: 29). The charge itself aims to divide—attempting to slander Jesus by claiming his allegiance to the enemy.

Jesus' initial response does not seem to answer the charge of collusion with the enemy. Instead, he draws on common knowledge to expose the absurdity of the opponents' claim. In effect, he asks, "How could I be in league with demons when everyone knows that a divided kingdom will fall?" Rather than defending his own exorcisms, he implicitly criticizes the accusers' behavior by pointing to the self-defeating effects of divisiveness itself. "Every *basileia* divided against itself is laid waste, and every house divided against itself will not stand." The general rule is proven in the specific case: "if Satan is divided against himself, how will his *basileia* stand" (v. 18a)?

While we might expect Jesus to turn the tables on his accusers, defining them as outsiders, he instead appeals to their common ground. "And if I cast out demons by Beelzebul, by whom do your sons cast them out" (v. 19)? This question links the evaluation of Jesus' exorcisms to those of the accusers' sons. Thus Jesus and the sons of his accusers stand on common ground against the demonic powers. If he casts out by Beelzebul, so do they. If they do not, then neither does he. Arland Jacobson rightly insists that "Q 11:19–20 implies that the other Jewish exorcists do indeed cast out demons by the power of God" (Jacobson: 163; see also, Piper: 123). The success of the argument rests squarely on the position that the accusers' sons and Jesus are on the same side. Both stand against Satan in their exorcisms. If the accusers grant this common ground, they must accept the proposition that follows in Q 11:20 that Jesus' exorcisms—like the sons' exorcisms—draw on the power of God.

Q 11:20 functions as a third conditional construction that clinches the refutation of the accusation: "But if it is by the finger of God that I cast out demons, then the *basileia* of God has come upon you." This verse echoes but reverses the accusation of 11:15 by replacing "by Beelzebul" with "by the finger of God" in the protasis. The apodosis then reverses the language about Satan's basileia in 11:17–18 to identify Jesus' actions with God's *basileia*. With the exorcisms of both Jesus and the sons of his accusers firmly located on the side of God's *basileia*, the text reverses the charge of Jesus' collusion with Beelzebul while also making a critique of those who would divide God's *basileia* with such slander. These sayings are followed by two parables (vv. 21–22 and 24–26) and one saying (v. 23) that all focus on the imagery of two competing *basileiai* and the victory ensured to the stronger one. Implicit is a plea for the solidarity of all those who are part of the *basileia* or household of God (see Johnson-DeBaufre 2005:154–64).

Communal Visions as Resistance

In both of these Q texts communal images are deployed rhetorically to counteract the divisive effects of in-group slander. If dominating powers benefit from the fragmentation and atomization of subordinate groups, these texts might represent both evidence of pressure towards fragmentation and "strategies by which subordinate groups manage to insinuate their resistance, in disguised forms, into the public transcript" (Scott: 136).

Scott's discussion of efforts to resist atomization among subordinate groups focuses chiefly on what he calls "often painful and ugly" forms of social control (131). These texts in Q suggest, however, that positive communal images or slogans such as "the children of *Sophia*" and the "*basileia* of God" also function to create solidarity and mutuality in the face of fragmentation. Scott confirms this possibility indirectly in his discussion of charismatic acts or speeches, which appear in the public discourse and which motivate people to common action or purpose. These are not merely occasions when subordinates are manipulated into thinking or behaving in a certain way. Rather, for Scott, they are times when the hidden transcript goes public in a way that subordinates can recognize their mutuality with each other. These moments can be a time when

> subordinates can fully recognize the full extent to which their claims, their dreams, their anger is shared by other subordinates with whom they have not been in direct touch.... Assuming they define themselves as acting within some larger frame of reference (for example, nationality, mother tongue, religion, and so on) they are likely to be susceptible to the same kinds of public acts, the same forms of symbolic assertion and refusal, and the same moral claims. (Scott: 223–24)

Within this framework, it is also possible that common religious "dreams" of reversal—such as the "*basileia* of God"—could emerge from the hidden transcript to promote the same social cohesion subordinates seek to achieve through divisive and ugly means such as slander and backbiting. While Scott warns against seeing such mutuality among subordinates as "some mystical link of human solidarity," he affirms that, "if there seems to be an instantaneous mutuality and commonness of purpose, they are surely derived from the hidden transcript" (223). While we should not idealize these common dreams of reversal, we also should not underestimate them since, as Scott notes, "the millennial theme of a world turned upside down, a world in which the last shall be first and the first last, can be found in nearly every major cultural tradition in which inequities of power, wealth, and status have been pronounced" (80).

Slogans such as "children of *Sophia*" and "*basileia* of God" can give us a glimpse of the common ground among Jewish social groups that might emerge as sites of mutuality under a situation of domination. Communal imagery is deployed even in the context of the distinctly negative imagery and tone of John's opening speech in Q (3:7–9, 16–17) and in the speech against the Pharisees (11:42–59). While the audience is charged to "bear fruit worthy of repentance" (3:8) and to attend to justice, mercy, and faithfulness (11:42), the appeals rest on common claims: as the children of Abraham (3:7) and as sharing a common tradition, exemplified here by tithing mint, dill, and cumin (11:42). Jesus does not reject the practices of the Pharisees, but urges them to continue without neglecting the practices of justice and mercy. There is a general consensus among Q scholars that the inscribed audience of these text is an "outsider" audience, whether unrepentant Jews, religious leaders, or all of Israel and that their negative depiction in Q resulted from the Q people's experience of rejection. By using a framework of subordinate groups resisting fragmentation in situations of domination, however, these appeals to common ground may suggest that Q is far less interested in presenting and defending its view of Jesus against opponents than in using the Jesus tradition to think with about communal identity and purpose.

In *The First Gospel*, Arland Jacobson suggests that the study of Q "requires of us some exegetical imagination to interpret it as a 'Jewish' rather than as a 'Christian' document, granted, of course, that 'Jewish' has no single meaning" (2). I have applied critical imagination (see Schüssler Fiorenza 2001:179–82) to Q 7:31–35 and Q 11:14–20, de-centering the identity of Jesus and the Jesus movement as the central interest of the text. If we begin with the assumption that Jesus and his accusers and the audience of Q and other Jews are subordinates within complex systems of imperial domination, then it becomes possible that these texts function rhetorically in historical situations other than group identity formation. I have argued that the problem being addressed in Q 7:31–35 is not resistance to John and Jesus but rather the judgmental in-fighting of the people of "this generation," who play a divisive game when they judge each other on the basis of different eating practices. Similarly, Q 11:14–20 defends Jesus' exorcisms as part of the realization of the *basileia* of God by granting that the sons of his accusers—other Jewish exorcists—are also on the side of God. The accusation of demon collusion itself is a divisive act that is countered by Jesus' reminder that a *basileia* divided against itself cannot stand.

Scott's insights on the atomizing logic of domination and the resistance of subordinates to such logic opens a space for re-reading conflict stories in the gospels for infrapolitical traces of the hidden transcript. I argue that these Q texts make as much if not more sense as internal struggles over the values and visions of the communities of first-century Palestine who dared to imagine alternatives to the prevailing notions of household and *basileia*. This may suggest that the Q community told this controversy story not to assert the singularity of Jesus or the superiority of their claim on the Israelite tradition but rather to make a case for the communal vision of the *basileia* of God over and against the *basileia* of Satan.

Claiming the Common Ground

Like Scott, many feminist and minority biblical interpreters have set out to recover nonhegemonic voices and to read against the grain of both the texts and the history of their interpretation. As mentioned above, Scott's book clearly sets out "to suggest how we might more successfully read, interpret, and understand the often fugitive political conduct of subordinate groups" (17). Beyond his interest in understanding the politics of resistance among Malay peasants (17), he does not further articulate why this is an important task to undertake. Are the quest for more accurate historiography and the solution to persistent intellectual problems sufficient reasons to read against the grain of the public transcript? Feminist and minority interpreters have made the important insight that the interests and social location of the interpreter have a significant impact on how one interprets the data and tells history. Our perspectives, experiences, and expectations shape what can be imagined when we write the history of early Christianity. Because of this, scholars must not only re-read the data as Scott and I have done, but also identify the frameworks that shape their interpretation and articulate their own social location and interests in the ongoing process of interpretation.

I locate my own attempt to re-read Q in the recognition that biblical interpretation is part of the ongoing public transcript of our time. As I have argued elsewhere, biblical scholarship on Christian origins participates in the larger contemporary debates about Christian identity in a diverse world (Johnson-DeBaufre 2005:27–42 and 115–30). Contemporary struggles over religious difference and the history of Christian anti-Judaism focus my own attention on aspects of the tradition that foster and give a history to voices of solidarity and common cause against systems of domination. This project thus becomes important not only historically but also ethically:

> Such an investigation is important particularly because of the frightening increase of neo-Nazism, racism, and antiforeign sentiments in the United States and Europe. The worldwide increase of the practice of hate and the language of oppression in the name of religion underscores the need for interreligious dialogues, especially between the so-called Abrahamic religions, Judaism, Islam, and Christianity. Such interreligious dialogues are, however, of interest not only to religious people. Since religion often plays a divisive role in nationalistic and antidemocratic struggles, interreligious dialogue must fashion an ethos and ethics that can contribute to the solution of hostilities rather than continuing to fuel national and international conflicts. (Schüssler Fiorenza 2000:67)

I propose these interpretations, therefore, not only because they are historically plausible and textually defensible, but also because they are ethically preferable. Although the disciplines of the academy often do not encourage such self-critical reflexivity among scholars, I suggest that Scott is a clear ally in this project of ethically engaged historical reconstruction.

The mythopoeic language of clashing *basileiai* and the call to choose sides may point to the social and historical experience of Jewish communities under the dehumanizing and divisive effects of foreign rule. The solidarity of God's people is envisioned by the text as necessary to the victory of God's *basileia*. In Q 11:14–20, Q's Jesus makes a case for common cause among those who attempt to expel the demonic forces that ravage the people. That common cause is the healing and liberating work of the *basileia*. It is significant, therefore, that when Q's Jesus does turn to delineating difference between people, it is precisely the values of the *basileia* of God that are at the center of the dispute. In Q 11:42–52, Jesus criticizes the Pharisees for what Alan Kirk convincingly calls "ostentatious displays of prestige and rank" (4). Thus for Q, the Pharisees' notion of the *basileia* of God or the "way things should be" too closely resembles the *basileiai* of the world (Q 4:5–6). According to Q, those valued the most in the *basileia* of God are the poor (6:20), the sick (7:22; 10:9), the least (7:28), and the weak (10:23). Those values stand in sharp contrast with the values of Roman imperial systems of domination. In this sense, we may hear a whisper of an ancient version of the kind of ideological reversal that Scott argues is "part and parcel of the religio-political equipment of historically disadvantaged groups" (91). If we have, it is not because the gospel texts or the history of interpretation have simply recorded or even amplified the voices of resistance, but because, for the sake of our future, we have made special efforts to hear them.

Response

The Work of James C. Scott and Q
A Response

William R. Herzog II

When applied to the New Testament, the work of James C. Scott has proven to be versatile and endurable as the essays in part two of this volume of Semeia Studies demonstrate. In light of the insights found in these essays, it might be useful to ask why Scott's work has been so fruitful even though his field research has been in peasant communities quite distinct from the villages of Galilee in the first century. In light of this fact, we could ask, What elements in his work transfer to such good effect?

Scott's work is relevant and valuable because he has conducted his field work in villages and social settings in advanced agrarian societies where the few dominate the many, and wherever power relations are asymmetrical, communication assumes more complex forms. If one uses Scott's work, it is no longer possible to assume that texts communicate in a straightforward way but may assume a variety of guises and disguises. Things are not what they seem, and it is often difficult to read between the lines and attend to the unspoken or submerged subtexts as well as the so-called "plain meaning" of the text. This situation, in turn, increases the difficulty of reading texts but promises to reveal some of their hidden meaning as well. Scott speaks about this situation in terms of public transcripts and hidden transcripts. The dominant control the content and use of public transcripts while peasant villagers and other marginalized figures nurture a very different version of events, history as seen from below and codified in hidden transcripts, that is, hidden from the eyes and ears of the elites who seek to impose their ideological will on their vulnerable villagers.

The reason for this situation lies in the nature of agrarian societies where the few dominate the many and choreograph the public relations between the dominant and the subordinated classes. In this context, the rulers use texts to communicate public transcripts, inscribing and privileging their views at the expense of the visions of the ruled. In a good deal of biblical scholarship, practitioners have been content to limit their inquiries and discussions of texts to the ways they function as expressions of the

211

public transcripts of the elites, reproducing their ideologies and repackaging their hegemony in varied forms of theological discourse.

But Scott has provided a model for listening to the same texts in order to capture some echoes of the hidden transcripts of the dominated. Such communication will always be compromised by the need to articulate its message within the seemingly limited confines of the public transcript but, human ingenuity being what it is, peasants find ways to express their reading of their context in terms that support their "little tradition" version of events, that is, a popular or folk version of the "great tradition" of the urban elites. Scott's work offers a hermeneutical tool for re-reading a public transcript text in such a way that it may reveal genuine aspects of the hidden transcripts of the oppressed.

Scott's hermeneutic affords contemporary interpreters of the Jesus traditions and Q materials with a distinctive opportunity to hear voices long silenced. These traditions read through the interpretive lens developed by Scott may allow us to hear the voices of the oppressed and the dominated who dwell in what Paulo Freire called "a culture of silence." The Jesus traditions and Q materials may provide a glimpse into history seen from below rather than provide just another variation of history seen from above. At the very least, Scott's approach creates a chance to hear a wider spectrum of voices and see a broader spectrum of visions than ever before. Since the materials in the Jesus traditions and the Q materials do not belong to the ruling elites, they afford a cache of resources that may enable us to glimpse some of the hidden transcripts that emerge from these materials. So, in an unexpected way, the biblical materials and the work of Scott are compatible with each other.

Two of the essays in this section illustrate the interpretive possibilities involved in taking seriously Scott's view of matters. Alan Kirk selects a particular moment in the scheme of things when we are confronted with a rarity, namely, "a public declaration of the hidden transcript." This is not a typical moment but an extraordinary moment when the rituals of decorum and subordination are abandoned in favor of a more direct challenge to the powerful. Usually, this occurs in response to new depredations directed against the peasant villages as the result of a colonial power asserting greater control over its domains or a subsistence crisis within the peasant village fomented by the escalating greed of the ruling class. Such moves usually require further stigmatization of peasants, a move which is resisted by the peasants who then declare their counter-stigmatizing campaign more openly than they normally would do. Kirk's subsequent reading of the Beelzebul controversy and the woes that follow provides a clear focus for his discussion and a good example of the strategies at work.

Kirk reads the controversy and its accompanying woes as an example of the management of stigmatizing and counter-stigmatizing. Since any public declaration of the hidden transcript threatens to upset the balance of power in an agrarian society, elites can be counted on to respond by stigmatizing and demonizing such expressions. This situation calls for a strong response in the form of counter-stigmatizing. All of this provides a context for understanding the Beelzebul controversy and the woes that follow. Through his use of Scott's interpretive work, Kirk has provided a fresh way of reading familiar passages.

Kirk has selected an extraordinary moment in the cycle of conflict when submerged grievances finally erupt like a volcano. While Scott's approach can certainly accommodate this moment into his framework, it does not capture the more subtle forms of everyday resistance that may also be identified by him. Still, the selection of an extraordinary moment in the pattern of domination and resistance may suggest ways to apply Scott's work to more ordinary ideological "weapons of the weak."

The same could be said of Melanie Johnson-DeBaufre's essay which adds an interest in feminist biblical interpretation to the work of Scott. Both Scott and feminist interpretation have a stake in reading texts against the grain in an effort to recover the voices of the silenced. For this reason, the work of Scott complements Johnson-DeBaufre's feminist reading. Gender issues do not figure prominently in Scott's writings so Johnson-DeBaufre adds both a complicating factor to Scott's reading and offers yet another dimension to the larger task that they share in common, hearing from the marginalized and the suppressed.

The issue on which Johnson-DeBaufre focuses her work is the struggle between fragmentation as a weapon of the powerful and solidarity as a counter-weapon of the weak. It is in the interests of the rulers to keep the dominated as fragmented as possible so that oppressed populations do not approach the crucial point where discovery of common issues might begin a movement toward more active expressions of discontent. Such fragmentation entails not only physical isolation but ideological and cultural fragmentation as well. These dynamics she finds played out in Q 7:31–35 and Q 11:14–20. In this case, the blend of feminist theory and Scott provides a framework for reading against the grain.

The textually centered discussions of Kirk and Johnson-DeBaufre are augmented by Milton Moreland's essay which integrates anthropological theory, Q studies and archaeology. Drawing on Scott's "moral economy of the peasant" rather than the more familiar works on hidden transcripts, Moreland summarizes peasant strategies for guaranteeing and maintaining their subsistence during a period of colonial occupation, especially as those colonial masters increase their demands on the peasant base. Yet, Moreland seems concerned that we may claim "the most extreme conditions for peasants" in early Roman Galilee and thereby exaggerate the exploitation and oppression of the peasantry. He finds support for this moderating view in the study of pottery distribution in Galilee by D. Adan

Bayewitz. Bayewitz discovered that pottery produced in the village of Kefar Hananya was found at Sepphoris and distributed throughout Galilee, and he concluded from this fact that a reciprocal relationship existed between urban centers and the villages of Galilee, something like a first century version of a market system mutually beneficial to urban elites and peasant villagers. As I have argued elsewhere, Bayewitz's conclusion confuses the means of production with the relations of production. Granted that the pottery made at Kefer Hananya was widely distributed in Galilee. But it does not follow that the potters in the village benefited in any extraordinary way from their cottage industry of making pottery. As Scott's own work suggests, if peasants had established a lucrative pottery production, it would be appropriated by elites who would take much of its profits for themselves. Even more to the point, peasant cultivators usually turn to other subsidiary activities like pottery production when their basic agricultural subsistence is threatened in some significant way. This would mean that the production of pottery was occurring precisely because the peasants' harvests were being subjected to ever more ruthless tribute. While Moreland is certainly able to argue the case for a less exploitive relationship between urban center and village, his arguments do not seem persuasive.

Moreland's more substantial contention is that the "ideology of the sayings of Jesus in Q, especially in their final literary form, do not correspond to the peasant subsistence ethic." Indeed, he contends that the ethic and values of the Jesus movement and the Q people generated very little peasant interest. Throughout his discussion of Q materials, he limits himself to their "final literary form," that is, the texts are treated as part of a public transcript alien to the more hidden transcripts of the villagers themselves. In light of the conditions prevailing in Galilee during the formation of the Jesus movement and the Q people, it would seem at least worth the effort to use Scott's hermeneutic to scout the materials for the presence of hidden transcripts in the sayings of Jesus and the Q community as Kirk and Johnson-DeBaufre have done so successfully. It stands to reason that Moreland's decision to work with the "larger compositional structures at work in the document" would reflect the ideology of the village scribes and, therefore, would yield forms of the Jesus tradition least palatable to peasant villagers. The scribes would be working toward the formulation of a sayings tradition that could conflict with the values of the little tradition current in the villages of Galilee. The more involved the inquiry with redactional layers of Q, the greater the distance between them and peasant life is likely to be.

Moreland sketches the very circumstances for the emergence of a hidden transcript when he focuses on the non-peasant non-elites who contribute to the growth of a hidden transcript by forming a "dissident subculture." They also provide the "power, assistance and supralocal organization that helps peasants act." It does not require a great deal of imagination to identify Jesus, the itinerating prophet, as just such a figure. If so, then his sayings and actions may be contributing to the formation and elaboration of a hidden transcript of resistance to Herodian, priestly and Roman rule.

Moreland's essay does a remarkable job of integrating disciplines that, in biblical studies, have not always coexisted in harmony and mutual appreciation. The level of integration of archaeology, anthropological theory and Q studies is enlightening and insightful.

These three essays are introduced by Richard Horsley's clear and concise programmatic essay that draws upon *The Moral Economy of the Peasant* and Scott's extensive on "Protest and Profanation." From this material, Horsley extracts a six-step approach for understanding peasant resistance and revolt. *Step 1.* Peasants believe that they have a basic right to a subsistence in which they can maintain their honorable standing in their villages. Whenever elites lay claim to the resources that insure this subsistence, their claims are judged to be invalid. *Step 2.* To ward off the threats that govern their lives, peasants develop their own forms of generalized reciprocity and a notion of mutuality, often mistaken for a form of egalitarianism. In effect, the peasant villagers develop their own model of "equity and justice" in the absence of any such concerns among the rulers. *Step 3.* When the rulers threaten peasants' subsistence, they will encounter increasing resistance as the villagers assert their right to a guaranteed subsistence, and they will pool their resources to aid villagers in serious trouble. *Step 4.* The economic demands of a colonial or imperial power bring increased pressure on both the land and labor of peasants, causing serious disintegration of the traditional "moral economy" of the villagers and introducing new insecurities into established relationships. *Step 5.* Peasants rarely revolt unless their basic subsistence is imperiled, but when they face the possibility that they will cross a downward threshold from free holder to tenant or from tenant to day laborer, they will escalate their resistance because the consequences are so grave. At this point, much depends on the power and ability of the colonial power to impose its will. *Step 6.* As the threat to the peasants' way of life increase, they will contemplate revolt, even if the prospects of success are slender. The very act of stirring a revolt unites peasants.

Horsley then applies his six-step approach to the Q materials suggesting that the speeches in Q may provide glimpses into the Israelite little tradition with its focus on covenantal community. Indeed, he argues that the "oral performance of the Q speeches may have provided both an ideology and motivation for the communities of the movement that heard them performed." Many of his correlations will be familiar to readers of Horsley's work but this essay provides a particularly clear framework for understanding the essays collected in this volume and for the use of Scott's hermeneutical lenses. His essay makes an excellent case for the value of Scott's work for New Testament studies.

These three essays and the introductory essay by Richard Horsley make a strong case for the value of Scott's work for biblical studies. It is to be hoped that these essays and others using Scott's approach will continue to make stimulating contributions to understanding the Gospels and the gospel traditions.

Bibliography

Achtemeier, John. 1990. *Omnes verbum somnat*: The New Testament and the Oral Environment of Late Western Antiquity. *JBL* 109:3–27.
Adan-Bayewitz, David. 1993. *Common Pottery in Roman Galilee: A Study in Local Trade*. Ramat-Gan, Israel: Bar-Ilan University Press.
Adan-Bayewitz, David, and Isadore Perlman. 1990. The Local Trade of Sepphoris in the Roman Period. *IEJ* 40:153–72.
Alföldy, Geza. 1985. *The Social History of Rome*. London: Croom Helms.
Allison, Dale. C. 1993. *The New Moses: A Matthean Typology*. Minneapolis: Fortress.
Amodio, Mark C. 2005. *Writing the Oral Tradition: Oral Poetics and Literate Culture in Medieval England*. Poetics of Orality and Literacy 1. Notre Dame, Ind.: University of Notre Dame Press.
Applebaum, Shimon. 1977. Judea as a Roman Province: The Countryside as a Political and Economic Factor. *ANRW* 2.8:386–95.
Arav, Rami, and Richard Freund, eds. 1995. *Bethsaida: A City by the North Shore of the Sea of Galilee*. Bethsaida Excavations Project 1. Kirksville, Mo.: Thomas Jefferson University Press.
Arnal, William E. 2001. *Jesus and the Village Scribe: Galilean Conflicts and the Setting of Q*. Minneapolis: Fortress.
Assmann, Aleida. 1983. Schriftlich Folklore: Zur Entstehung und Funktion eines Überlieferungstyps. Pages 175–94 in *Schrift und Gedächtnis: Beiträge zur Archäologie der literarischen Kommunikation*. Edited by Aleida Assmann, Jan Assmann, and Christof Hardmeier. Munich: Fink.
Aviam, Mordechai. 2004. *Jews, Pagans and Christians in the Galilee*. Land of Galilee 1. Rochester, N.Y.: Institute of Galilean Archaeology, University of Rochester.
Bagnall, Roger S. 1976. *The Administration of the Ptolemaic Possessions outside of Egypt*. Leiden: Brill.
Bagnall, Roger S., and Bruce W. Frier. 1991. *The Demography of Roman Egypt*. Cambridge: Cambridge University Press.
Baltzer, Klaus. 1971. *The Covenant Formulary*. Philadelphia: Fortress.
Bauman, Richard. 1977. *Verbal Art as Performance*. Prospect Heights, Ill.: Waveland.
Becker, Howard S. 1963. *Outsiders: Studies in the Sociology of Deviance*. New York: Free Press; London: Collier-Macmillan
Bediako, K. 1990. *Jesus in African Culture (A Ghanian Perspective)*. Accra: Asempa.
———. 1992. *Theology and Identity: The Impact of Culture upon Christian Thought in the Second Century and in Modern Africa*. Carlisle, England: Regnum.
Ben Yehuda, Nachman. 1990. *The Politics and Morality of Deviance. Moral Panics, Drug*

Abuse, Deviant Science, and Reversed Stigmatization. Albany: State University of New York Press.

Botha, Pieter J. J. 1991a. Mark's Story as Oral-Traditional Literature: Rethinking the Transmission of Some Traditions about Jesus. *Hervormde Teologiese Studies* 47:304–34.

———. 1991b. Living Voice and Lifeless Letters: Reserve towards Writing in the Greco-Roman World. *Hervormde Teologiese Studies* 49:742–59.

———. 1992. Greco-Roman Literacy as Setting for New Testament Writings. *Neot* 26:206.

———. 1993. The Social Dynamics of the Early Transmission of the Jesus Tradition. *Neot* 27:205–31.

———. 2001. Cognition, Orality-Literacy, and Approaches to First-Century Writings. Pages 37–63 in *Orality, Literacy, and Colonialism in Antiquity*. Edited by J. A. Draper. SemeiaSt 43. Atlanta: Society of Biblical Literature.

Bowman, Alan K., and Greg Woolf. 1994. *Literacy and Power in the Ancient World*. Cambridge: Cambridge University Press.

Boyarin, Daniel. 1993. Placing Reading: Ancient Israel and Medieval Europe. Pages 10–37 in *The Ethnography of Reading*. Edited by Jonathan Boyarin. Berkeley and Los Angeles: University of California Press.

Bradbury, Nancy Mason. 1998. Traditional Referentiality: The Aesthetic Power of Oral Traditional Structures. Pages 136–45 in Foley 1998b.

Brown, D. 1998. *Voicing the Text: South African Oral Poetry and Performance*. Cape Town and Oxford: Oxford University Press.

———, ed. 1999. *Oral Literature and Performance in Southern Africa*. Oxford: Currey.

Cancian, Frank. 1989. Economic Behavior in Peasant Communities. Pages 127–70 in *Economic Anthropology*. Edited by Stuart Plattner. Stanford, Calif.: Stanford University Press.

Chafe, W. L. 1980. The Deployment of Consciousness in the Production of a Narrative. Pages 9–50 in *The Pear Stories: Cognitive, Cultural, and Linguistic Aspects of Narrative Production*. Edited by W. L. Chafe. Norwood, N.J.: Ablex.

———. 1994. *Discourse, Consciousness, and Time: The Flow and Displacement of Consciousness Experience in Speaking and Writing*. Chicago: University of Chicago Press.

Chancey, Mark. 2002. *The Myth of a Gentile Galilee*. SNTSMS 118. Cambridge: Cambridge University Press.

Clanchy, M. T. 1979. *From Memory to Written Record: England, 1066–1307*. London: Arnold; Cambridge: Harvard University Press.

Cope, Trevor. 1968. *Izibongo: Zulu Praise-Poems*. Oxford: Clarendon.

Cotter, Wendy J. 1987. The Parable of the Children in the Market-Place, Q (Lk) 7:31–35: An Examination of the Parable's Image and Significance. *NovT* 29:295–302.

Cotton, Hannah M. 1998. The Rabbis and the Documents. Pages 167–79 in *Jews in a Greco-Roman World*. Edited by Martin Goodman. Oxford. Oxford University Press.

Crawford, J. R. 1970. The Consequences of Allegation. Pages 305–18 in *Witchcraft and Sorcery: Selected Readings*. Edited by Max Marwick. Harmondsworth, England: Penguin.

Crossan, John Dominic. 1991a. *The Historical Jesus: The Life of a Mediterranean Jewish Peasant*. San Francisco: HarperSanFrancisco.

———. 1991b Lists in Early Christianity: A Response to Early Christianity, Q, and Jesus. *Semeia* 55:235–43.
———. 1994. *Jesus: A Revolutionary Biography*. San Francisco: HarperSanFrancisco, 1994.
———. 1998. *The Birth of Christianity: Discovering What Happened in the Years Immediately after the Execution of Jesus*. San Francisco: HarperSanFrancisco.
Crossan, John Dominic, and Jonathan Reed. 2001. *Excavating Jesus: Beneath the Stones, Behind the Texts*. San Francisco: HarperSanFrancisco.
Dewey, Joanna. 1980. *Markan Public Debate: Literary Technique, Concentric Structure, and Theology in Mark 2:1–3:6*. SBLDS 48. Chico, Calif.: Scholars Press.
———. 1989. Oral Methods of Structuring Narrative in Mark. *Int* 53:32–44.
———. 1992. Mark as Aural Narrative: Structures as Clues to Understanding. *STRev* 36:45–56.
———. 1994. The Gospel of Mark as an Oral-Aural Event: Implications for Interpretation. Pages 248–257 in *The New Literary Criticism and the New Testament*. Edited by Elizabeth Struthers Malbon and Edgar V. McKnight. Sheffield: Sheffield Academic Press.
Doane A. N. 1991. Oral Texts, Intertexts, and Intratexts: Editing Old English. Pages 75–113 in *Influence and Intertextuality in Literary History*. Edited by Jay Clayton and Erid Rothstein. Madison: University of Wisconsin Press.
Douglas, Mary. 1970. Introduction. Pages xi–xxxvii in *Witchcraft Confessions and Accusations*. Edited by Mary Douglas. London: Tavistock.
———. 1991. Witchcraft and Leprosy: Two Strategies of Exclusion. *Man*, n.s., 26:723–36.
Downing, F. G. 1994. A Genre for Q and a Socio-cultural Context for Q: Comparing Sets of Similarities with Sets of Differences. *JSNT* 55:3–26.
Draper, Jonathan A. 1994. Jesus and the Renewal of Local Community in Galilee: Challenge to a Communitarian Christology. *JTSA* 87:29–42.
———. 1996. Confessional Western Text-Centred Biblical Interpretation and an Oral or Residual-Oral Context. *Semeia* 73:61–80.
———. 1997. "Less Literate Are Safer": The Politics of Literacy and Orality and the Bible in the South African Context. Paper given at the Association of Anglican Biblical Scholars, San Francisco, November 1997. Published in *AThR* 84 (2002) 303–18.
———. 2000a. The Bishop and the Bricoleur: Bishop John William Colenso's *Commentary on Romans* and Magema kaMagwaza's *The Black People and Whence They Came*. Pages 415–56 in *The Bible in Africa: Transactions, Trajectories, and Trends*. Edited by G. O. West and M. W. Dube. Leiden: Brill.
———. 2000b. Recovering Oral Tradition Fixed in Text. The Case of Q3:7, 4:1–13. Pages 85–111 in *Orality, Memory, and the Past: Listening to the Voices of Black Clergy under Colonialism and Apartheid*. Edited by Phillipe Denis. Pietermaritzburg: Cluster.
———. 2002. The Bible as Onion, Icon, and Oracle: Reception of the Printed Sacred Text in Oral and Residual-Oral South Africa. *JTSA* 112:39–56.
DuBois, Thomas A. 1995. *Finnish Folk Poetry and the "Kalevala."* New York: Garland.
———. 1998. Ethnopoetics. Pages 123–35 in Foley 1998b.
Dunn, James D. G. 1988 Matthew 12:28/Luke 11:20: A Word of Jesus? Pages 29–49 in *Eschatology and the New Testament: Essays in Honor of George Raymond Beasley-Murray*. Edited by W. Hulitt Gloer. Peabody, Mass.: Hendrickson.

Edwards, Douglas. 1988. First Century Urban/Rural Relations in Lower Galilee: Exploring the Archaeological and Literary Evidence. Pages 169–82 in *Society of Biblical Literature 1988 Seminar Papers*. Atlanta: Scholars Press.

———. 1992. The Socio-Economic and Cultural Ethos of Lower Galilee in the First Century: Implications for the Nascent Jesus Movement. Pages 53–73 in *Studies on the Galilee in Late Antiquity*. Edited by Lee Levine. New York: Jewish Theological Seminary.

Eilberg-Schwartz, Howard. 1990. *The Savage in Judaism: An Anthropology of Israelite Religion and Ancient Judaism*. Bloomington: Indiana University Press.

Elmer, Peter. 1996. "Saints or Sorcerers": Quakerism, Demonology, and the Decline of Witchcraft in Seventeenth-Century England. Pages 145–79 in *Witchcraft in Early Modern Europe: Studies in Culture and Belief*. Edited by Jonathan Barry et al. Cambridge: Cambridge University Press

Fiensy, David. 1991. *The Social History of Palestine in the Herodian Period*. Lewiston, N.Y.: Mellen.

Filter, H., and S. Bourquin. 1986. *Paulina Dlamini: Servant of Two Kings*. Durban: Killie Campbell Africana Library; Pietermaritzburg: University of Natal Press.

Finley, Moses I. 1973. *Ancient Economy*. Berkeley and Los Angeles: University of California Press.

Finnegan, Ruth 1970. *Oral Literature in Africa*. Oxford: Clarendon.

———. 1977. *Oral Poetry: Its Nature, Significance, and Social Context*. Cambridge: Cambridge University Press.

———. 1988. *Literacy and Orality: Studies in the Technology of Communication*. Oxford: Basil Blackwell.

Foley, John Miles. 1986. *Oral Tradition in Literature: Interpretation in Context*. Columbia: University of Missouri Press.

———. 1990. *Traditional Oral Epic: The Odyssey, Beowulf, and the Serbo-Croatian Return Song*. Berkeley and Los Angeles: University of California Press. Repr., 1993.

———. 1991. *Immanent Art: From Structure to Meaning in Traditional Oral Epic*. Bloomington: Indiana University Press.

———. 1995. *The Singer of Tales in Performance*. Bloomington: Indiana University Press.

———. 1998a. The Impossibility of Canon. Pages 13–33 in Foley 1998b.

———, ed. 1998b. *Teaching Oral Traditions*. New York: Modern Language Association.

———. 1999a. *Homer's Traditional Art*. University Park: Pennsylvania State University Press.

———. 1999b. Epic Cycles and Oral Tradition: Ancient Greek and South Slavic. Pages 99–108 in *Euphrosyne: Festschrift for Dimitris Maronitis*. Edited by Antonios Rengakos. Stuttgart: Steiner.

———. 2002. *How to Read an Oral Poem*. Urbana: University of Illinois Press. eCompanion at www.oraltradition.org/hrop.

———, ed. and trans. 2004a. *The Wedding of Mustajbey's Son Beirbey as Performed by Halil Bajgori*. Folklore Fellows Communications 283. Helsinki: Academia Scientiarum Fennica. eEdition at www.oraltradition.org/zbm.

———. 2004b. Epic as Genre. Pages 171–87 in *The Cambridge Companion to Homer*. Edited by Robert Fowler. Cambridge: Cambridge University Press.

———, ed. 2005. *A Companion to Ancient Epic*. Oxford: Blackwell.

Foucault, Michel. 1979. *Discipline and Punish: The Birth of the Prison.* New York: Vintage.
Freyne, Seán. 1980. *Galilee from Alexander to Hadrian 323 B.C.E. to 125 C.E.: A Study of Second Temple Judaism.* Wilmington, Del.: Glazier.
———. 1988a. Bandits in Galilee: A Contribution to the Study of Social Conditions in First Century Palestine. Pages 50–68 in *The Social World of Formative Christianity and Judaism.* Edited by Jacob Neusner and Peder Borgen. Philadelphia: Fortress.
———. 1988b. *Galilee, Jesus, and the Gospels: Literary Approaches and Historical Investigations.* Philadelphia: Fortress.
———. 1994. The Geography, Politics, and Economics of Galilee and the Quest for the Historical Jesus. Pages 75–121 in *Studying the Historical Jesus: Evaluations of the State of Current Research.* Edited by Bruce Chilton and Craig Evans. Leiden: Brill.
———. 2000. The Galilean World of Jesus. Pages 113–35 in vol. 1 of *The Early Christian World.* Edited by Philip Francis Esler. New York: Routledge.
Gal, Zvi. 1992. *Lower Galilee during the Iron Age.* Translated by M. R. Josephy. Winona Lake, Ind.: Eisenbrauns.
Gee, J. P. 1996. *Social Linguistics and Literacies: Ideology in Discourses.* 2nd ed. London: Taylor & Francis.
Gerhardsson, Birger. 1961. *Memory and Manuscript: Oral Tradition and Written Transmission in Rabbinic Judaism and Early Christianity.* ASNU 22. Uppsala: Gleerup.
Goodman, Martin. 1991. Babatha's Story. *Journal of Roman Studies* 81:69–75.
Goody, Jack R. 1977. *The Domestication of the Savage Mind.* Cambridge: Cambridge University Press.
———. 1987. *The Interface between the Written and the Oral.* Cambridge: Cambridge University Press.
Golomb, Louis. 1988. Supernaturalist Curers and Sorcery Accusations in Thailand. *Social Science and Medicine* 27:437–43.
Goffman, Erving. 1963. *Stigma: Notes on the Management of Spoiled Identity.* Englewood Cliffs, N.J.: Prentice-Hall.
Grant, Frederick C. 1926. *The Economic Background of the Gospels.* London: Oxford University Press.
Green, William Scott. 1989. Writing with Scripture: The Rabbinic Uses of the Hebrew Bible. Pages 7–23 in *Writing with Scripture: The Authority and Uses of the Hebrew Bible in the Torah of Formative Judaism.* Edited by Jacob Neusner. Minneapolis: Fortress.
Gunner, Elizabeth A. W. 1984. Ukubonga Nezinbongo: Zulu Praising and Praises. Ph.D. thesis. School of Oriental and African Languages, London.
——— 2002. *The Man of Heaven and the Beautiful Ones of God = Umuntu Wasezulwini Nabantu Abahle Bakankulunkulu: Writings from Ibandla Lamanazaretha, A South African Church.* Studies on Religion in Africa 24. Leiden: Brill.
Halliday, M. A. K. 1978. *Language as Social Semiotic: The Social Interpretation of Language and Meaning.* Baltimore: University Park Press.
Harris, William V. 1989. *Ancient Literacy.* Cambridge: Harvard University Press.
Harnack, Adolf von. 1908. *The Sayings of Jesus.* New York: Putnam's Sons. Translation of *Sprüche und Reden Jesu: Die zweite Quelle des Matthäus und Lukas.* Vol. 2 of *Beiträge zur Einleitung in das Neue Testament.* Leipzig: Hinrichs, 1907.

Hanson, K. C. 1997. The Galilean Fishing Economy and the Jesus Tradition. *BTB* 27:99–111.

Hanson, K. C., and Douglas E. Oakman. 1998. *Palestine in the Time of Jesus: Social Structures and Social Conflicts.* Minneapolis: Fortress.

Harnack, Adolf von. [1907] 1908. *The Sayings of Jesus.* New York: Putnam's Sons. Translation of *Beiträge zur Einleitung in das Neue Testament*, vol. 2: *Sprüche und reden Jesu. Die zweite Quelle des Matthäus und Lukas.* Leipzig, 1907.

Haslam, Michael W. 2005. The Physical Media: Tablet, Scroll, Papyrus. Pages 142–63 in Foley 2005.

Havelock, Eric A. 1963 *Preface to Plato.* Cambridge: Harvard University Press.

Heilbroner, Robert, and William S. Milberg. 2001. *The Making of Economic Society.* 11th ed. Upper Saddle River, N.J.: Prentice Hall.

Herzog, William R. II. 2005. Why Peasants Responded to Jesus. Pages 47–70 in vol. 1 of *Christian Origins: A Peoples History of Christianity.* Edited by Richard A. Horsley. Minneapolis: Augsburg Fortress.

Hexham, I. 1994. *The Scriptures of the amaNazaretha of EKuphaKameni: Selected Writings of the Zulu Prophets Isaiah and Londa Shembe.* Edited by Irving Hexham. Translated by Londa Shembe and Hans-Jürgen Becken. Calgary: University of Calgary Press.

Hezser, Catherine. 2001. *Jewish Literacy in Roman Palestine.* Tübingen: Mohr Siebeck.

Hohmeier, Jürgen. 1975. Stigmatisierung als sozialer Definitionsprozeß. Pages 5–24 in vol. 1 of *Stigmatisierung: Zur Produktion gesellschaftlicher Randgruppen.* Neuwied, Germany: Luchterhand.

Honko, Lauri. 1998. *Textualising the Siri Epic.* Folklore Fellows Communications 264. Helsinki: Academia Scientiarum Fennica.

———, ed. 2000. *Textualization of Oral Epics.* Berlin: de Gruyter.

Hopkins, Keith. 1991. Conquest by Book. Pages 133–58 in *Literacy in the Roman World.* Edited by Mary Beard. JRA Supplement 3. Ann Arbor: University of Michigan Press.

Horsley, Richard A. 1984. Popular Messianic Movements around the Time of Jesus. *CBQ* 46:471–93.

———. 1985. "Like One of the Prophets of Old": Two Types of Popular Prophets at the Time of Jesus. *CBQ* 47:435–63.

———. 1987. *Jesus and the Spiral of Violence: Popular Jewish Resistance in Roman Palestine.* San Francisco: Harper & Row. Minneapolis: Fortress, 1995.

———. 1989. *Sociology and the Jesus Movement.* New York: Crossroad.

———. 1991a. Q and Jesus: Assumptions, Approaches, and Analyses. *Semeia* 55:175–209.

———. 1991b. Logoi Propheton: Reflections on the Genre of Q. Pages 195–209 in *The Future of Early Christianity: Essays in Honor of Helmut Koester.* Edited by Birger A. Pearson et al. Minneapolis: Fortress.

———. 1995. *Galilee: History, Politics, People.* Valley Forge, Pa.: Trinity Press International.

———. 1996. *Archaeology, History, and Society in Galilee: The Social Context of Jesus and the Rabbis.* Valley Forge, Pa.: Trinity Press International.

———. 1999. Jesus and Galilee: The Contingencies of a Renewal Movement. Pages 57–74 in *Galilee through the Centuries.* Edited by Eric M. Meyers. Winona Lake, Ind.: Eisenbrauns.

———. 2005. Jesus Movements and the Renewal of Israel. Pages 23–46 in vol. 1 of *Christian Origins: A People's History of Christianity*. Edited by Richard A. Horsley. Minneapolis: Augsburg Fortress.
———. 2007. The Languages of the Kingdom: From Aramaic to Greek, Galilee to Syria, Oral to Oral-Written. Forthcoming in Sean Freyne Festschrift.
Horsley, Richard A., and Jonathan A. Draper. 1999. *Whoever Hears You Hears Me*. Harrisburg, Pa.: Trinity Press International.
Horsley, Richard A., with John S. Hanson. 1985. *Bandits, Prophets, and Messiahs: Popular Movements in the Time of Jesus*. Minneapolis: Winston.
Horst, Pieter W. van der. 1997. "The Finger of God": Miscellaneous Notes on Luke 11:20 and Its *Umwelt*. Pages 89–130 in *Sayings of Jesus: Canonical and Non-canonical: Essays in Honor of T. Baarda*. Edited by William Petersen et al. Leiden: Brill.
Humphries, Michael. 1999. *Christian Origins and the Language of the Kingdom of God*. Carbondale: Southern Illinois University Press.
Hymes, Dell. 1981. *"In Vain I Tried to Tell You": Essays in Native American Ethnopoetics*. Philadelphia: University of Pennsylvania Press.
———. 1989. Ways of Speaking. Pages 433–51 and 473–74 in *Explorations in the Ethnography of Speaking*. Edited by Richard Bauman and Joel Sherzer. 2nd ed. Cambridge: Cambridge University Press.
———. 1994. Ethnopoetics, Oral-Formulaic Theory, and Editing Texts. *Oral Tradition* 9:330–70.
Jacobson, Arland. 1992. *The First Gospel: An Introduction to Q*. Sonoma, Calif.: Polebridge.
Jaffee, Martin. 1998. The Oral-Cultural Context of the Talmud Yerushalmi: Greco-Roman Rhetorical Paideia, Discipleship, and the Concept of Oral Torah. Pages 27–61 in *The Talmud Yerushalmi and Graeco-Roman Culture I*. Edited by Peter Schaefer. Tübingen: Mohr Siebeck.
———. 2001. *Torah in the Mouth*. Oxford: Oxford University Press.
Jeffreys, Elizabeth, and Michael Jeffreys. 1971. *Imberios and Margarona*: The Manuscripts, Sources, and Edition of a Byzantine Verse Romance. *Byzantion* 41:122–60.
Johnson-DeBaufre, Melanie. 2002. It's the End of the World as We Know It: Eschatology, Q, and the Construction of Christian Origins. Th.D. diss. Harvard University.
———. 2003. Bridging the Gap to "This Generation": A Feminist-Critical Reading of Q 7:31–35. Pages 214–33 in *Walk in the Ways of Wisdom*. Edited by Shelly Matthews, Cynthia Kittredge, and Melanie Johnson-DeBaufre. Harrisburg, Pa.: Trinity Press International.
———. 2006. *Jesus among Her Children. Q, Eschatology, and the Construction of Christian Origins*. HTS 55. Cambridge: Harvard University Press.
Jousse, Marcel. [1925] 1990. *The Oral Style*. Translated by E. Sienaert and R. Whitaker. New York: Garland. [*Le Style oral rhythmique et mnémotechnique chez les verbo-moteurs*.]
———. [1931–50] 1997. *The Anthropology of Geste and Rhythm: Studies in the Anthropological Laws of Human Expression and Their Application in the Galilean Oral Style Tradition*. Edited and translated by E. Sienaert and J. Conolly. Durban: Centre for Oral Studies, University of Natal. [*L'Anthropologie du Geste*.]
Kautsky, John H. 1982. *The Politics of Aristocratic Empires*. Chapel Hill: University of North Carolina Press.

Kearney, Michael. 1996. *Reconceptualizing the Peasantry: Anthropology in Global Perspective*. Critical Essays in Anthropology. Boulder, Colo.: Westview.
Kelber, Werner. 1983. *The Oral and Written Gospel*. Philadelphia: Fortress.
———. 1989. Sayings Collections and Sayings Gospel: A Study in the Clustering Management of Knowledge. *Language and Communication* 9:213–24.
———. 1994. Jesus and Tradition: Words in Time, Words in Space. *Semeia* 65:139–67.
Kelly, C. M. 1994. Later Roman Bureaucracy: Going through the Files. Pages 161–76 in *Literacy and Power in the Ancient World*. Edited by Alan K. Bowman and Greg Woolf. Cambridge: Cambridge University Press.
Kennedy, George A. 2003. *Progymnasmata: Greek Textbooks of Prose Composition and Rhetoric*. Writings from the Greco-Roman World 10. Atlanta: SBL.
Khumalo, C. V. 2003. The Class of 1856 and the Politics of Cultural Production(s) in the Emergence of Ekukhanyeni, 1855–1910. Pages 207–41 in *The Eye of the Storm: Essays on the 150th Anniversary of His Consecration as Bishop of Natal in 1853*. Edited by J. A. Draper. London: T&T Clark.
Kirk, Alan 1998 *The Composition of the Sayings Source: Genre, Synchrony, and Wisdom Redaction in Q*. Leiden: Brill.
———. 2001. Breaching the Frontier: Going Public with the Hidden Transcript in Q 11. Paper presented at the Society of Biblical Literature Annual Meeting, Denver.
———. 2004. Administrative Writing, Oral Tradition, and Q. Paper presented at the Q Section, Society of Biblical Literature Annual Meeting, San Antonio.
Kloppenborg, John S. 1987. *The Formation of Q: Trajectories in Ancient Wisdom Collections*. Studies in Antiquity and Christianity. Philadelphia: Fortress.
———. 1989. The Formation of Q Revisited: A Response to Richard Horsley. Pages 201–15 in *Society of Biblical Literature 1989 Seminar Papers*. Atlanta: Scholars Press.
———. 1991. Literary Convention, Self-Evidence, and the Social History of the Q People. *Semeia* 55:77–102.
———. 1993. The Sayings Gospel Q: Recent Opinion on the People behind the Document. *CurBS* 1:9–34.
———. 2000. *Excavating Q: The History and Setting of the Sayings Gospel*. Minneapolis: Fortress; Edinburgh: T&T Clark.
Koester, Helmut. 1971a. GNOMAI DIAPHOROI: The Origin and Nature of Diversification in the History of Early Christianity. Pages 114–57 in Robinson and Koester 1971.
———. 1971b. One Jesus and Four Primitive Gospels. Pages 158–204 in Robinson and Koester 1971.
———. 1990a. Q and Its Relatives. Pages 49–63 in *Gospel Origins and Christian Beginnings*. Edited by J. E. Goehring et al. Sonoma, Calif.: Polebridge.
———. 1990b. *Ancient Christian Gospels: Their History and Development*. Philadelphia: Trinity Press International.
Kolsti, John S. 1990. *The Bilingual Singer: A Study in Albanian and South Slavic Oral Epic Traditions*. New York: Garland.
Krapp, George Philip, and Elliott van Kirk Dobbie, eds. 1966. *The Exeter Book*. The Anglo-Saxon Poetic Records 3. New York: Columbia University Press.
Lendon, J. E. 1997. *Empire of Honour: The Art of Government in the Roman World*. Oxford: Oxford University Press.

Lenski, Gerhard E. 1984. *Power and Privilege: A Theory of Social Stratification*. 2nd ed. Chapel Hill: University of North Carolina Press.
Lenski, J., and G. E. Lenski. 1985. *Human Societies: An Introduction to Macrosociology.* New York: McGraw-Hill.
Lewis, Naphtali, ed. 1989. Greek Papyri. In *The Documents from the Bar Kokhba Period in the Cave of Letters.* Judean Desert Studies 2. Jerusalem: Israel Exploration Society, Hebrew University of Jerusalem, Shrine of the Book.
Lipp, Wolfgang. 1975. Stigmatisierung. Pages 25–53 in vol. 1 of *Stigmatisierung: Zur Produktion gesellschaftlicher Randgruppen.* Neuwied, Germany: Luchterhand.
———. 1977. Charisma—Social Deviation, Leadership, and Cultural Change: A Sociology of Deviance Approach. *Annual Review of the Social Science of Religion* 1:57–77.
———.1985. *Stigma und Charisma: Über soziales Grenzverhalten.* Berlin: Reimer.
———.1993. Charisma—Schuld und Gnade, soziale Konstruktion, Kulturdynamik, Handlungsdrama. Pages 15–32 in *Charisma: Theorie–Religion–Politik.* Edited by Winfried Gebhardt et al. Berlin: de Gruyter.
Lord, A. B. 1960. *The Singer of Tales.* Cambridge: Harvard University Press.
Lührmann, Dieter. 1969. *Die Redaktion der Logienquelle.* Neukirchen-Vluyn: Neukirchener.
Macadam, Henry Innes. 1983. Epigraphy and Village Life in Southern Syria during the Roman and Early Byzantine Periods. *Berytus* 31:103–15.
Mack, Burton. 1988. The Kingdom That Didn't Come. Pages 608–35 in *Society of Biblical Literature 1988 Seminar Papers.* Atlanta: Scholars Press.
———.1988. *A Myth of Innocence: Mark and Christian Origins.* Philadelphia: Fortress.
Mack. Burton L., and Vernon Robbins. 1989. *Patterns of Persuasion in the Gospels.* Sonoma, Calif.: Polebridge.
Malina, Bruce J. 1993. *The New Testament World: Insights from Cultural Anthropology.* Rev ed. Louisville: Westminster John Knox.
Malina, Bruce J., and Jerome H. Neyrey. 1988. *Calling Jesus Names: The Social Value of Labels in Matthew.* Sonoma, Calif.: Polebridge.
Maluleke, T. S. 1996. Black and African Theologies in the New World Order: A Time to Drink from Our Own Wells. *JTSA* 96:3–19.
———. 2000. The Bible among African Christians: A Missiological Perspective. Pages 87–112 in *To Cast Fire upon the Earth: Bible and Mission Collaborating in Today's Multicultural Global Context.* Edited by T. Okure. Pietermaritzburg: Cluster.
Marwick, Max. 1970. Witchcraft as a Social Strain Gauge. Pages 280–95 in *Witchcraft and Sorcery: Selected Readings.* Edited by Max Marwick. Harmondsworth, England: Penguin.
———. 1967. The Sociology of Sorcery in a Central African Tribe. Pages 101–26 in *Magic, Witchcraft, and Curing.* Edited by John Middleton. Austin: University of Texas Press.
Moreland, Milton. 2004. The Galilean Response to Earliest Christianity: A Cross-Cultural Study of the Subsistence Ethic. Pages 37–48 in *Religion and Society in Roman Palestine: Old Questions, New Approaches.* Edited by Douglas R. Edwards. London: Routledge.
Muller, C., ed. 1996. The Hymns of the Nazaretha. Composed by Isaiah and Galilee Shembe. Translation and explanation by Bongani Mthethwa. Introduced and edited by Carol Muller.

Nash, Manning. 1967. Witchcraft as a Social Process in a Tzeltal Community. Pages 127–33 in *Magic, Witchcraft, and Curing*. Edited by John Middleton. Austin: University of Texas Press
Neyrey, Jerome H. 1996. Clean/Unclean, Pure/Polluted, and Holy/Profane: The Idea and the System of Purity. Pages 80–104 in *The Social Sciences and New Testament Interpretation*. Edited by Richard L. Rohrbaugh. Peabody, Mass.: Hendrickson.
Niditch, Susan. 1996. *Oral World and Written Word*. Louisville, Ky.: Westminster John Knox.
O'Keeffe, Katherine O'Brien. 1990. *Visible Song: Transitional Literacy in Old English Verse*. Cambridge: Cambridge University Press.
Ong, Walter J. 1967. *The Presence of the Word: Some Prolegomena for Cultural and Religious History*. Minneapolis: University of Minnesota Press.
———. 1982. *Orality and Literacy: The Technologizing of the Word*. London: Methuen.
Opland, Jeff. 1983. *Xhosa Oral Poetry*. Cambridge: Cambridge University Press.
Parker, D. C. 1997. *The Living Text of the Gospels*. Cambridge: Cambridge University Press.
Parry, Milman. 1930. Studies in the Epic Technique of Oral Verse-Making. I: Homer and Homeric Style. *Harvard Studies in Classical Philology* 41:73–147. Repr. as pages 266–324 in *The Making of Homeric Verse*. Oxford: Clarendon, 1971.
———. 1971. *The Making of Homeric Verse: The Collected Papers of Milman Parry*. Oxford: Clarendon.
Penfield, J. 1983. *Communicating with Quotes: The Igbo Case*. Westport, Conn.: Greenwood.
Piper, Ronald A. 1989. *Wisdom in the Q-Tradition*. Cambridge: Cambridge University Press.
Pitt-Rivers, Julian. 1977. *The Fate of Shechem*. Cambridge: Cambridge University Press.
Popkin, Samuel L. 1979. *The Rational Peasant: The Political Economy of Rural Society in Vietnam*. Berkeley and Los Angeles: University of California Press.
Redfield, Robert. 1956. *Peasant Society and Culture*. Chicago: University of Chicago Press.
Reed, Jonathan L. 1999. Galileans, '"Israelite Village Communities," and the Sayings Gospel Q. Pages 87–108 in *Galilee through the Centuries*. Edited by Eric Meyers. Winona Lake, Ind.: Eisenbrauns.
———. 2000. *Archaeology and the Galilean Jesus: A Re-examination of the Evidence*. Harrisburg, Pa.: Trinity Press International.
Reichl, Karl. 1992. *Turkic Oral Epic Poetry: Traditions, Forms, Poetic Structure*. New York: Garland.
Richardson, Peter. 1996. *Herod the Great: King of the Jews and Friend of the Romans*. Columbia: University of South Carolina Press.
Rivière, Peter. 1970. Factions and Exclusions in Two South American Village Systems. Pages 245–55 in *Witchcraft Confessions and Accusations*. Edited by Mary Douglas. London: Tavistock.
Robbins, Vernon K. 1989. Rhetorical Composition and the Beelzebul Controversy. Pages 161–93 in *Patterns of Persuasion in the Gospels*. Edited by Burton L. Mack and Vernon K. Robbins. Sonoma, Calif.: Polebridge. Online: http://www.religion.emory.edu/faculty/robbins/composition/composition86.html.
———. 1997. Orality as a Social Location in The Gospel of Thomas. Pages 86–114 in *Society of Biblical Literature 1997 Seminar Papers*. Atlanta: Scholars Press. Online:

http://www.religion.emory.edu/faculty/robbins/composition/composition86.html.

———. 2004. Where Is Wuellner's Anti-hermeneutical Hermeneutic Taking Us? From Schleiermacher to Thistleton and Beyond. Pages 105–25 in *Rhetorics and Hermeneutics: Wilhelm Wuellner and His Influence*. Edited by James D. Hester and David Hester. Emory Studies in Early Christianity 9. New York: T&T Clark.

Robinson, James M. 1971. Logoi Sophon: On the *Gattung* of Q. Pages 71–113 in Robinson and Koester 1971. Originally published as Logoi Sophon: Zur Gattung der Spruchquelle Q. Pages 77–96 in *Zeit und Geschichte: Dankesgabe an Rudolf Bultmann zum 80. Geburtstag*. Edited by E. Dinkler. Tübingen: Mohr Siebeck, 1964.

Robinson, James M., Paul Hoffman, and John S. Kloppenborg, eds. 2000. *The Critical Edition of Q*. Hermeneia. Louvain: Peeters; Minneapolis: Fortress.

———. 2000. History of Q Research. Pages xix–lxxi in *The Critical Edition of Q*. Edited by James M. Robinson, Paul Hoffmann, and John S. Kloppenborg. Minneapolis: Fortress; Louvain: Peeters.

Robinson, James M., and Helmut Koester. 1971. *Trajectories through Early Christianity*. Philadelphia: Fortress.

Rohrbaugh, Richard. 1984. Methodological Considerations in the Debate over the Social Class Status of Early Christians. *JAAR* 52:519–46.

Sanders, E. P. 1985. *Jesus and Judaism*. Philadelphia: Fortress.

Sanneh, L. 1989. *Translating the Message: The Missionary Impact on Culture*. Maryknoll, N.Y.: Orbis.

———. 1990. The Gospel and Culture: Ramifying Effects of Scriptural Translation. Pages 1–23 in *Bible Translation and the Spread of the Church: The Last Two Hundred Years*. Edited by P. Stine. Leiden: Brill.

———. 1994. Translatability in Islam and in Christianity in Africa: A Thematic Approach. Pages 23–45 in *Religion in Africa: Experience and Expression*. Edited by T. D. Blakely, W. E. A. van Beek, and D. L. Thomson. London: Currey.

Satlow, Michael. 1993. Reconsidering the Rabbinic *ketubbah* Payment. Pages 133–51 in *The Jewish Family in Antiquity*. Edited by Shaye J. D. Cohen. BJS 289. Atlanta: Scholars Press.

Schur, Edwin M. 1980 *The Politics of Deviance: Stigma Contests and the Uses of Power*. Englewood Cliffs, N.J.: Prentice-Hall.

———. 1971. *Labeling Deviant Behavior*. New York: Harper & Row.

Scott, Bernard Brandon, and Margaret Dean. 1993. A Sound Map of the Sermon on the Mount. Pages 672–725 in *Society of Biblical Literature 1993 Seminar Papers*. Atlanta: Scholars Press.

Scott, James C. 1976. *The Moral Economy of the Peasant: Rebellion and Subsistence in Southeast Asia*. New Haven: Yale University Press.

———. 1977. Protest and Profanation: Agrarian Revolt and the Little Tradition. *Theory and Society* 4:1–38, 211–46.

———. 1985. *Weapons of the Weak: Everyday Forms of Peasant Resistance*. New Haven: Yale University Press.

———. 1987. Resistance without Protest and without Organization: Peasant Opposition to the Islamic *Zakat* and the Christian Tithe. *Comparative Studies in Society and History* 29:417–52.

———. 1990. *Domination and the Arts of Resistance: Hidden Transcripts*. New Haven: Yale University Press.

———. 2005. Afterword to "Moral Economies, State Spaces, and Categorical Violence." *American Anthropologist* 107:395–402.
Schröter, Jens. 1997. *Erinnerung an Jesu Worte: Studien zur Rezeption der Logienüberlieferung in Markus, Q und Thomas*. WMANT 76. Neukirchen-Vluyn: Neukirchener.
———. 2001. *Jesus und die Anfänge der Christologie: Methdologische und exegetische Studien zu den Ursprüngen des christlichen Glaubens*. Biblisch-Theologische Studien 47. Neukirchen-Vluyn: Neukirchener.
Schüssler Fiorenza, Elisabeth. 2000. *Jesus and the Politics of Interpretation*. New York: Continuum.
———. 2001. *Wisdoms Ways: An Introduction to Feminist Biblical Interpretation*. Maryknoll, N.Y.: Orbis.
Shanin, Theodor, ed. 1987. *Peasants and Peasant Societies: Selected Readings*. 2nd ed. New York: Basil Blackwell.
———. 2000. *Jesus and the Politics of Interpretation*. New York: Continuum.
Sienaert, Edgard. 1990. Marcel Jousse: The Oral Style and the Anthropology of Gesture. *Oral Tradition* 5:91–106.
———. 1999. On the Rhythmographic Representation of an Oral-Style Text. Unpublished paper.
Sienaert, E., N. Bell, and M. Lewis, eds. 1991. *Oral Tradition and Innovataion: New Wine in Old Bottles*. Durban: University of Natal Oral Documentation and Research Centre.
Sienaert, E., and J. Conolly. 2000. Marcel Jousse on "Oral-Style," "Memory," and the "Counting-Necklace." Pages 65–84 in *Orality, Memory, and the Past: Listening to the Voices of Black Clergy under Colonialism and Apartheid*. Edited by Phillipe Denis. Pietermaritzburg: Cluster.
Scott, Bernard Brandon, and Margaret E. Dean. 1993. A Sound Map of the Sermon on the Mount. Pages 672–725 in *Society of Biblical Literature 1993 Seminar Papers*. Atlanta: Scholars Press.
Sjoberg, Gideon 1960. *The Pre-industrial City*. New York: Free Press.
Small, Jocelyn Penny. 1997. *Wax Tablets of the Mind: Cognitive Studies of Memory and Literacy in Classical Antiquity*. London: Routledge.
Smith, Jonathan Z. 1982. Toward a Rediscription of Canon. Pages 36–52 in *Imagining Religion: From Babylon to Jonestown*. Chicago: University of Chicago Press.
Ste. Croix, G. E. M. de. 1981. *The Class Struggle in the Ancient Greek World: From the Archaic Age to the Arab Conquests*. London: Duckworth.
Stock, Brian. 1983. *The Implications of Literacy: Written Language and Models of Interpretation in the Eleventh and Twelfth Centuries*. Princeton: Princeton University Press.
———. 1990. *Listening for the Text: On the Uses of the Past*. Baltimore: Johns Hopkins University Press.
Strange, James. 1992. First-Century Galilee from Archaeology and from the Texts. Pages 23–59 in *What Has Archaeology to Do with Faith?* Edited by James Charlesworth and Walter Weaver. Valley Forge, Pa.: Trinity Press International.
Strickert, Fred. 1998. *Bethsaida: Home of the Apostles*. Collegeville, Minn.: Liturgical Press.
Taylor, Vincent. 1959. The Original Order of Q. Pages 95–118 in *New Testament Essays: Studies in Memory of T W. Manson*. Edited by A. J. B Higgins. Manchester, England: Manchester University Press.

Tedlock, Dennis 1971. On the Translation of Style in Oral Narrative. *Journal of American Folklore* 84:114–33.
———. 1985. *Popol Vuh: The Mayan Book of the Dawn of Life and the Glories of Gods and Kings*. New York: Simon & Schuster.
Theissen, Gerd. 1973. Wanderradikalismus: Literatursoziologische Aspekte der Überlieferung von Worten Jesu im Urchristentum. *ZTK* 70:245–71.
———. 1978. *Sociology of Early Palestinian Christianity*. Philadelphia: Fortress.
Thomas, Rosalind. 1989. *Oral Tradition and Written Record in Classical Athens*. Cambridge: Cambridge University Press.
———. 1992. *Literacy and Orality in Ancient Greece*. Cambridge: Cambridge University Press.
Thompson, Dorothy J. 1994. Literacy and Power in Ptolemaic Egypt. Pages 67–83 in *Literacy and Power in the Ancient World*. Edited by Alan K. Bowman and Greg Wools. Cambridge: Cambridge University Press.
Tuckett, Christopher M. 1991. Q and Thomas: Evidence of a Primitive "Wisdom Gospel"? A Response to H. Koester. *Ethl* 67:346–60.
———. 1996. *Q and the History of Early Christianity*. Edinburgh: T&T Clark.
Turner, E. G. 1978. Writing Materials for Businessmen. *BASP* 15:163–69.
Tyler, Stephen A. 1986. On Being Out of Words. *Cultural Anthropology* 1:131–37.
Ulrich, Eugene. 1999. *The Dead Sea Scrolls and the Origins of the Bible*. Grand Rapids: Eerdmans.
Vaage, Lief. 1994. Q and Cynicism: On Comparison and Social Identity. Pages 199–229 in *The Gospel behind the Gospels*. Edited by R. A. Piper. NovTSup 75. Leiden: Brill.
Vansina, Jan. 1985. *Oral Tradition as History*. Madison: University of Wisconsin Press.
Wolf, Eric. 1966. *Peasants*. Eaglewood Cliffs, N.J.: Prentice-Hall.
Woolf, Greg. 1994. Power and the Spread of Writing in the West. Pages 84–98 in *Literacy and Power in the Ancient World*. Edited by Alan K. Bowman and Greg Woolf. Cambridge: Cambridge University Press.
———. 2002. *Cambridge Ancient History* 9:892.
Wuellner, Wilhelm. 1989. Hermeneutics and Rhetorics: From "Truth" and "Method" to "Truth" and "Power." *Scriptura* 3:1–54.
Wylie, Alison. 2002. *Thinking from Things: Essays in the Philosophy of Archaeology*. Berkeley and Los Angeles: University of California Press.
Yeivin, Z. 1993 Chorazin. Pages 301–4 in vol. 1 of *The New Encyclopedia of Archaeological Excavations in the Holy Land*. Edited by Ephraim Stern. New York: Simon & Schuster.
Youtie, Herbert C. 1971a. *Agrammatos*: An Aspect of Greek Society in Egypt. *Harvard Studies in Classical Philology* 75:161–76.
———. 1971b. *Bradeos grafon*: Between Literacy and Illiteracy. *Greek, Roman, and Byzantine Studies* 12:239–61.
———. 1975. *Hypografeus*: The Social Impact of Illiteracy in Graeco-Roman Egypt. *Zeitschrift fuer Papyrologie und Epigraphie* 17:201–21.

Printed in the United States
80302LV00004B/22